D1366614

Praise for *Market Upside Down*

"Vinh Tran's deep knowledge of global economic events and his skill as a market participant shine through in *Market Upside Down*, wherein he illuminates the structural problems that exist in the U.S. economy and the ongoing risks these problems pose to investors. The book gives investors practical strategies for thriving in turbulent times and is important for anyone who wants to understand the new normal of the investing landscape."
— **Tony Crescenzi,** Strategist and Portfolio Manager, PIMCO and Author of *Investing from the Top Down* and *The Strategic Bond Investor*

"*Market Upside Down* makes a case against consensus wisdom, which holds that in spite of two devastating bear markets in stocks in 2000 and 2008, stocks should remain the cornerstone of investment portfolios, even for retirees and conservative investors. The author argues that the current financial crisis means that future returns in stocks are highly problematic. He goes on to outline alternate strategies designed to preserve capital and produce absolute returns. This is a provocative and well-documented book, full of interesting ideas. It deserves your attention."
— **Annette Thau, Ph.D.,** Author of the bestselling *The Bond Book*

"There are lots of these books that purport to understand the current credit crisis and even claim to have seen the severity of it ahead of time. Vinh Tran's book, on the other hand, is very clear and understated in its accurate analysis of not only what happened, but the consequences of this crisis to investors and markets going forward. The language is clear and precise, even if the subject matter is murky and complex. He is to be heartily congratulated for demystifying the mess we're in."
— **Lawrence J. Longua,** Director, REIT Center, NYU Schack Institute of Real Estate

"The fall in real estate values, credit market crises, and the stock market crash of 2008 and their effects worldwide put into question all that we have learned about investing. Vinh Tran provides the first best guide to making investment decisions for the future."
— **Ronald W. Sellers,** Chairman, CEO, Atlantic Asset Management

"*Market Upside Down* gives a well-written, strong case as to why our economy may not easily recover the financial crisis. The book also suggests how we can invest to reduce our risks. I may not agree with everything, but it is a good read!"
— **Roger G. Ibbotson,** Chairman and CIO, Zebra Capital Management, LLC and Professor in Practice at Yale School of Management

"*Market Upside Down* is a cautionary tale of the evils of debt. Our economic woes won't end with the resolution of the mortgage-backed securities crisis. Investors are facing a new crisis caused by massive government debt. But, fear not, Vinh Tran doesn't leave his readers unprotected. In his insightful book, he shares his strategies for profiting in down markets by investing in assets that promote liquidity, are diverse, help preserve capital, and manage unforeseen risks."
— **Thong Nguyen,** Group Executive, Fiduciary Solutions, Bank of America, Global Wealth and Investment Management

Market Upside Down

Market Upside Down

How to Invest Profitably in a Shrinking Economy

Vinh Q. Tran

Vice President, Publisher: Tim Moore
Associate Publisher and Director of Marketing: Amy Neidlinger
Executive Editor: Jeanne Glasser
Editorial Assistant: Myesha Graham
Development Editor: Russ Hall
Operations Manager: Gina Kanouse
Senior Marketing Manager: Julie Phifer
Publicity Manager: Laura Czaja
Assistant Marketing Manager: Megan Colvin
Cover Designer: Chuti Prasertsith
Managing Editor: Kristy Hart
Project Editors: Julie Anderson and Jovana San Nicolas-Shirley
Copy Editor: Gill Editorial Services
Proofreaders: Apostrophe Editing Services and Water Crest Publishing
Indexer: Lisa Stumpf
Compositor: Jake McFarland
Manufacturing Buyer: Dan Uhrig

© 2010 by Pearson Education, Inc.

Publishing as FT Press

Upper Saddle River, New Jersey 07458

FT Press offers excellent discounts on this book when ordered in quantity for bulk purchases or special sales. For more information, please contact U.S. Corporate and Government Sales, 1-800-382-3419, corpsales@pearsontechgroup.com. For sales outside the U.S., please contact International Sales at international@pearson.com.

Company and product names mentioned herein are the trademarks or registered trademarks of their respective owners.

Printed in the United States of America

First Printing February 2010

ISBN-10: 0-13-704486-0
ISBN-13: 978-0-13-704486-3

Pearson Education LTD.
Pearson Education Australia PTY, Limited.
Pearson Education Singapore, Pte. Ltd.
Pearson Education North Asia, Ltd.
Pearson Education Canada, Ltd.
Pearson Educatión de Mexico, S.A. de C.V.
Pearson Education—Japan
Pearson Education Malaysia, Pte. Ltd.

Library of Congress Cataloging-in-Publication Data

Tran, Vinh Quang, 1946-
  Market upside down : how to invest profitably in a shrinking economy / Vinh Q. Tran.
    p. cm.
  Includes bibliographical references.
  ISBN 978-0-13-704486-3 (hbk. : alk. paper) 1. Investments—United States. 2. Investments. 3. Recessions—United States. 4. United States—Economic conditions—2009- I. Title.
  HG4910.T73 2010
  332.60973—dc22
                                                                                    2009040422

To my wife Nhung,
Our son Thuy, and daughter Heather

Contents

Acknowledgments

It was like an accident happening in slow motion. You saw it coming; you screamed for people to get out of its way. But your gesticulations were looked at in puzzlement.

To clients, friends, and colleagues who listened and encouraged me to write this book, I wish to extend special thanks.

I am also indebted to friends and colleagues who read the manuscript and offered suggestions and comments: Thong M. Nguyen and Brian L. Seidman at Bank of America's Global Wealth Management; Joseph Pignatelli at Archstone Partners; Roger C. Ibbotson at Zebra Capital Management and Yale School of Management; Ronald W. Sellers, Duane Roberts, Fowad Sheikh, and Michael Dineen at Atlantic Asset Management Partners; Lawrence J. Longua at New York University; Bridget Lyons, Ralph W.H. Lim, and Lucjan T. Orlowski at Sacred Heart University; Vikas Agarwal at Georgia State University. They were most generous with their time and support. Any errors, however, are all mine.

This book would not come to life without my editor, Jeanne Glasser, executive editor of FT Press/Wharton School Publishing, who is ever patient and indulging; and Julie Anderson, of the editorial staff, who is meticulous, exacting, and yet forgiving of my demands.

My wife has put up with my many acts of disappearance as only a writer with a day job could inflict on his family. I owe her a debt of gratitude for her support and love. And to my son, thanks for his reverse parenting; and my daughter, thanks for the love only a devoted daughter can give.

About the Author

Dr. Vinh Q. Tran has spent more than 20 years as a money manager for global financial institutions including Morgan Stanley, Bank of America, and Aetna Life & Casualty, where he managed global investments, hedged equities and alternative investments, and advised wealthy individual and institutional investors. Throughout his career, Dr. Tran has earned high acclaim for his investment performance from *Fortune, The New York Times, Morningstar*, and others.

Dr. Tran has taught advanced investment as adjunct professor of Finance at NYU's Stern School of Business. He holds a Ph.D. and MBA in Finance from George Washington University, and graduated magna cum laude in both Accounting and Political Science from the University of Dalat, Vietnam.

Dr. Tran is the author of *Evaluating Hedge Fund Performance* and *Foreign Exchange Management in Multinational Firms*. He resides in Greenwich, Connecticut with his wife and two children.

Introduction

In investing, pessimism is your friend, euphoria is the enemy.

—Warren Buffet
CNBC, Interview, July 3, 2009

In autumn 2008, the U.S. stock market crashed to the lows seen only at the depth of the tech stock bubble burst during 2000–2002, then it plunged even further a few months later.

The Dow Jones Industrial Average had just made historic highs the previous year. Euphoria still hung in the air. No one expected to see record lows again—not another bear market, not so soon. Yet, within 12 months, precipitated by house price declines and subprime mortgage defaults, the Dow Jones Industrial Average saw half of its value evaporate. Almost in a flash, investors saw their gains from U.S. stocks in the past decade disappear—all the fruits of their patient long-term investing.

As a result, the United States experienced a systemic crisis that rapidly spread from its bankrupt or near-insolvent financial institutions to all sectors of its economy and every corner of the world.

To prevent its economy from sliding into a cycle of depression and deflation like Japan in the 1990s, the American government and its counterparts abroad undertook aggressive interest rate cuts and initiated massive bailout programs aimed at averting the global banking system from collapse.

Like Japan in the 1990s, the Federal Reserve cut its Fed funds rate to near zero, and the Treasury injected huge amounts of capital to bolster the banks in the hope that they would resume lending to ease the liquidity crunch. But the banks, teetering on the precipice of bankruptcy, held on to the government funds instead of lending the money, fearful of losses from making bad loans in a recessionary economy.

And stocks kept plunging. By the time President Barack Obama launched his $787 billion stimulus program on the heels of his election to the presidency, accompanied by high approval ratings and soaring speeches, stocks had crashed through the lows of October crisis levels and had surpassed the 2000 bear market bottom.

Although not immediately greeted by the stock market with loud cheers, those rescue measures nevertheless stemmed the tide of economic setbacks and stabilized stock prices. Reinforced with stimulus programs like "cash for clunkers," a host of economic statistics stopped deteriorating by mid-2009, and the stock market was flushed with a renewed sense of confidence in the beginning of a new bull market— as some well-known Wall Street strategists have asserted. Robert J. Shiller, the Yale University professor and originator of the S&P/ Case-Shiller house price index, however, was puzzled:

> The global signs of a recovery in economic confidence seem puzzling.
>
> It is a large and diverse world, after all, so why should confidence have rebounded so quickly in so many places? Government stimulus and bailout packages have generally not been big enough to have such a profound effect. What happened?...For a fuller explanation, look beyond the traditional economic links and think of the world economy as driven by social epidemics, contagion of ideas, and huge feedback loops that gradually change world views....
>
> All of this suggests that a social epidemic is supporting renewed confidence. This confidence can keep growing by contagion, as a kind of self-fulfilling prophecy, and we may see the markets and the economy recover further. But in an economy that is still unstable, the stories could also morph into different forms, the price feedback could turn downward, and the dynamic could turn ugly again—just as it has in the past.[1]

Thus, it is not impossible to imagine that the rally from the March 2009 lows could turn into a lengthy extension, like the bounces in the aftermath of previous crashes. The Federal Reserve can keep money cheap for far longer than expected; it has the Bank of Japan's near-zero interest rate policy as a model. And the federal government can offer up one after another of the cash-for-clunkers programs it copied from a program two-and-a-half-times as big that was started in Germany. It is the sovereign power of printing money and deficit spending. Although current equity valuation is hardly a bargain, stocks are often bought for no other reason than because prices are expected to go higher. "An upward movement in stock prices generates its own upward feedback," as Robert Shiller put it.[2] We saw this phenomenon in Japan during the several years before the 1989 peak and numerous times again during Japan's 20 years of slumber. We saw it prior to the tech bubble burst in 2000. The multiyear market advance before the collapse in 2008 was built on an upside-down pyramid scheme of easy credit and inflated house prices. Before the collapse of Lehman Brothers Holdings and its abandonment by the Treasury and the Federal Reserve in September 2008, the stock market was almost oblivious to the subprime debacle and the pending banking collapse.

But when the recognition came, everyone in the crowd tried to exit by the narrow door.

However, another crash of the equity market and the resulting depressive impacts on savers and the economy may not be easily reversed this time by lowering interests, quantitative easing, or public spending programs. Interest rates will have been too low to be reduced for effect, and the Fed balance sheet is already stressed out. The government should find that its budget deficits and record debt load make it difficult, if not impossible, to get a trillion dollars here, another there for bailout and stimulus spending. The banks that have recently reported profits on the back of subsidized capital provided by taxpayers while retaining toxic assets on their balance sheets may find their financial strength inadequate to absorb new write-offs and loan defaults. In the meantime, American households are hardly in a position to take another hit after losing trillions of dollars in equities and real estate, amid rising job losses and low savings rates.

The reality is that the United States and its citizens are deep in debt. The country is now in far worse shape than Japan was at the start of its two-decade decline; the latter's stock market is still mired near the bottom with no end in sight. How long can an economy grow and its stock market rise on unsustainable debt and reliance on for-eigners' largess to fund its relentless spending? How many fabricated booms and busts can a country absorb before its paper money loses its international standing and its social fabric is torn apart?

When the next crisis comes, where will the United States and its citizens find the resources to combat and recover? The Federal Reserve may crank up the printing press at full speed, but the global markets have ways to express their displeasure through soaring inter-est rates, the dollar's collapse, and sell-offs of stock prices. By the time the next crisis rears its head, when the effects of "the massive shots in the arm" have worn off, the pain and patience of real people may have reached their limits. Confidence may be replaced by recognition and fear of even darker days ahead. Without confidence and optimism, the values of the stock certificates will simply evaporate.

Optimism and hope may be created by sound bites on television, but they are not sustainable for too long.

For savers and long-term investors, there must be better ways to save and invest than hoping for the stock market to go up.

* * *

This book is not about doomsday. Nor is it about predicting the future, because forecasting, especially that of stock prices, is a haz-ardous business, besieged with mistaken signs and distorted rearview mirrors, made foggier with the passage of time and emotion. But the more confusing the outlook, the clearer one thing is: The equity investing game is becoming less favorable, the odds are increasing, and winning is questionable and much less assured than it was in the 1980s and '90s. We discuss these issues in Chapters 1 through 6. In the first three chapters, we take a close look at the conditions leading to the government policies following the stock market and real estate collapses in the United States in 2008 and in Japan following their respective peaks in 1989 and 1991. In the next three chapters, we examine the factors framing the prospects of future stock prices and the risks of equities to savers and long-term investors.

This book is about opportunities for savers and long-term investors who diligently save and invest to prepare for their retire-ments and for those who are already retired. The book sets the stage for you to assess your goals and objectives in an upside-down stock market; to think about the critical facets of risks of stocks, and the potential devastating impacts of risks and stock losses on your financial well-being and futures; to explore investment opportunities that may be better positioned to provide liquidity and income; and to seek a safer approach than investing in only traditional stocks and betting on stock prices to keep rising. We explore and discuss these issues in Chapters 7 through 9, with a focus on the absolute return approach to save and build wealth for the long term.

My goal is not to draw a map of the future but to lay out the landscape of the prospects of the U.S. economy and the stock market to help you discern the contours of a vague outline, what the stock market must deal with in the long term and what savers and long-term investors should be aware of, and what you might be able to do to protect your life savings and your family's financial future. My purpose is rooted in the view that, unless the weather is fine, the journey to sea is not worth taking for savers and investors who rely on their investments for retirement income and support. There are other ways to save, perhaps at a tortoise's speed, but these ways are dependable and, in the long term, potentially more rewarding. In Chapters 10 and 11, we discuss these opportunities and strategies that can generate returns while their risks of losses are better managed and contained within the margins you can afford.

Hopefully, when another stock market crash comes, savers who follow this approach will not see the results of their years of hard work and deprived cravings devastated, and retirees will not have to look for work to put food on the table. At the most euphoric moments, when TV commentators and market sages predict higher and higher stock prices and years of bull market, investors should remember the unprecedented and growing mountain of debt and leverages that support the American economy and its stock market while the United States relies on foreign governments of questionable dependability for support of its public and consumer spending habits. And remember, too, how savings were damaged and financial futures undermined in the aftermath of the 2008 stock market crash!

To paraphrase an old saying, wariness is the mother of prevention.

1

Black Swan Octobers

The infamous Black Monday of October 19, 1987 has been remembered in the United States as the worst-ever one-day stock market decline. In merely one day, the market bellwether, the Dow Jones Industrial Average, dropped 508 points, losing 22.6 percent of its market value from the previous Friday's closing. However, as heart-stopping as it was to watch the selling chaos minute by minute—if Wall Street believers in long-term equity investing stayed true to their preaching, the event might have hardly warranted more than a footnote.

Black Monday

That same day turned out to be the best buying opportunity for the next decade (see Figure 1.1). The 1987 bear market[1] that followed Black Monday lasted less than a month, although it recorded a stunning loss of 34 percent. Less than two months earlier, the Dow had recorded a new historic high at 2,746.7—and that was after five years of relentless rise from the August 1982 bottom, bringing up the Dow by a stupendous average of 28.5 percent a year. After the Black Monday crash, this index went back and forth above the low close of 1,738.7; then it subsequently took off for a new record high three years later. All in all, for those three years, the average annual return exceeded 20 percent, not even counting dividends! It was not such a bad reward for a gut-wrenching day of watching the market seemingly free-fall!

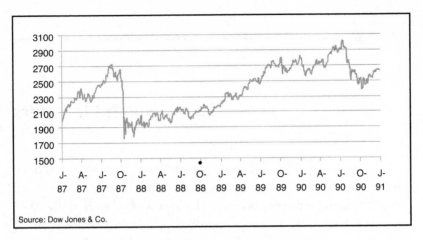

Figure 1.1   Dow Jones Industrial Average 1987–1990

Then, after a brief pause lasting less three months in 1990 that gave back 21 percent in the process, the Dow embarked on a spectacular bull run that did not end until 2000.

That the bull run lasted for 18 years starting in 1982 (interrupted only briefly by the short-lived, although large and dramatic, decline in 1987 and the slightly longer 20-percent corrections in 1990 and 1998) only reinforced the argument that stocks would eventually go up. All you have to do is hold on to them long enough. As for market declines, they would not last long and would not really affect your portfolios, because they are only paper losses anyway. In fact, so the argument goes, you might even take advantage of the downturns to buy more.

The rise of the stock market in those 18 years also served to bolster the pitch to unwary investors about the high return potential of stocks and the "you-can't-lose" proposition of the buy-and-hold strategy that depends on the market going ever upward.

The 2000 Bear Market

The 2000 tech bubble burst punctured a hole in this strategy. The three-year bear market exposed the fundamental risk in stocks; that is, the market cannot go up and up forever. In fact, stock market losses can cause substantial damage to an investor's wealth for prolonged periods. A result of this realization is that many investors looked for strategies that somehow provided equity-like returns without the usual risks of equities. That Bernie Madoff's massive Ponzi scheme and other lesser scams could happen and last for years only serves to highlight investors' deep-seated need for an investment paradigm that does not depend solely on the stock market going steadily up and up.

The 2000 bear market did not end as quickly or register any dramatic October movements (see Figure 1.2). In fact, in all those years, October was an up month, a Black Swan in white disguise, running counter to the down trends of the prior months in a prolonged bear market (see the section "What Is Black Swan?"). Each time, the rally looked like it signaled the end of the bear's hug. The trading was characterized by high volume and price formations such as key reversal days, which chart technicians use to detect a change in direction of the market's trends.

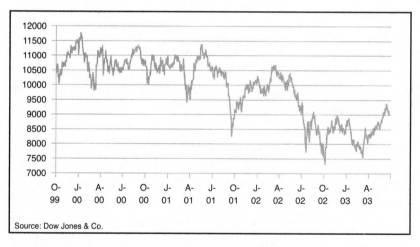

Figure 1.2   Dow Jones Industrial Average 2000–2003

For two years, the Dow went up and down violently. From the high in 2000, it recorded a loss of 30 percent by September 2001. But by mid-March of 2002, it recovered and was a mere 9.3 percent below the 2000 peak.

What Is Black Swan?

In the language of markets, Black Swan refers to an event that is unpredicted and unpredictable but has large consequences. It is similar to the "tail" risk that mathematicians use to describe events that have little chance of occurring—although similar events may have happened in the past—but the potential losses are unusually large. Black Monday and the 9/11 attack are examples. The Black Swan theory was postulated by Nassim Nicholas Taleb in his 2007 book, *The Black Swan*. Taleb argues that just because some event did not happen does not mean it cannot happen in the future. When it does happen, losses will be devastating. Taleb points out that trading and financial firms are especially vulnerable to Black Swan events for which they are unprepared, despite their sophisticated but flawed mathematical models.[2]

But, in the end, the result was far worse than the 1987 drop. It lasted for 39 months, including the round-trip return in March 2003 back to the lows of the previous year; it was longer than the 1929 depression. In between, the Dow registered two bear market periods: between May 21 and September 21, 2001 and then again between March 19 and October 9, 2002. Both times, the Dow went down by more than 30 percent, almost as bad as the loss in 1987. Additionally, there were three other periods—each lasting for a month or two—during which the Dow lost from 12 to 16 percent that easily qualified as severe corrections.

The market went down, each time punctuated by false hopes of rallies and reversals. Quickly after each new low was reached, the index would rally strongly to the cheers of market commentators, while pundits went on television proclaiming the bear market was over, only to see the gains given up and the market drop to fresh new lows.

After the Dow hit the cycle's lows in October 2002, it scored a couple of months of strong rallies—exceeding 22 percent—that seemed to signal the bear market had already ended. But then these lows came back a mere six months later.

How many investors were sucked into these fake-out violent moves? Overall, from high to low, the Dow recorded a loss of 37.9 percent from its peak in December 2000. That wasn't much larger than the drop in 1987. But long-term holders of equities saw their net worth decline to the 1997 level, leaving them in waste after six years of roller-coaster rides, while long-term savers put in additional investments during market rallies only to see losses multiply. Flows of Funds accounts (FFA), published by the Federal Reserve, showed that the values of equities held by households and nonprofit organizations declined in 2002 to $10.6 trillion, from $17.2 trillion in 1999, for a loss of $6.6 trillion or 38.3 percent. This loss was far greater the 27 percent drop of the Dow in those three years.

The 2008 Market Crash

The financial crisis and market crash of 2008 started in October (again!) of 2007.

As shown in Figure 1.3, in the early months, it looked like it would be no more than a normal correction. Declines were followed by rallies that broke through the previous resistance levels, even after the collapse of the venerable investment bank Bear Stearns in March that shook the very foundation of the U.S. financial system and the world. It seemed the worst was over when JP Morgan Chase, the third largest U.S. bank at the time, stepped in at the behest of the Federal Reserve in coordination with the Treasury to bail out Bear Stearns by buying all its assets for a pitiful $2 per share—which months later was raised to $10 per share amid intense complaints that JP Morgan got it too cheap. The market recovered and sailed through some key resistance points, coming close to being even for the year.

But it was not to be the end.

All in one frantic weekend in mid-September, Lehman Brothers Holdings was abandoned to bankruptcy despite its management's desperate pleas for a lifeline from the Treasury and the Federal Reserve. It was also a day of reckoning for Merrill Lynch. Its CEO hurriedly went on the prowl looking for a buyer, lest it would follow Lehman's fate when the market reopened on Monday. In what was later revealed to be a rushed and ill-advised acquisition concluded in less than 24 hours in December, Bank of America ended up the new owner of Merrill Lynch. To top off the whirlwind of the weekend, the government took over the global insurance giant American International Group, leaving a mere 20 percent stake to its shareholders, who already had seen the stock's value virtually wiped out.

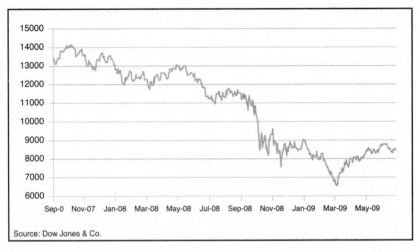

Source: Dow Jones & Co.

Figure 1.3   Dow Jones Industrial Average October 2007–June 2009

It dawned on market participants that this was not a run-of-the-mill market correction. With this realization, the market crashed. October 2008 showed up as a Black Swan, losing 27 percent, most of it in the first week.

It was presidential election time, and Washington became frenetic with talks of bankrupt banks and financial bailouts for them—with cries for help from the Big Three automobile makers thrown in for good measure. A $700 bailout plan was hastily put together by the Bush administration to stave off the banks from going under, amid posturing by the presidential candidates and partisan cries among congressmen and senators.

All this didn't seem to matter much to the stock market; it kept going lower. By the time President Obama was sworn in and the ink on his $787 billion fiscal stimulus plan was hardly dried, the Dow had made fresh new lows in the second week in March 2009. By then, the losses had climbed to 54 percent from the market's peak in 2007, rivaling the damage in the 1929 Depression in just as short a period of time.

As usual, the market staged a bounce in the next three months amid statistics showing the economic deterioration was not accelerating— that is, the economy was still getting worse, but at a slower pace! Seizing on these figures, the former Federal Reserve chief Alan Greenspan claimed "...we are finally beginning to see the seeds of a bottoming,"[3] while Chairman Ben Bernanke testified to the Congress in June that he was more confident than a month ago of an economic recovery by year-end.[4] Market pundits were only too eager to join the chorus and vied with TV hosts to make bold predictions of the economy and the market. Stock analysts also joined the newfound party; they raised the number of "buy" ratings for the first time since the bear market began.[5]

The euphoria was short lived, and the gloom quickly returned when the reality of rising unemployment hit the market in early July. To top it off, as if timing for effect, Vice President Joe Biden said the administration had "misread how bad the economy was."[6] At the same time, calls for an additional $300 billion of stimulus were bubbling up from the official circle—from the House Majority Leader Steny Hoyer to Laura D'Andrea Tyson, an economic adviser to the president—although only a fraction of the first $787 billion stimulus funds had been spent at that time and would not be fully committed until 2010.[7]

In response to all this talk of additional stimulus, "stocks fell to their lowest level in 10 weeks on Tuesday as talk of a second government stimulus plan heightened fears that the economy is not yet on the path to recovery...," Reuters reported.[8] Wall Street economists and market strategists dismissed the idea as "likely to do little to boost the stock market."[9] The respected strategist David Rosenberg was more emphatic, saying that an additional round of government stimulus was likely to have little more impact than "cushioning the blow."[10] More forthcoming after having left Merrill Lynch, he added that the market was currently only halfway through a bear market that could last another nine years.[11] Art Cashin, the long-serving director of floor operations at UBS Financial Services, chimed in, "It's like the Biblical story of the fat and lean years. During the fat, you can throw a dart at the wall, and anything you buy goes up."[12] He was referring to the 17.6-year cycle, counting the current one to have started in 2000.

Never before has this sort of grim comments come from these mainstream market veterans. Why this gloom?

Why the difference now? Why was the decline in 1987 so short, barely longer than the blink of an eye? And why did the 2000 bear market last for three years? Why was the crash in 2008 so virulent, causing more damage to investors' wealth than in 1987 and 2000–2003, wiping out the value of more than 10 years of patient investing in a matter of only a few months, with the end not yet in sight, possibly for many years to come? How about two decades?

The Prospects Beyond

The 2008 market crash and the ensuing financial crisis started with the collapse of house prices and the resulting widespread defaults of subprime mortgages. Soon it rapidly spread throughout the world and to every corner of the U.S. economy. It was not confined in one sector like the tech stocks in 2000, or to one industry like the savings and loan associations in the 1970s, or to one influential financial player like Long Term Capital Management in 1998; nor was it a short-lived price correction of an overheated stock market's quick trigger reaction to former Fed chairman Alan Greenspan's "irrational exuberance" jawboning like in 1987. In the 2008 disaster, what Warren Buffett called "economic Pearl Harbor," the damages to the banking system of the United States and the world and the global economy were far more substantial than in previous downturns, and the government actions intended to fix the system and stimulate economic growth were much more far-reaching. The intervention measures were massive in scale, unprecedented in scope, and so thoroughly intrusive in the running of businesses that those businesses that received the government's help became like government-owned enterprises.

It was all started because the largest, most valuable assets an American family has—its house and its American dream—suddenly declined in value. Starting in 2006, house prices began to decline after several years of sharp rise. Millions of homes became worth less than what their owners had paid for them. But more alarming, the houses were worth less than what their owners owed to the banks that had lent them the money. Unable to pay back their loans, or seeing no reason to keep on paying for an asset that was worth less than the borrowed money, many people walked away from their obligations, devaluing the mortgage-backed securities that had made it possible to issue the mortgage loans to the now-defunct homeowners.

The banks that in one form or another had participated in these mortgage-backed securities, either as issuers or investors, suddenly found their balance sheets devastated by these devalued assets. The banks' stock prices went down; their own survival was at stake.

In quick succession, once-impregnable financial institutions had to be rescued by the federal government.

In one form or another, with the Fed leading the charge by opening the liquidity spigot in unprecedented fashions, the government tried to prop up the financial system.

But the result was just the same. One after another, venerable banking institutions ceased to exist. Bear Stearns was forced into a government-arranged merger with JP Morgan Chase. Lehman Brothers, the 158-year-old and third-largest investment bank, was left to go bankrupt. Merrill Lynch sold itself to Bank of America during a frantic weekend of negotiations monitored by regulatory authorities to avoid a bankruptcy filing on the following Monday. The specter of the bank run on Britain's Northern Rock loomed large (see the following excerpt).

Northern Rock Customers Crowd Branches, Withdraw Cash

Sept. 14 (Bloomberg)—Hundreds of Northern Rock Plc customers crowded into branches in London today to pull out their savings after the mortgage-loan provider sought emergency funding from the Bank of England.

"It's scary," said Peter Pye, 60, a retired university lecturer standing in a line of about 30 people outside the Moorgate branch in the financial district. "I have my life's savings in Northern Rock." He said he would withdraw a "six-figure" sum and leave 5,000 pounds in the account.

The Bank of England said it will provide emergency cash to Northern Rock, Britain's third-largest mortgage provider, in the nation's biggest bailout of a financial institution in 30 years. The rising cost of credit left the lender unable to make new loans and stoked concern among customers about their money.

Northern Rock, which has 1.4 million retail depositors and 800,000 mortgage customers, hasn't imposed any special limits on withdrawals, spokesman Don Hunter said. The Newcastle, England-based company, which traces its roots back to 1850, had to restart its Internet banking site "over a period of time" today after unusually high usage froze the service, he said.

"No Risk."

"There is no risk," said James Hamilton, an analyst at Numis Securities in London. "The Bank of England said Northern Rock is solvent." Hamilton said that "as credit turmoil will return to normal, Northern Rock's business will." The British Bankers' Association said there's "no reason for either mortgage customers or savers to worry." The group provides London interbank offered rates, or Libor, a benchmark for money-market rates in the dollar, the euro and 11 other currencies.

"Why leave your money in a bank that obviously has some major problems?" said Michael Ribotham, 74. "I'm not young and don't have a chance to make it back again." Ribotham was waiting at Moorgate for about 40 minutes.

Excerpt from Bloomberg.com, "Northern Rock Customers Crowd Branches, Withdraw Cash," September 17, 2009

The market's reaction to the government's rescue efforts was a huge sell-off. In the first two weeks of October 2008, the Dow lost almost 3,000 points before recovering slightly. The stock of the investment bank Morgan Stanley, which had just reported a strong third quarter, went into a free fall by September and faced a possible run-on-the-bank—despite a balance sheet with plenty of liquidity—as hedge funds and its other clients abandoned it in droves. Goldman Sachs, the only other investment bank left standing of the once much-envied investment banking fraternity of five, fared little better. As disclosed in September 2008, its CEO Lloyd Blankfein had approached Citigroup—the wounded and loss-suffering bank that had once been the world's number-one global banking powerhouse—for a possible merger. Uncharacteristically, Goldman Sachs, the world's largest and most successful investment bank, the white shoe firm of the smartest and best investment bankers, was turned down. No one wanted to touch an investment bank—with its billions of dollars of assets in little-understood and toxic securities and counterparty risk obligations—at least not without government guarantees, after the Lehman fiasco.

Facing a total collapse of the world banking system and a global depression, the U.S. Treasury and Federal Reserve engineered unprecedented rescue measures in coordination with other foreign governments to bail out the biggest and the not-so-big financial institutions of the world. In the United States, the Treasury and the Fed announced plans for a huge bailout fund of $700 billion to inject capital and buy toxic assets from the banks. The Dow rallied almost 1,000 points on the news, only to lose all and more in subsequent days as Congress fought bitterly over the bill while the presidential candidates postured to gain advantage and President Bush made speeches but otherwise stood by helplessly as his party's congressional members went their own different ways.

When the bill was finally passed, the Dow again lost steam and dropped below the crisis level on October 10. The stock market did not believe the measures were sufficient to shore up the system!

Clearly, other measures were needed to stem the bloodletting. It was now the Fed's turn to step up by cutting interest rates—and it did, more aggressively than it had ever before. By November 5, the Fed funds rate had been cut to 1 percent, as low as at the depth of the 2000 bear market. Before Christmas, it was brought down to 0.25 percent, even lower than Japan's 0.5 percent discount rate at its economic lowest point in the 1990s. Significantly, the Fed also announced it would print as much money as necessary—through quantitative easing and purchase of Treasury and mortgage securities—to thaw the frozen credit markets and revive the economy.

Other world central banks had already reduced interest rates, but none matched the large cut of 1.5 percent reduction by the Bank of England on November 6. The Dow promptly lost 444 points on the same day! The previous day, it had lost 486 points.

Fiscal stimulus plans have also been put forth throughout the world. Japan put up a $51.5 billion package, while Germany moved on a $30 billion plan of tax breaks and loans. The stunner was a program worth $586 billion unveiled by the Chinese government on November 10, dwarfing stimulus measures up to that time by any other country in the Group of 20 largest economies.

When the Chinese plan was announced, the Asian markets rallied sharply, but the Dow, which opened with close to 200-point gains, promptly lost ground and ended the day down by almost 1 percent.

And so it went with each anticipated or announced rescue measure, here in the United States or abroad: Initial excited hope quickly faded away. By the time President Obama was sworn in, the Dow had dipped back down to the October crisis level—despite his high approval ratings and soaring speeches. Even when his budget-busting $787 billion stimulus plan was passed into law, the Dow reached new lows and soon surpassed the 2000 bear market bottom.

Japan had similarly experienced a devastating real estate price collapse in 1989. Its government embarked on all measures both monetary and fiscal to shore up its banking system and its economy— to little long-term effect. Since then, the Japanese economy has languished, and its stock prices have continued to decline, although not without repeatedly faltered attempts to rally (see Figure 1.4). After 20 years, its key stock market index, the Nikkei 225, had declined repeatedly to new lows, and its economy was entering a fresh new recession.

But America in 2008 was different from Japan two decades earlier, just as America's economic conditions in 2008 were much different from any previous crisis.

Figure 1.4   Japan's Nikkei 225 1984–2009

The United States Is in Much Worse Shape

The United States was in much worse shape going into this crisis than Japan was in 1989. Unlike the Japanese in the late 1980s, Americans had little savings. The savings rate in the United States was 1.4 percent at the end of 2007; it had been declining steadily from approximately 10 percent in the early 1980s. Compared to Americans, the Japanese were frugal; they saved at a rate of 13 percent in 1990 when Japan started its decline. At the national level, the U.S. total debt was reaching 400 percent of GDP, compared to Japan's 260 percent at the beginning of its two-decade slumber.

The baby boomers were retiring, and most didn't have much money put aside to support their old age. Medicare, already operating on a deficit, expected its trust fund to run dry in seven years, and the Social Security system is projected to run out of money by 2037, and possibly sooner. What can the retirees do in their old age without retirement savings and medical care?

Fifteen million U.S. workers had lost their jobs as of the end of June 2009, and the unemployment roll was still rising. Many of those still employed were deep in debt, living from paycheck to paycheck and seeing their income falling, even before this crisis.

For those who had saved, primarily through IRA and 401(k) accounts, stock market losses wiped out some $8.4 trillion from their savings in 2008 alone, while their net worth declined by $10.9 trillion. Adding to the woes, millions of homeowners were forced into foreclosures and bankruptcy. Others could no longer tap into their home equity to support buying habits made easy by rising home prices, liberal credit, and cheap imports now that, according to the Flows of Fund accounts of the Federal Reserve, the value of their real estate holdings had lost a staggering $4 trillion since house prices peaked in 2006.

The U.S. manufacturing base is in shambles—unlike Japanese companies, which continued to be highly competitive in the 1990s, even at the worst of Japan's economic downturn. Many products that American firms manufacture are of poor quality and are more expensive than those made by Sony, Samsung, Hyundai, or Toyota, or they're simply less desirable. Even those sold by U.S. companies under their name brands, such as computers or micro chips, are actually manufactured somewhere else in the emerging economies. Starting with textile and apparel, and then consumer goods and electronics, U.S. manufacturing is a shadow of what it used to be a mere quarter-century ago.

Even the U.S. automobile companies, once the envy of the world, are in danger of disappearance. Chrysler has disappeared as an independent company, whereas General Motors emerged from bankruptcy at a much smaller size. The latter's gorgeous Pontiac Solstice Coupe is another epitaph of great hopes and unmet promises. Ford, founded by the inventor of the Model T, has been struggling.

The Last Pontiac

This new targa-top Solstice is the last of the Pontiacs, the final breath of a brand that failed to adapt to a changing world.

It could become something of a collector's item.

Here is a car that essentially matches my definition of a doomed romance. Its drop-dead gorgeous exterior made me yearn for a fling that would turn meaningful, but a week of companionship revealed a list of quirks that included nearly every imaginable character flaw. A love-hate relationship, I suppose, was inevitable.

The spartan cabin, finished in unrelenting black on my test car, was especially noteworthy: I believe it could be the first automotive interior styled entirely by an accounting department. The only minimum-security prison I have ever visited (honest, it was only to interview an inmate) had more luxurious appointments.

Despite its many faults, the shapely little coupe is a sexy attention-getter, another beauty designed by Franz von Holzhausen when he was a rising star at General Motors. (Mr. von Holzhausen subsequently left for Mazda and is now at Tesla.) Outward visibility is atrocious, but that's the price of being so stylish. If you can't live with that, buy an old Volvo wagon.

So what sort of epitaph, if any, does the Solstice GXP coupe suggest for the once-mighty Pontiac nameplate? In many ways, it is a rolling testament of GM's shortsightedness: a pinch of pizazz, a dash of panache, all mixed into a package of unmet promise.

Excerpt from Jerry Garrett, "The Last Pontiac," The New York Times, *July 2, 2009*

In the meantime, the U.S. federal budget was so extended that the federal government was living like its citizens: by borrowing. Its outstanding debts were over $11 trillion. The deficit was $1.4 trillion in fiscal 2009—almost $1 trillon more than in 2008. And, unlike Japan in the 1990s, which continued to grow its trade surplus to add to its foreign currency reserve and to finance its government debt, the U.S. trade deficits had been unrelenting, piling on more debts to foreign countries, including those unfriendly to it. Similarly, across the country, state and local governments—from Atlanta to Sacramento, from Pennsylvania to Florida—faced budget shortfalls and were clamoring for federal bailouts. California paid its bills by printing money in the form of IOUs.

Americans were living on borrowed money—and borrowed time.

In October 2008, they became broke.

And the Crisis Is Worldwide

The Japanese debacle was pretty much an isolated situation, confined solely to Japan. From the start, Japanese equity investors suffered alone while the world's stock markets embarked on a decade-long climb with spectacular gains until 2000.

With the U.S. crash of 2008, not a single country was untouched:

- From tiny Iceland, better known for its fisheries than leveraged lending, to the mighty Russia, of oil wealth and newfound confidence as a global power but now facing dwindling foreign exchange reserves and a potentially unstoppable run on its currency

- From the canyon of Wall Street, littered with defunct banking fortunes, to the small towns in Norway that faced budget cutbacks due to losses from investments in American-issued mortgage-backed securities

- From the bailouts of HBOS, Lloyds, and Royal Bank of Scotland in the UK to the nationalization by tiny Latvia of its second-largest bank.

Even Australia's economy, which had escaped the recession, began to stall, with its exports dropping to a 14-month low. "The full brunt of the deepest and most synchronized post-war global recession has yet to fully bear down on Australia," said a senior economist at RBC Capital Markets. However, "[E]xport income, the terms of trade, and business investment are all set to move substantially lower...."[13]

In the United States, 7.2 million workers had lost their jobs since the start of the recession in December 2007. The Gross Domestic Product (GDP) in the fourth quarter of 2008 had contracted by 5.4 percent, followed by a decline of 6.4 percent in the first quarter of 2009, the fastest rate of contraction since 1982. The unemployment rate had reached 9.5 percent by mid-2009 but was widely expected to go higher, possibly surpassing the 10.8 percent rate in 1982. Oil and commodity prices were continuing to drop, giving relief to U.S. consumers but depressing the economies and stock markets of Brazil, Venezuela, and other resource producers. However, the savings from lower gas prices gave little boost to U.S. retailers, many of whom filed for bankruptcy.

China faced a slowdown and injected massive stimulus into its system to bring its economic growth back to the 8-percent level needed to absorb new workers in the labor force, or the regime would face potential social unrest. Other countries in Asia shared the same or worse fate; cosmopolitan Singapore's GDP plunged 16.4 percent in the fourth quarter.

Lessons Not Learned

As the crisis spread throughout the world, the actions of the United States and other countries eerily resembled the measures undertaken by the Japanese government to keep its banks afloat. Forgotten, however, was how ineffective these actions were in reversing the Japanese stock market's long-term decline.

The crash in Japan began in January 1990. This should have caused many business failures, resulting in a severe economic depression. It didn't happen! Why?

The reason was that Japanese banks had been lending massive amounts of money throughout the 1990s to companies that otherwise would have gone out of business, often from reckless property and stock speculation in the boom years. These loans prevented weak companies from failing but put many banks into insolvency. But the structure of the Japanese banking system was such that the government would prop up any bank that looked destined to fail. Several major banks did fail in November 1997 and early 1998, and they were promptly nationalized and saved.

The Japanese banks also carried on their books massive loans they had made to finance overvalued real estate purchases in Japan and marquee commercial buildings elsewhere in the world, including leveraged buyouts like that of RJR Nabisco. And they were not required—in fact, were discouraged for tax reasons—to set aside reserves for bad loans. In 1991, Japanese banks carried total loans of 450 trillion yen, with only 3 trillion yen in reserves for bad debts.

When real estate prices plunged, the collaterals of these loans dipped in value often to less than 20 percent of the amounts of the loans. But many of the loans were carried on the banks' books as if there were little impairment. This charade was made possible by such practices as continued bank lending to the owners of the properties used as collaterals so that the borrowers could continue to make interest payments, or the property owners transferring the properties to corporate affiliates at valuations that bore little relation to real market conditions.

The Japanese banks survived, although their ability to do business, to make loans to corporations that were in dire need of capital, was severely curtailed.

The Nikkei also survived, but its value was promptly cut in half. And it has not stopped falling. Not that the Japanese government has not tried to stop the fall, with such artifacts as using money from government pension funds to buy stocks and pressuring big investors not to sell shares, in addition to concealing the full impact of the debacle on the banks from the public.

Fast forward to 2008. The U.S. bank bailout is a response to similar circumstances. With greater speed and innovations, the government's rescue plans required greater amounts to keep the ailing institutions afloat but their long-term effectiveness remains to be seen.

In addition to cutting interest rates, the Federal Reserve embarked on an emergency loan program to supply liquidity to the banking system. Under this program, it accepted low-quality securities from the banks as collaterals, as opposed to Treasuries as it had heretofore required. As a result, the Fed's balance sheet soared to $2 trillion, a rise of 140 percent in the seven weeks since it relaxed the collateral standards on September 14, 2008. By year-end 2008, its balance sheet had ballooned further, reaching $3 trillion, and its authority stretched to new limits following what Dallas Fed President Richard Fisher called "Bagehot on steroids" actions—referring to the nineteenth-century English banker Walter Bagehot's advice to banks to lend to each other to avert crises. Additionally, in March 2009, the Fed launched a $1.2 trillion program to purchase up to $300 billion worth of government debt over the next six months and to boost purchases of mortgage securities and debt from Fannie Mae and Freddie Mac.

At the same time, the list of companies lining up for government bailout funds grew by the day—from the automakers to American Express, which got authority from the Fed to become a bank holding company without the normal 30-day waiting period. Hartford Insurance, Genworth, and other insurers also queued up for federal aid. The rescue of AIG had tallied close to $200 billion by then, more than double the original $85 billion price tag, and the U.S. government had become its 80 percent owner. Its stock price had lost so much value that the company had to do a 10-to-1 reverse split to attract institutional investors. Citigroup, the very model of a financial supermarket giant, had gone back twice to the government for assistance. The second time, it received an additional $20 billion of fresh capital, bringing the total to $45 billion, plus a 90-percent backstop guarantee on $306 billion of its toxic assets. The securities under the government's guarantee, however, were but a sliver of Citigroup's $3 trillion of assets, more than one-third of which were off balance sheet assets of questionable valuation; among them were $667 billion of mortgage-related securities. The government had become its largest shareholder with a 36-percent equity stake; its stock was trading for just a few dollars (see Figure 1.5). At the same time, Bank of New York Mellon had been affected by the recession, but it had steered clear of the mortgage-backed securities disaster; therefore, its stock turned in a performance much different from Citigroup.

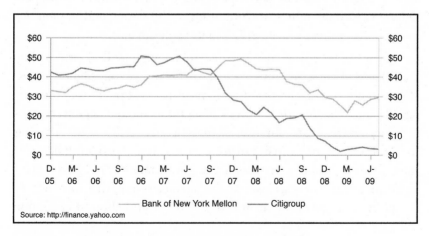

Figure 1.5   Citigroup versus Bank of New York Mellon

The Treasury backtracked on its plan to buy toxic mortgage securities from banks, the very source of the threat to the banking system. Instead, it shifted its focus to buying auto loans, credit card debts, and other such consumer borrowings. Later it came up with the Public-Private Investment Program (PPIP) to take the toxic assets off the banks' books, only to leave that program idle for months. To make the plan work, the multibillion-dollar PPIP called for private investors, through a group of select investment firms, to buy the toxic assets with government subsidies, but on a leveraged basis—as if the system needed more leverage—to make the return more attractive to investors. When it was finally announced in July of 2009, nine investment firms, including some of the largest as well as minority- and women-owned firms to meet legislators' demand, were selected to set up funds with seed money coming from the government, and additional capital to be raised from private investors such as foreign government-owned sovereign wealth funds and others. But the $30 billion amount provided by the government was significantly less than what was originally envisioned as the center piece of a plan targeted at taking $1 trillion of bad assets off the ailing banks. Also, a huge part of the plan was cut out—the part that had intended for the Federal Deposit Insurance Corporation to buy up to $500 billion of the banks' troubled assets. Adding to the drama, the huge bond manager Pacific Investment Management Co., which had been widely expected to be a leading participant in the PPIP, withdrew from participation in June, citing "uncertainties of the design and implementation of the program," according to its spokesman.[14]

Anyway, the banks had become reluctant to sell at prices they considered too low, and investors were unwilling to pay higher prices. Why should the banks refuse to sell these assets at pennies to the dollar? Because the government had given them enough capital to withstand any further deterioration of these assets, besides guaranteeing to reimburse them for parts of their losses! If the economy deteriorated further causing more losses, the government would have to bail them out again! This was just like the Japanese banks that were not let to fail by their government, much to the consternation of economic experts from America who blamed this policy as a key reason for Japan's economic slumber.

At any rate, a bigger problem may lie in the huge residential and commercial loans the banks hold on their books, which may face massive defaults if the recession runs longer. "The real hit lies in the trillions of dollars in residential home loans and commercial loans banks hold in whole-loan form on their balance sheets," a managing director of the investment bank Westwood Capital LLC commented.[15] In that event, there would not be enough money for the government to avert a deeper crisis.

In the meantime, like the Japanese banks, U.S. banks continue to restrict lending. Their explanation? They said they would resume lending to good credits. In an economic recession, which is rapidly spreading and may be longer than anyone has thought, along with mounting personal and corporate bankruptcies, where are the banks going to find good credits? While the banks play the waiting game, credit and mortgage spreads remain high, despite aggressive easing by the Fed, discouraging even qualified borrowers.

With the Treasury backtracking on the plan to buy toxic securities to get them off the banks' balance sheets, the United States is walking down the same slippery road traveled by Japan. Injecting capital into the banks may help them deal with further losses from these securities but would not prevent these losses from harming their bottom lines, thus undermining their stock prices. The troubled assets—from mortgage-backed securities to residential and commercial loans to the tune of trillions of dollars—are also clogging the banks' books, to the extent that these discourage banks from adding additional loans to their balance sheets.

No wonder the banks have been reluctant to dole out credits.

The banks' behavior can have enormously adverse effects on the Fed's easy monetary policy to stimulate economic growth. As explained by the president of the Federal Reserve Bank of Dallas, Richard W. Fisher, "[t]he rates that matter most for the economy's recovery—those paid by businesses and households—rose rather than fell [with the Fed's reduction of interest rates]. Those banks with the greatest toxic asset losses were the quickest to freeze or reduce their lending activity. Their borrowers faced higher interest rates and restricted access to funding when these banks raised their margins to ration the limited loans available to reflect their own higher cost of funds as markets began to recognize the higher risk that [these] banks represented."[16] The detrimental impacts on the economy have been noted by Meredith Whitney, a keen observer and respected analyst of the credit scene. "Anyone counting on a meaningful economic recovery will be greatly disappointed. How do I know? I follow credit, and credit is contracting. Access to credit is being denied at an accelerating pace. Large, well-capitalized companies have no problem finding credit. Small businesses, on the other hand, have never had a harder time getting a loan."[17]

The Uncanny Parallel

Several years into the Nikkei crash, a Japanese professor said, "In the late 1980s, people were living in a dream. They did not understand reality. Right now, in a sense, we're in a state of chaos because of that."[18]

Americans have lived in such a dream life since the 1990s. When the tech bubble burst, it took the Fed cutting interest rates to 1 percent to induce a recovery, after the NASDAQ had lost 80 percent of its value.

But the low interest rates were kept low for too long and became the engine driving up housing demand so that every family could realize the American dream. Along came the invention of subprime mortgages to finance the house-buying sprees all around the world. Then came the securitization of mortgage loans and the huge leverages used to issue more of them. This was followed by the ballooning of these mortgage-backed securities on banks' balance sheets because they produced so much profits but also depressed their Tier I capital. Finally, the mortgage-backed securities were sold to unwary investors as safe investments, allowing the banks to issue even more of them. When the collaterals that held this house of cards together—the houses paid for by subprime mortgages—tumbled in value, the structure unraveled.

Not that the U.S. government stood by while the party celebrating ever-higher house prices went on. It encouraged more lending to unqualified buyers with low or no down payments. It deregulated the banking industry by abolishing the Glass-Steagall Act, which was legislated after the 1929 crash to separate commercial from the riskier investment banking activities. And it turned the federal budget into deficits from a surplus of hundreds of billions of dollars just a few years earlier.

Just like Japan of the 1990s, the United States frantically tried later to prop up the banks and other businesses by injecting money it didn't have. Also like Japan, it resorted to the favorite budget expenditure of politicians of all creeds—spending for infrastructure public works. In the process, it strained the central bank's balance sheet and ran up federal budget deficits to be well past the $1 trillion mark.

And the Prospects Look Worse

Japan has continued to enjoy favorable trade balances all these years in the hope of exporting itself out of the morass. Although the trade surpluses were insufficient to bring Japan out of its economic slumber, the United States has no such luxury; its trade deficits have been persistent over the past 30 years (see Figure 1.6). In 2009, the U.S. trade balance deficit has narrowed somewhat since the recession slowed down its imports. However, its trading partners also experienced economic slowdowns or recessions, in many cases even more so than in the United States; as a result, U.S. exports to them declined. In fact, the Euro area economies were expected to contract by more than 4 percent according to the International Monetary Fund, while Japan could shrink by more than 6 percent. Among the emerging markets, growth in China and India would also be slower. The economies of Brazil and Russia would likewise contract. Russia's growth rate swung to a –6 percent in 2009, compared to a growth rate of 8.1 percent in 2007.

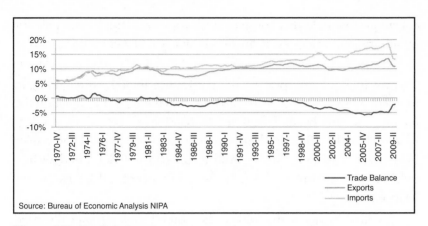

Figure 1.6   Trade balances

At the same time, while the Japanese real estate crash brought down the Nikkei, it did not bring about economic recession.

The U.S. economy, brought down by the subprime mortgage debacle and home price declines, has been in a recession since December 2007, and the prospects of growth have been pared down with each new estimate. Gross domestic product (GDP) had declined for four quarters in a row since the third quarter of 2008, with the worst decline in the first quarter of 2009 at an annual rate of –6.4 percent. The second quarter's performance gave hopes that the recovery had begun, yet it still declined by –0.7 percent, despite increases in federal, state, and local government spending (see Figure 1.7). By all accounts, 2009 was the first annual contraction since the recession in 1991. We will return to this subject in greater detail in Chapter 4, "The New Economic Reality."

Meanwhile, it is important to underscore the Japanese experience indicating that a depression need not happen to drive stock prices lower, to fractions of their highs. Japan's economy did not experience year-on-year contraction until 1998, and there were no two consecutive quarterly declines until the second and third quarters of 1993. All it would take was for the stock market to realize that lower rates of economic growth would prevail for prolonged periods of years.

The discounting mechanism of future prices took Japan's stock market lower.

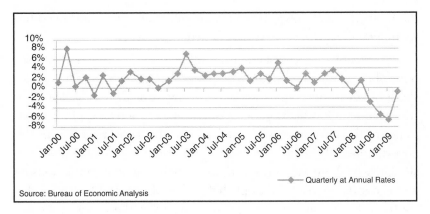

Figure 1.7   GDP quarterly growth rates

Japan and the U.S. Stock Market: Discounting the Economy's Future

Japan's GDP growth did not decelerate significantly for a couple of years following the Nikkei's peak in 1989. In fact, the growth rate was 5.2 percent in 1990, about the same as the previous year. However, the Nikkei lost 46 percent of its value by December 1990! In the eight years following the Nikkei's peak, Japan's GDP still grew at a pace that would make Europe envious. From 1990–1997, Japan's growth rate was a respectable 2.3 percent, but that was a slowdown from an average of 4.7 percent during 1985 and 1989.

That growth continued didn't matter much to the Japanese stock market. By September 1998, the Nikkei had declined an additional 46 percent from the December 1990 level. Overall, although growth continued in the intervening years, the Nikkei lost 68 percent between the peak in December 1989 and an interim low in October 1998. Although the subsequent rally was impressive in terms of percentage, it was short lived and took the Nikkei only to a level of 20,830. It was followed by another stunning loss of 66 percent amid the 2008 global crisis.

What was so remarkable about the Japanese market in those years was that the decline occurred amid economic growth as well as sharply and steadily rising stock prices worldwide—a tailwind that was not available to the United States in its current downturn. Also, the moves up and down were violent, with each rally short lived but seemingly suggesting the worst was over.

Nevertheless, the stock market reflected that the Japanese economy had seen its best growth periods! The U.S. equity market should likewise discount the years of slow growth that lie ahead in America. That it is likely to be so can be seen by a review of the experience of the Japanese real estate bust and the measures taken by the government of Japan to cure its ailing economy to little effect, and the similarity of those measures to the U.S. policy actions in the housing and economic debacle. Except that, as discussed, the United States started off 2009 in worse shape than Japan at the onset of its two decades of economic malaise.

The next chapter turns to the Japanese experience to see how it is analogous to the U.S. stock market.

2

Japan: The Setting Sun

The Japanese believed in their divine destiny as children of the Sun Goddess. Like the sun that rises in the East, it was the natural order of things.

A few years after the end of the Civil War, the enfeebled Tokugawa shogunate's fiefdoms collapsed and the Japanese were united in 1868 under the restored imperial rule of the Meiji dynasty. Like the newly independent America, Japan prospered and modernized its economy by adopting technologies from Europe including railway and communications, banking, and modern weaponry from rifles to cannons, and especially warships.

In 1895, Japan's victory over feudal Qing Dynasty's China, during the conflict to gain control of Korea, completed its transformation from an agrarian economy to an industrial power capable of facing down the West, which it did. In 1904–05, when Japan defeated Russia's Army in Manchuria and destroyed the latter's Navy fleet in "the greatest naval battle since Trafalgar," the Japanese felt that their nation had become a Great Power.

Rising from the Ashes

Japan now was well on its way to becoming a great colonial master, with vast occupied territories in Asia, from Manchuria to the Philippine islands. Then came its disastrous confrontation with America at Pearl Harbor and the ensuing humiliating defeat in

World War II. But the resulting utter destruction only interrupted Japan's momentum. Like the proverbial phoenix rising from the ashes, Japan soon became the second-largest economy of the world, with riches far surpassing any time in its past—certainly more than any of its victors, except the occupying United States. And despite setbacks and slow growth in the past two decades, while its neighbors near and far enjoyed strong economic growth, Japan is still the second-largest economy on earth. Its trade surplus has continued strong as it has sold more and more of its high-tech products to the world, especially America, while collecting income and dividends from its investments in the rest of the world. Its international payments position, though, has deteriorated but remained positive, unlike the United States and several other countries in the Group of 7 economies (see Figure 2.1). In 2009, amid the worst global economic recession in almost a century, Toyota emerged from being a maker of cheap cars to become the world's largest automobile company.

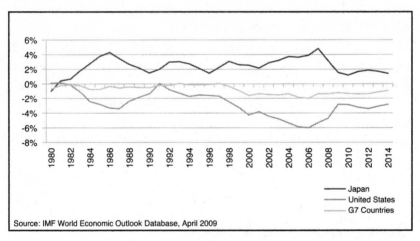

Source: IMF World Economic Outlook Database, April 2009

Figure 2.1   Current account balance: Japan and G7 countries

Products manufactured in Japan have invaded every consumer market in the world, first as cheap imitators of things made in America, France, Britain, and elsewhere in Europe, but in short order as preferred alternatives to their better-known competitors. By the 1980s, Japanese exports had taken over entire industries that heretofore were mainstay manufacturing bases of Western Europe and America, from television and consumer electronics to cameras and watches. Made-in-Japan was no longer a mark of cheap stuff but a stamp of quality and dependable products. That has remained so to this day.

Foreigners, especially Americans, began to bow to the idea that Japan could do no wrong. Management experts, engineers, and everyone else tried to learn from the Japanese business models, from just-in-time inventory to efficient management practices. Entire factories in America were set up to mimic these newfound techniques. General Motors set up the Saturn division to build small fuel-efficient cars—with much fanfare, but forgettable results—vowing to use the much-heralded Japanese management methods to compete head on with the Japanese car manufacturers, although European car makers have been masters at small car manufacturing for decades.

Japan's trade surpluses and treasury soared, its currency up appreciated, and the country became a net creditor to America and the world. And so it remains today. In the process, Japan's economic growth has skyrocketed. In 1988, its GDP growth reached 6.8 percent, 40 percent faster than the other two largest economies: the United States and Germany.

Concurrently, the Japanese stock market climbed up almost in a straight line, fueled by the growing riches, overseas capital from foreign investors eager for profit, and not least of all, speculation by Japanese corporations, many of whose businesses had nothing to do with trading in the stock market. Between 1985 and 1989, the Nikkei 225 index more than tripled for an average of 27.5 percent a year. Its stock market's valuation was outrageously high; its price-to-earnings (P/E) multiples were five times or more of the U.S. market. But lacking an explanation based on more conventional yardsticks (like relationships between expected earnings, which most analysts forecasted to be moderating, and stock prices, which kept rising), many a great prominent Wall Street strategist attributed the high prices to the ample liquidity in the Japanese market. It's like saying that because you have so much money to spend, you should pay more for what you buy. Someone else will surely soon come along and pay higher prices for the same thing! The argument sounded credible enough coming from Wall Street sages that the Japanese index kept rising, incited by streams of liquidity from foreigners, as well as by a fear among the professional investor class of missing the good time and losing out to the competition.

Real estate ownership, or rather speculation, joined the party and prices soared, with plenty of assistance from the banks. In 1990, approximately 22 percent of the mortgages in Japan were held by banks. The banks also made loans to small businesses, amounting to 75 percent of their lending; many of these small business loans were backed by properties. As in the United States, the Japanese government stepped in to promote homeownership, with the Housing Loan Corporation providing low-rate subsidized mortgage rates. Leveraging with real estate was also rampant, as properties were used as loan collaterals with the same assets used to back loans of many times their values from multiple lenders.[1]

Facing the specter of bubbles in the stock and real estate markets, the Bank of Japan quickly raised interest rates. Between 1989 and 1990, the central bank raised the discount rate five times, to 6 percent. It thus reversed the easy-money posture it had taken between 1986 and 1987, whereby it cut by half the discount rate, which is the interest rate it charged on loans it makes to member banks, from 5 percent to 2.5 percent.

The Collapse of the Nikkei

The climb of stock prices stopped, and real estate soon followed.

In 1989, the Nikkei hit the high of 38,957 on the last trading day of the year. This level was never seen again. In the meantime, the Japanese economy went into a slumber, although its GDP did not experience year-on-year contraction in the years following the Nikkei peak. In fact, its growth rate was not that different from Europe's (see Figure 2.2). Compared to the United States, Japan continued to enjoy strong economic growth for a couple of years following the Nikkei peak. In 1990, Japan's GDP grew almost 5.2 percent, followed by a growth rate of 3.35 percent in 1991 when the U.S. economy went into recession. Furthermore, on a quarter-to-quarter basis, Japan's GDP did not record consecutive declines in any two quarters until the second and third quarters of 1993, and those declines were relatively small: –0.67 percent and –0.69 percent, respectively.

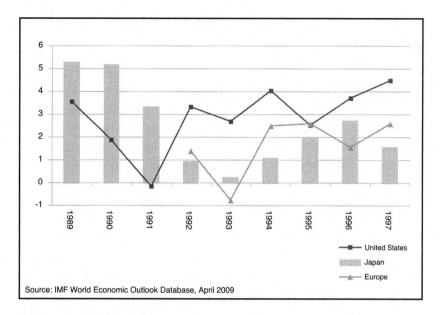

Figure 2.2   Japan's GDP

But Japan's stock market remained range-bound and depressed and lost some 80 percent from the 1989 peak—over the course of 20 years.

Much has been written about the circumstances leading to the crash in December 1989, its aftermath, and the policy measures taken or not taken by the Japanese government to stimulate its economy and revive the stock market. However, for some years, the interest on finding a "cure" for the Japanese enigma seemed to have waned.

Why? As the Nobel laureate Paul Krugman put it, "Western pundits, having once placed Japan on a pedestal, now either prefer not to discuss the subject or to see Japan's failures mainly as an occasion for smug self-congratulation." That would be fine if Japan was [sic] a banana republic. But, Krugman continued, "It's not just that we are talking about a huge economy here, an economy whose woes can drag down a lot of smaller countries with it. What really disturbs me is this: If we don't really understand what has gone wrong in Japan, who's to say the same thing can't happen to us?"[2]

It can't! That has been the consensus even at the high of the
housing craze in the United States. Typically, the discussion would
start with the recognition of the existence of a speculative bubble
similar to Japan's. The concerns then would be brushed off along the
lines summed up by a *Wall Street Journal* reporter:

> In the U.S., investors have begun speculating in the residen-
> tial market by snapping up condominiums and rental proper-
> ties in hot markets like Miami, Las Vegas, Phoenix, Los
> Angeles, and New York. Though regulators and economists
> worry that those markets are especially vulnerable to a down-
> turn, they don't believe a correction will affect the overall
> U.S. housing market. And there hasn't been a major land grab
> in the U.S. by corporations.
>
> "What's more, Japan's boom and bust triggered a banking cri-
> sis. When the bubble burst, borrowers couldn't repay their
> loans, and the banks were stuck with hundreds of billions of
> dollars of dud loans on their books.
>
> While defaults on home mortgages were low, says Barclays
> Capital banking analyst Jason Rogers, "the killer was the loans
> to corporations—to property developers."[3]

Although the article was published in 2005, these words could be
used in 2009 to describe what happened in the United States, except
that the trouble in the U.S. commercial real estate had only just
begun to make its appearance. Such feelings in 2005, however, could
be forgiven, for it would take another three years for the U.S. housing
bubble burst to register on the overall economy. More memorable
were the convictions of many even when the banking crisis in the
United States had already started brewing, as reported in a *USA
Today* article in January 2008:

> U.S. banks also were in stronger financial condition them-
> selves at the outset of the crisis, though they have been forced
> subsequently to swallow massive, multibillion-dollar losses on
> mortgage-linked investments.
>
> "If you look back at Japan, and you think to yourself what was
> their monetary policy like and why did that happen, I don't
> think this is an analogous situation," says Robert Rubin,
> chairman of Citigroup's executive committee and U.S. Trea-
> sury secretary in the late 1990s.[4]

As events have revealed, what had led to the collapse of the Nikkei and the Japanese government's measures to tackle the slump were being repeated here in the United States—albeit with arguably greater speed and sense of urgency. Will that alone make a difference?

Collapse of Real Estate

As bubbles went, the rise of real estate prices in Japan in the 1980s was not unique, in that those who participated in it—from speculators, homeowners, and the regulators and the banks who financed their loans—believed the inflated prices would last forever, or at least until they could sell their speculative purchases with huge profits to someone else coming along later. So the banks kept on extending financing to their customers, and the buyers scrambled to get into the game before prices went higher.

Whether the inflated prices were justified was not at issue.

They bought because they believed prices would go higher and they could unload the assets at higher profits. For those who followed the real estate frenzy in California, Florida, and Las Vegas, this theme sounds familiar. In these markets, people queued up in long lines for the first chance to buy. Sections of subdivisions were often sold out the first day of opening. Their developers then issued lottery tickets to those who had been "unlucky" for not being "selected" for a chance at the other sections the developers would offer to sell, but the offerings were never enough to meet the demand of anxious buyers.

In Japan, prices kept rising to absurd levels. From 1985 to the peak in 1991, house prices in Tokyo more than tripled. Choice properties in the prime Ginza district sold for some $100,000 a square foot in 1989. In Tokyo's other districts, prices were only marginally lower. Overall, real estate prices in Japan's six largest cities increased by 168.5 percent from 1985 to the peak. Adding to the folklore, the small piece of land, about 850 acres, under the Imperial Palace in Tokyo at one time was valued at more than the entire real estate of the state of California. It probably could have been sold for much higher if it had been put up for sale, with potential buyers only too eager to bid up for a trophy property.

Although these numbers made for great headlines, they distracted from the fact that overall Japan's national real estate prices did not rise that dramatically (see Figure 2.3). For all of Japan, the prices rose by 51 percent from 1985 to 1991, as compared to nearly 170 percent in the six big cities. In fact, during the 12 years between 1980 and 1991, the rate of appreciation averaged only 6.6 percent a year.

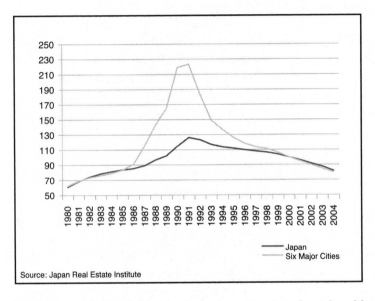

Figure 2.3   Residential land prices: Japan versus six major cities

Additionally, when land prices were dissected into commercial, residential, and industrial segments, the increases in home prices looked more modest by comparison (see Figure 2.4). From 1985 to the peak, home prices in the six cities rose 2.6 times. But the Japan Real Estate Institute commercial index for the six major cities jumped four times, from 128.9 in 1985 to 519.4 in 1991! Also, most of the mortgage defaults were on commercial properties, less so on residential dwellings.

However, what often failed to make newspaper headlines was that, in important measures, the real estate bubble in Japan in the 1980s was more subdued than the current house price bubble burst in the United States—if that were at all possible!

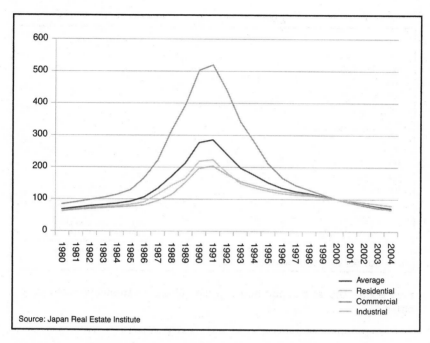

Figure 2.4   Land prices: commercial versus residential

In Japan's big cities, prices rose faster than the average, as one might expect, just the same as prices in the U.S. coastal cities. However, in terms of average home prices, between 2000 and the peak in 2006, average home prices in the United States across 50 states and the District of Columbia as measured by the Federal Housing Finance Agency's House Price Index rose by 61 percent, compared to Japan's 51 percent rise in the national figure (see Figure 2.5). During the same six-year period, the S&P/Case-Shiller indices of home prices show the Composite index of the ten largest cities (Composite 10) rose by 125 percent, and the Composite 20 increased by 106 percent (see Figure 2.6).

From 2000 to 2006, Los Angeles home prices increased by 178.3 percent, according to S&P/Case-Shiller Home Price Indices, only a bit less than price increases in Tokyo. But it was not just one city in the United States that enjoyed the real estate bubble. On the list of cities with real estate prices that inflated as much as the six big Japanese cities were Los Angeles, Miami, Las Vegas, and New York City (see Figure 2.7). And there were more homes in these cities than in Tokyo.

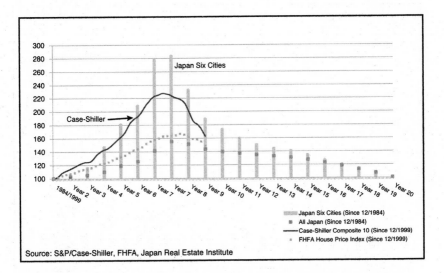

Figure 2.5   U.S. and Japan house price bubbles: national versus major cities

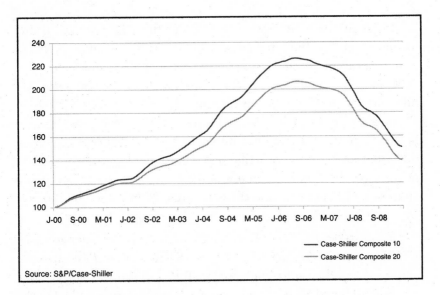

Figure 2.6   U.S. home prices

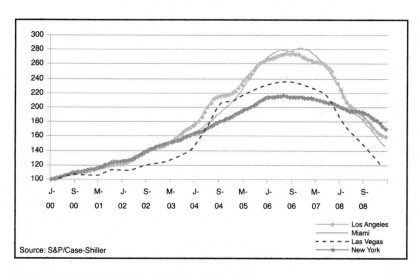

Figure 2.7   Home prices in major U.S. cities

Compared to Japanese commercial properties, the United States commercial real estate enjoyed no less a spectacular rise. Figure 2.8 tracks the returns of the indices representing the United States and Japanese commercial real estate sectors: Japan Real Estate Institute commercial index for the six major cities, the All REIT and Mortgage REIT indices published by the National Association of Real Estate Investment Trusts (NAREIT). Mortgage REITs provide debt financing through their investments in mortgages and mortgage-back securities. Equity REITs own and manage commercial properties; currently they account for some 83 percent of the 134 publicly traded U.S. REITS. The All REIT index includes both types of REITs, as well as the hybrid version across all major property sectors and major geographic regions.

The growth of the REIT industry is relatively recent. After the crash in the late 1980s and "market-stabilizing structural changes," as recounted in a *Harvard Business Review* article in January 2006, real estate experts believed "the industry's transformation...drained considerable risk out of a once notoriously unstable market."[5] The

REIT industry was now in a position to take advantage of investment funds looking for an alternative to equities after the tech stock debacle. "After the tech bust, people wanted real assets they could see and touch and real dividends," said Stephen Lebovitz, president (at the time) of a major shopping mall REIT.[6] So prices rose. "Prices are at levels I never would have guessed a few years ago," said the president of a real estate investment advisory company, which manages some $43 billion of assets.[7]

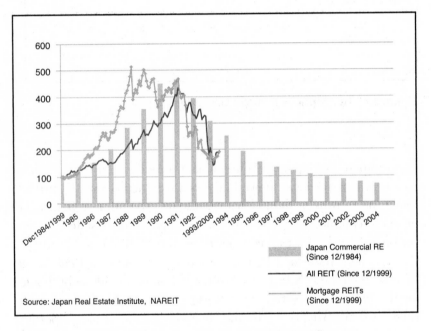

Figure 2.8   Commercial real estate: Japan and United States

Figure 2.8 speaks volumes of what followed. In Japan, commercial real estate began to take off in 1985, only to reach the peak in 1991. In the United States, REITs embarked on a steep rise beginning in 2000 pretty much at the same pace as Japan's and topped out exactly seven years later. Commercial real estate prices have not stopped falling in Japan. In the United States, prices have been declining for several years at a faster rate than commercial properties in Japan.

Industry veterans feared that commercial real estate in the United States could be the "second shoe" to drop in hurting the economy, as Daniel Tishman, chairman and CEO of the Tishman Construction Corporation told CNBC. "We're getting through the single housing real estate market OK but the numbers involved in commercial real estate in all sectors are staggering," he said. "Trillions of dollars are involved in commercial loans. The roll over of those loans in the next 5–7 years is going to happen and the money just isn't there for refinancing."[8]

Since the peak in 2006, U.S. real estate prices of both residential and commercial properties were coming back to the 2003 levels. In Japan, the declines were no less spectacular than the rises, and the fall still continued. Nationally, by 2006, land values had collapsed by 55.9 percent from the peak in 1991, thus wiping out the gains made since 1985. In the biggest six cities, the losses amounted to three-quarters of the values recorded in 1991. For the retail property sector, the damage was even more pronounced, at 86.9 percent.

The Stock Market and Real Estate

In Japan, the Nikkei 225 index reached its historic high on the last day of 1989, but the run-up in real estate prices pressed on for another two years.

In the United States, the tech bubble burst during 2000–2002 hardly affected house prices. If anything, investors shunned equities and piled on to buy real estate, borrowing beyond their capability, while lenders were only too happy to oblige. Once the equity market began its rally in 2003 and went on to make new highs, the twin bull markets of real estate and stocks fed on each other, with no insignificant help from the Federal Reserve, which continued to keep interest rates low.

As in Japan, prices of real estate and stocks in the United States were spoon-fed on air; see Figure 2.9. In Japan, the *Keiretsu*, with interlocking ownership among associated companies helped maintain the artificially inflated prices, while easy credit allowed the owners to delay the recognition of the lower market prices.

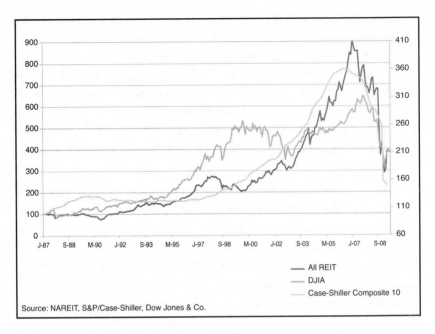

Figure 2.9   U.S. stocks versus real estate

In the United States, home prices rose on the back of accommodating real estate appraisers who never valued a property below the
prices indicated in the mortgage applications. Lenders, for their part,
were ready to accept what was claimed, often without documenta-
tion, much less verification of the veracity of the claims. Why? The
lenders only acted in their best interest, for they could immediately
get the mortgages off their balance sheets to financial firms that were
eager to convert them into mortgage-backed securities, and then sell
them off to ready buyers, from banks to institutional investors and
municipalities.

This process was made possible by the creative minds on Wall
Street, many of whom graduated from top universities with degrees
in mathematics, engineering, and computer sciences. Using obscure
math and computer modeling that even their superiors hardly understood, and backed by assumptions that were on the edge of reality
and historical probabilities, the mortgages underwritten and sold by
banks and mortgage lenders were sliced and diced into securities that
received top triple-A ratings but were paying higher yields than comparable corporate bonds.

Everyone came out a winner! The rating agencies received lucrative fees from those who issued the securities ("please your customers!"), the white-shoe bankers got their huge fees, and the lenders got the mortgages off their books while retaining the profits—all profits and no risks. Also, the investors got the bond yields higher than the yields that top ratings normally command.

Or did they?

Although the rating agencies professed the integrity of their process, while getting paid by those whom they rated, the worthiness of the securities was based entirely on the assumptions that home prices would go on rising and the home buyers would be able to pay the monthly installments until their mortgages were paid off—albeit with the proviso that a small number of them, well within the margin of tolerance by the mortgage issuers and the rating agencies, could default.

However, history never indicated that home prices would keep on rising while fewer and fewer people could afford them, especially when renting was cheaper than ownership.

Many of the prospective home buyers could not qualify for the mortgages in the first place. No matter. Urged on by the mortgage brokers and encouraged by the lenders, those who dreamed to have a house of their own were talked into believing that they could afford to buy the houses of their dreams. The buyers did not need to come up with a down payment; in fact, they could borrow more than the house's price, pocketing the difference for spending on a new car or such American birthrights. Interest rates were too high for them to get the loans? No problem. The mortgage would start with an artificial rate, based on short-term maturities as if the mortgage would be paid off in a few years. These initial rates would be significantly lower than the market rates for mortgages of conventional 30-year maturities, thus allowing the borrowers to qualify. The borrowers also could elect to make payments less than the required amounts, adding the differences to their principals. Also, payments toward the principals were accordingly delayed.

When the aptly named "teaser" rate expired, the mortgage rate would be reset. Unfortunately, the reset rate would be much higher, if the then-prevailing market rates were higher. Also, a large margin would be added to the market rates prevailing at the time of the reset;

the less credit-worthy a borrower, the higher the margin. Additionally, payments toward the principal would be added. The principal could also be higher than it was originally due to the addition of unpaid interest stemming from the difference between the "teaser" rates and the higher prevailing market rates.

Suddenly, the home buyers found themselves unable to pay the monthly mortgage installments, which often trebled the initial payments upon the rate reset. With little savings to make up for the difference, or jobless, as increasingly numbers of homeowners found themselves, the home buyers defaulted.

The dominoes began to fall. There were more homes on the market than willing buyers, many of which sat in partly finished developments covered with weeds and pillaged by vandals.

But if the unwitting buyers were the only ones who had to pay the price for their naiveté, the real estate bust in America may have been contained among the unfortunate few.

In fact, until two years after home prices had peaked in 2006, the pundits and market sages still predicted that the real estate market would soon recover and higher prices would return. The stock market dutifully followed the prognosis and made new historic highs in October 2007 while the Federal Reserve kept raising interest rates to prick the real estate bubble that had already begun to leak. Indeed, the Fed raised the key Fed funds rate until the last rate hike in July 2006, and it kept the rate at 5.25 percent until September 2007 when it was hurriedly cut by 0.5 percent, instead of the usually more measured pace of 0.25 percent. In retrospect, the economic recession was dated to have begun in the fourth quarter of 2007.

The stock market climb helped conceal the deterioration of the securities that were created from the mortgages backed by the values of the homes, whose prices were coming down. And these securities declined in value as if they were "junk" bonds, despite their top ratings, as larger numbers of mortgage borrowers were unable to make the monthly payments. It turned out that a lot of people had bought these securities because they had been considered safe, with their very top ratings, better than the debts of countries like Italy and some others in Europe.

From small towns in far-away Norway to little banks in Iceland that had grown bloated from unchecked lending, from municipalities in the United States to pension plans of government workers and corporate employees alike, people had bought these mortgage securities because they had been rated as safe by the rating agencies. Importantly, banks in America and many other countries, especially in Europe, had stocked up on these securities.

When it came time to assign values to these securities, the banks and everyone else found there were no bidders and their values, intricately linked to home values, were fast declining. Many municipal governments found themselves unable to meet their budget obligations. But the fate of the banks was more ominous.

As soon as it became known that the mortgage securities—now called toxic assets, as if they were the chemicals dumped into the Love Canal in upstate New York—carried on the banks' books faced huge write-offs, the banks' very solvency and the viability of the global banking system were called into question.

The transfer of the losses of real estate prices in Japan to its economy and stock market 20 years ago hardly differed from America's more recent experience. If anything, the Japanese sufferers of the debacle were in better shape to weather the storm than their American counterparts nowadays.

Whereas it was the securitization of home mortgages that linked home values and the weak borrowers directly to the U.S. banks and the rest of the economy, in Japan it was the corporations that speculated in real estate and the interlocking relationships in the *kereitsu* that brought the plight of real estate speculators to the banks that lent to them.

The Keiretsu are a metamorphosis of the traditional and powerful family-owned conglomerates called *Zaibatsu* that the occupying American authorities had attempted to dissolve. In its reincarnation, the Kereitsu consists of groups of companies with interlocking ownerships and business dealings. The affiliated companies in each group own each other's stocks, and each company shares ownership in all companies in the group. They provide financing to one another and make investments together, and their officers are appointed to serve on the other group members' boards of directors. The cross-holding of shares and interlocking business dealings with each other characterize them not much less than sister companies of U.S. conglomerates. In fact, it was the failure of the Americans to dissolve the Zaibatsu effectively that spawned the Keiretsu to replace their predecessors without changing the ways they did business.

As a fast-growing economy in a country with limited land availability, real estate has been considered a prized possession by the Japanese. When a company wanted to dispose of a piece of property, the buyer would be another member of the Keiretsu, who considered real estate a trophy possession. And, of course, the sale price would be transacted at a higher value than what the seller had paid. The left hand took off what the right hand was holding, recording a profit at the same time!

As real estate prices climbed, corporate Japan issued stocks and borrowed extensively to invest in real estate and booked the profits by selling to their corporate brethren, at higher and higher prices after each transaction. The real estate properties, which were valued at higher prices, were used as collateral for more borrowings and speculation.

These interlocking relationships and intra-group pricing transfers of real estate transactions help explain why real estate prices kept on rising for two years after the Nikkei 225 had reached its peak in December 1989. Although the values of the stocks held by the Keiretsu declined, their real estate holdings were circulated within their group members at artificial prices, thereby continuing the appearance of healthy valuation.

In the United States, the mortgage securities backed by the inflated home prices ended up on the books of every major financial institution as well as on the books of pension plans, endowments and foundations, municipalities, and individuals, both here and abroad. The linkage was widespread throughout the United States and the global economy, and once the unraveling started, no one sector was left unaffected. However, unlike Japan, the trading of these securities was transacted at arm's length and at prevailing market prices. Also, the values of these securities were marked to market, and losses were supposed to be disclosed at quarterly earnings announcements.

The relative transparency of the American markets led to a dire consequence—that is, losses in home prices were quickly reflected in mortgage default rates. As it became apparent that the default rate was rising rapidly, the values of the mortgage securities were marked down, and the losses suffered by the financial institutions prompted their stock prices to crash and their capital depleted to the point of insolvency.

Thus, in the United States, the decline of home prices led to the twin crash of the entire real estate sector and the stock market, wiping out trillions of dollars of net worth of financial firms as well as the wealth of individuals. All of these losses occurred within about a year, with real estate prices peaking in 2006, while stocks reached historic highs in October 2007. Within five quarters, the Dow Jones Industrial Average lost 54 percent. This was a significantly larger loss in the same time frame experienced by the Nikkei 225; by May 1991, it had lost only 34 percent from the peak. It would take the Nikkei more than a year later, until August 1992, to record a loss similar to the Dow's at its worst level. From this low, the Nikkei enjoyed a substantial rally, rising 47 percent in a little more than a year. The Dow also benefited from a rally after the low in March 2009, gaining an impressive 30 percent in three months.

Thus, two world-shaking events, which happened some twenty years apart, precipitated by similar circumstances although not entirely identical, have so far resulted in losses, financial and otherwise, of similar magnitudes. For the United States, the question is to avoid a similar loss of time. But apart from forecasts, hopes, and pontifications from market sages, government officials, and politicians alike, the United States is following the same prescriptions that have not kept Japan from its fate, nor helped it recover from the two decades' slumber.

Fixing the System

The Bank of Japan's conduct of its monetary policy after the twin crash of its stock and real estate markets has been subject to much criticism. As the economy grew sluggish, the Bank started to cut the discount rate in January 1986, to 4.5 percent from 5 percent. That year the economy recorded a gain of only 3 percent, slowing from 5 percent in 1985, and lagging the United States at 3.5 percent. And the bank kept on reducing rates, in part, reportedly, at the U.S. urging to spur investments in Japan and help attract imports from the United

States in an effort to reduce the two countries' trade imbalance. In fact, the Plaza Accord in 1985 engineered by the U.S. government to reverse the rising trend of the U.S. dollar had led to the rapid appreciation of the yen—indeed the fall of the dollar across the board—and badly hurt Japan's exports and cut into its economic growth. The increasingly monetary easing did not stop until the discount rate had reached 2.5 percent in February 1987, but it did help the economy grow at a faster rate of 3.8 percent in 1987, just slightly ahead of the much bigger U.S. economy at 3.4 percent. The overheating, however, set in soon thereafter as the Nikkei and real estate prices raced higher.

Ironically, this was the same easy monetary regime under Federal Reserve Chairman Alan Greenspan that helped create the real estate rush in the United States after the 2000 recession. Although operating under different circumstances, including fear of a prolonged recession after the 9/11 attack, the Fed did keep interest rates low for too long, even after signs of overheating in the housing market were palpitating.

In May 1989, Bank of Japan reversed course. For the first time in over two years, it hiked the discount rate. Once started, it kept raising rates upward right through the Nikkei's crash in December 1989, and it did not stop until August 1990 when the discount rate reached 6 percent. By then, the Nikkei had already lost 40 percent, and the economy has slowed markedly. However, the Bank of Japan kept the discount rate static until July 1991, when it was cut to 5.5 percent.

This slow action by the Bank of Japan has been the focus of criticism and has been blamed for the lengthening of Japan's economic malaise. A prominent critic of the Bank of Japan's "exceptionally poor monetary policymaking" was a U.S. economist who blamed the failure to lower interest rates in the early 1990s for the country's economic malaise and its deflationary environment. Now, as chairman of the Federal Reserve, the former Princeton economist Ben Bernanke wants to make sure that the same mistakes are not repeated in the United States.

Be that as it may, the fact was, Japan's economy did not fall into a recession in accordance with the technical definition of two consecutive quarters of negative growth until the second half of 1993 (see Figure 2.10). By then, the discount rate had dropped to 2.5 percent. In September 1995, it was further reduced to 0.5 percent, helping the Nikkei to rise by some 20 percent in a year's time, even though before then, starting in early 1994, the U.S. Federal Reserve had sharply tightened up its monetary stance. Nevertheless, the Bank of Japan stayed the course and cut its discount rate to 0.1 percent in September 2001, as the Fed serially reduced interest rates in the United States. In contrast, the U.S. economy had fallen into a recession even before the housing bubble burst was recognized and the banking crisis became apparent. Since the start of the recession dated at December 2007, the United States has seen only one quarter of positive GDP growth and four quarters of consecutive declines, as shown in Figure 2.10.

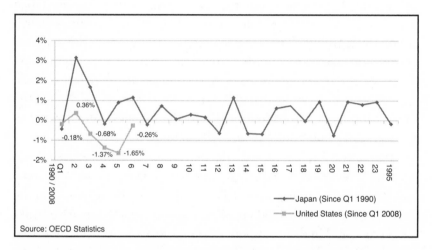

Source: OECD Statistics

Figure 2.10   Japan and United States: post-bubble GDP growth (quarter-on-quarter percent changes)

The loans taken on by the banks during the real estate bubble, however, were let to stay on the Japanese banks' balance sheets, just as the toxic mortgage-backed securities still remain on the U.S. banks' books. As the values of the underlying real estate properties used as their collaterals fell, the loans turned sour. By 1995, Japan's banks reported $280 billion of nonperforming loans; however, this figure turned out to be vastly understated. Between 1995 and 2003, $318 billion of nonperforming loans was written off. But new ones kept appearing, and by March 2002, nonperforming loans had reached $330 billion, or 8.4 percent of total lending.

By 1997, the Japanese banking system was in full crisis. In response, the government injected capital to the banks through a series of actions over the next two years. It also bought out the bankrupt Long Term Credit Bank and Nippon Credit Bank. In total, through a variety of measures, the Japanese government spent $495 billion, or 12 percent of its GDP, for the bailout of its banks.[9]

Japan's government stimulus had started soon after the real estate bubble burst. In 1994, it cut income taxes; again in 1998, it temporarily cut taxes by 2 trillion yen. Between 1992 and 1995, the government attempted six different spending programs worth about half-trillion U.S. dollars. For the second half of the decade, Japan launched a series of stimulus and public works programs worth another half-trillion dollars. All told, in the aftermath of the twin real estate and stock market crash, the Japanese authorities embarked on all measures of monetary easing, as well as fiscal policies worth approximately 28 percent of its GDP in the 1990s—about twice the total of the fiscal and bailout programs the United States has put in the works to combat the banking crisis and its aftermath.

If this brief recounting of the Japanese banking crisis and the resulting government responses sounds familiar, it is because they have been the same measures taken by the U.S. government and the Federal Reserve in the 2008 banking debacle. As the Japanese banks have recovered and their nonperforming loans have decreased to a reported 3.5 percent of total lending, the largest U.S. banks also have showed signs of stabilization, although their renewed profitability has been in large part due to the subsidized capital from taxpayers while lending standards have remained restricted. Furthermore, smaller local banks have continued to struggle, and bankruptcies have risen among them, including some large regional institutions like Colonial BancGroup, Inc. of Montgomery, Georgia.

Significantly, the Bank of Japan has kept its discount rate at 0.1 percent throughout these years. Its economic growth has resumed, but only at a moderate pace, averaging 2.1 percent between 2002 and 2007. In 2008, the economy contracted at an annual rate of 0.6 percent, and the contraction has accelerated in 2009 along with the global economy. In the real estate market, prices have continued to languish, in both commercial and residential sectors, as shown in

Figure 2.11. Commercial properties in Tokyo, Osaka, and Nagoya began to show some life in 2005 and continued with a gain of 8.9 percent in 2006, while residential land prices rose 2.8 percent. But outside of these cities, property values have continued to drop, falling for the fifteenth consecutive year by 2.8 percent.[10] Then 2008 came with the global real estate bust, and land prices fell 5.5 percent, with Tokyo losing 6.5 percent.

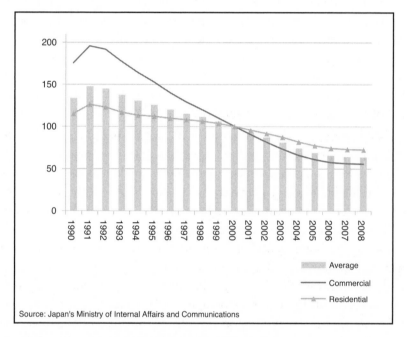

Source: Japan's Ministry of Internal Affairs and Communications

Figure 2.11   Japan: real estate prices continue to drop

That Japan's economy was weakened and its stock and real estate markets remained in a slump during the first half of the 1990s may have been in part attributable to Japan's purported policy mistakes. But, in the subsequent years, the Bank of Japan's zero interest rate policy and the government's huge stimulus programs could be hardly held accountable for the stubbornly continuing weakness of its economy and asset markets, especially amid a strong global expansion. If anything, Japan's policy measures have produced two decades of short but violent cycles of booms and busts in the stock market, with disappointingly little positive effect on its economy and asset prices. In fact, as observers of the Japanese economy have increasingly grown frustrated at the lack of explanation for the persistence of the Japanese malaise, some have resorted to exogenous factors like the aging of the population, the Japanese tendency to save rather than spend like Americans, or just simply the unwillingness to spend.

Or maybe there is a simpler explanation. That is, Japan is a mature economy that will not grow by application of Keynesian and traditional stimulus economic policies. Like a person who has eaten to his fill and cannot absorb more food intake, the limit of growth has come to Japan. Any increase in income will be hoarded, not spent. Also, the point may have been reached where the desire to hoard is no longer a powerful enough motivation for Japan to produce the incremental rate of growth that was the norm when it was repairing from war damages and the country was still poor. And the stock market of Japan has simply reflected this reality.

Of course, this explanation is hardly applicable to the open U.S. economy where getting rich is ingrained in the culture. But it also suggests that the actions of economic policy makers may face similar structural changes that may only evolve slowly before the U.S. economy can return to a stronger foundation on a sounder balance sheet and healthier economic growth. Intervention by the government and monetary authorities can only distort the business cycles, creating artificial booms inevitably followed by busts, precipitated often by realization in the official circles that they may have done too much interfering with the natural dynamics of a global open market economy, whether by keeping interest rates too low for too long or stimulating demand through tax cuts and deficit spending.

In summary, we have noted that when artificial stimulation of the economy, by way of easy monetary policy, was coupled with a speculative craze in real estate and the stock market, the combined brew produced only disasters. This is what happened to Japan in the 1980s, which no measures of fiscal or monetary cures have so far reversed. In the 2008 crash, the real estate bubble in the United States that was more inflated than Japan's was further fueled, in addition to monetary easing, by federal budget deficit spending, unchecked financial speculation with mortgage-backed securities, and unprecedented leveraging in all sectors of the economy. The resulting collapse in

U.S. stock prices has been faster and larger than what Japan experienced immediately following the 1989 peak. The U.S. government has so far responded to the crisis with measures similar to those of Japan, albeit with arguably greater speed. Will that be enough to make the difference? And what does that mean to savers and long-term investors?

These are the topics to be discussed in the next two chapters.

3

The Root Causes: Leveraging and Excess

Remember the implosion of the hedge fund firm Long Term Capital Management (LTCM) in 1998? Led by the defunct Salomon Brothers' famed trader John Meriwether, and with a roster of Nobel laureates and celebrity Harvard professors as well as a former Federal Reserve Board vice chairman among its leadership, LTCM was a practitioner of fixed income arbitrage. Its expertise was investing in fixed income securities that carried higher yields, and it hedged with short positions in lower-yielding bonds. No matter that the higher-yielding bonds were also among the riskiest—the difference in the yields of the two types of securities accounted for the profits of the trades. Because the yield differentials were small, a typical arbitrage of this type required leverages. To obtain a return in the low double-digit percentage (say, 10–12 percent annually), often a leverage of 20 to 30 times of capital is necessary.

For a few years, LTCM was able to generate much greater returns. In 1995—its first full year of operation—it produced returns of an eye-popping 43 percent after all fees and expenses. In the next year, it recorded a profit of 41 percent by leveraging to far greater extents through borrowings from its brokers and banks as well as using derivatives.

In 1998, with an investment capital of $4.8 billion, LTCM held $200 billion of securities in different fixed income assets. It further leveraged its holdings with derivatives worth $1.2 trillion in notional values.

The bets that LTCM made were on a fairly diversified portfolio of securities, ranging from U.S. Treasuries to mortgage-backed securities and international bonds issued by foreign governments, including

Russia, as well as equity index options and merger risk arbitrage. Then the Asian economic crisis came in 1997, followed by a speculative attack on Russia's currency, the ruble. The Central Bank of Russia attempted to defend its currency, losing $6 billion in the process in November 1997 alone. Its effort was in vain. In August 1998, Russia devalued its currency and defaulted on its domestic debt, some of which was owned by LTCM; furthermore, Russia placed a moratorium on payment to foreign creditors. These supposedly "can't-happen" world events led to a broad-based decline in value of fixed income assets across the globe and brought down the values of the securities underlying LTCM-leveraged portfolios, just like the mortgage-backed securities in the 2008 crisis.

These rare world events, although catastrophic, were not enough to be fatal to LTCM. It was the huge leverages that precipitated LTCM's collapse. One of the trades that it had on its books was long/short on off-the-run bonds against on-the-run treasuries. At the end of September 1998, the spread between these two securities had widened out from 5 basis points or five hundredths of 1 percent to 15 basis points. It was a big move, but it was not fatal on an unleveraged portfolio of $4.8 billion. The loss would have been a mere $4.8 million, or one-tenth of 1 percent. But multiplied by the amounts of leverage combined with other worse-performing positions, like the default of the Russian bonds, the losses were gargantuan. On August 21, LTCM reportedly lost $550 million. On September 21, the firm was said to have lost an additional $500 million.

LTCM was now caught in this avalanche of lower marking-to-market of the values of its holdings. This was like the financial institutions in 2008, which had to mark their toxic assets to the much lower market values. Thus marked to market, these securities were worth less as collaterals for the loans taken out to leverage the firm's capital. Furthermore, much of LTCM's portfolio was in illiquid securities, which were difficult to price and even more difficult to sell. It had to come up with additional capital to make up for the marked-to-market losses to meet collateral obligations on its borrowings and derivatives. Failing that, it would have to liquidate its assets in a fire sale. In that event, it was feared that other financial institutions holding similar assets could be thrust into financial trouble, creating a systemic breakdown of the entire banking system.

LTCM was a negligible presence in the then-$9 trillion U.S. economy. It was not even the largest hedge fund among the hundreds of them. Certainly, it was a dwarf compared to the investment bank Lehman Brothers Holdings, the very institution that was abandoned to bankruptcy in 2008 by Henry Paulson, President Bush's newly appointed Secretary of the Treasury, fresh from his perch as Chairman and CEO of Goldman Sachs. Yet its failure was feared to have such dire consequences on the U.S. banking system and the economy that the Federal Reserve had to assemble a consortium of leading banks—including Goldman Sachs—to bail it out, and in the process, put LTCM out of business.

As the mortgage debacle of 2008 unfolded, the entire U.S. economy was a leveraged investment of giant and unprecedented proportions. It was not just one hedge fund. Every sector of the U.S. economy was leveraged: Not only the homeowners who bought houses they couldn't afford and without down payments, but also the banks that originated the mortgages and securitized them into trading instruments, and, in particular, the entire network of global banks. These institutions now found themselves regretful owners of what became called toxic assets, from Bear Stearns to Wachovia Bank, Lehman Brothers and Citigroup, Bank of America, to Royal Bank of Scotland of the UK and a host of other international banks. Unlike LTCM, however, the U.S. economy made leveraged bets not on diversified portfolios of securities but on the viability of only one asset: the subprime mortgages taken out by borrowers who were deemed uncreditworthy. And the leveraging was even much higher.

The LTCM film clip was replayed in 2008.

How it came to be that the mortgages on relatively low-priced homes brought the entire United States and the global banking system to the brink of collapse has been blamed on many things, including the greedy bankers and their creed. However, what has mostly *not* been pointed out was that the root causes were the leveraging and excess accumulation of risks that were built on these innocuous securities that had well served the expansion of housing opportunities to millions of Americans. While Wall Street created them, the bankers acted on the opportunities they saw in response to the insatiable demand for housing ownership. The subprime borrowers bought the houses they couldn't afford because homeownership was encouraged by government policies. Isn't it part of the American dream? And, of course, there were those speculators who flipped houses for profits. Aren't there always speculators?

In all of this, the participants were aided by the Federal Reserve (and its counterparts abroad), who indulged in an easy monetary regime despite visible signs of a bubble in the real estate market, and the federal government pumping money into the system with rising budget deficit spending.

In 2008, the excess and leverages that fed off Wall Street's profit motives and government policies collided with the collapse of home prices and drove the U.S. banking system to the brink of bankruptcy. In the process, the U.S. and global economies were pushed into a deep recession, and stock markets worldwide sank into the worst equity bear market since the 1929 depression.

Housing as Leveraged Securities

Real estate was not supposed to have such a dire impact on stock prices. The year before and after the Black October crash in 1987, home prices continued to advance at an annualized rate of about 8 percent. During the tech bubble burst, home prices rose about 9.3 percent a year. Conversely, while stocks quickly recovered after the October 1987 crash and then embarked on a spectacular run-up until 2000, housing went into a slump between 1990 and 1993 with prices declining cumulatively by some 8 percent.

Home prices bottomed out by early 1994 but continued to languish near the bottom for three years amid an equity bull market (see Figure 3.1). During these years, home prices edged up by a negligible rate of about 1 percent a year, hardly compensating for inflation and borrowing costs. Overall, home prices were stagnant for more than 8 years after the peak was recorded in October 1989. During this time, the Dow almost tripled in value, appreciating at an annualized rate of 14.3 percent!

That real estate and stocks moved in their own ways reflects the different factors that drive their prices up or down. Stock prices are determined primarily by expectations of future company earnings.

Thus, the prices of individual stock certificates bearing the share of fractional ownership in a company will typically rise or fall as investors form their views—and the extent of their confidence in these views— about the future rate of growth in the earnings of a company.

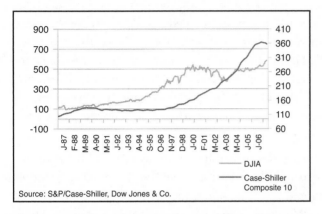

Figure 3.1   U.S. stocks versus home prices 1987-2006

For real estate, which over time is a depreciating asset due to wear and tear, inflation and demand are key drivers. In periods of high inflation, costs of construction and land values rise. In times of high employment, wages tend to rise and workers have more confidence in their jobs. These factors normally drive up demand and prices. Although overlapping to some extent, these different fundamental drivers permit real estate to have low correlation with movements in the stock market. In some periods, they even move in opposite directions, as they did in the 1970s; during this time, stocks stagnated while home prices marched upward.

Following the tech stocks' burst in 2000, housing was transformed into a profit-making machine for financial firms and a source of outsized bonuses for Wall Street deal makers. Houses became a kind of security, like stocks and bonds, that could be traded, bought, and sold, as well as leveraged like any other securities. The mechanism for this transformation is the securitization of home mortgages, which are structured into leveraged securities whose values depend on house prices and whose default risks depend in many cases on borrowers with poor credit histories.

The Securitization of Home Mortgages

It used to be that the neighborhood banks and mortgage lenders would retain the mortgage loans on their books after they had made the loans to their customers. They collected the interest and payments against the principal amounts and performed other functions to service the loans until they were paid off. More recently, these tasks are being parceled out to different players in the mortgage industry. In particular, the firms that originate the loans are not keeping the mortgages; they quickly sold to other investors. The mortgages are thus securitized and become mortgage-backed securities (MBS). Like other bonds, these securities pay interest out of the combined mortgage payments from homeowners.

Mortgage securitization was a useful innovation. Through intermediaries like pension plans and mutual funds, it allowed other investors, institutional and individual alike, to supply funds to the housing industry, making more loans available to home buyers. However, investors in these investment vehicles can be many layers of labyrinth-like intermediation removed from the mortgage originators. Also, by shipping off the risks of the mortgages to other investors, the originators' profit motive turned to making as many loans as possible. Previously they were concerned with not getting paid for the loans. It now becomes a worry of others, supposedly sophisticated investment bankers, traders, and investors who know what they were doing.

The securitization started with the originators of the mortgages selling them to a third-party institution. Such third parties could be a private-sector bank, such as Countrywide Financial or Lehman Brothers, or the government-sponsored entities (GSEs) Fannie Mae and Freddie Mac. These institutions collect mortgages and package the mortgages of like characteristics together into mortgage-backed securities. As the coupon and principal payments are made on the mortgages, they are passed through to the MBS holders.

The MBS issuers don't keep the mortgages either. The mortgages are repackaged and sold to other investors, who may hold them or again repackage them to sell to yet other repackagers. Unknown to the home buyers, in intricate ways, their homes have been bought and sold many times over, although the names on the ownership deeds may not have changed. The prices of the houses had better keep going up; otherwise, the last MBS buyers will be left empty handed, as they eventually were.

Subprime and Other Borrowers

Not all mortgages are created equal. Depending on underwriting standards and borrowers' credit histories, mortgages are differentiated in various ways. Principally, they are divided into four categories:

- **Prime** mortgages conform to standards set by Federal National Mortgage Association (Fannie Mae) and Federal Home Loan Mortgage Corporation (Freddie Mac) in terms of the loan amount, down payment, income, credit history, and property condition. These are conforming mortgages.

  The nonconforming mortgages are jumbo, Alt-A, and subprime.

- **Subprime** mortgages are loans to people with poor credit histories.

- **Alt-A** mortgages are loans to borrowers presumably with good credit, but the underwriting allows such terms as no income verification and little or no down payment; they are sometimes referred to as "liars' loans."

- **Jumbo** mortgages are those to prime borrowers that exceed the then-prevailing limit of $417,000.

At the start of the housing boom, mortgage activity was mostly concentrated in conforming loans. In 2001, conforming mortgages accounted for 68 percent of mortgage origination. Of the nonconforming loans, only 39 percent was securitized into MBS. In 2006, the ratios were reversed: 59 percent of mortgage origination was in nonconforming loans, of which 96 percent turned into MBSs.

Of the $1.3 trillion of MBS issuance in 2001, 73 percent was conforming. In 2006, total mortgage issuance had jumped by 53 percent, but conforming mortgages declined 16.8 percent, with the discrepancy made up entirely of nonconforming loans. By then, nonconforming MBS issuance had more than quatrupled to $1 trillion, from only $240 billion in 2001, and accounted for 53.3 percent of all MBS issuance (see Figure 3.2).

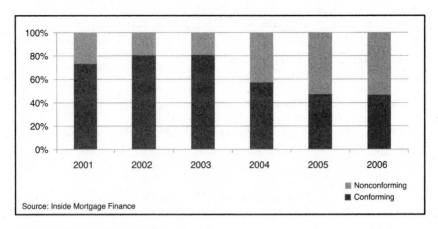

Figure 3.2   Mortgage issuance

Of the nonconforming mortgages, subprime jumped by 415 percent from the 2001 amount and rose to 43.4 percent of nonconforming MBS issuance from 35 percent in 2001 (see Figure 3.3). Combining with Alt-A mortgages, MBS issuance collaterized by mortgages issued to borrowers with poor credit rose by 727 percent between 2001 and 2006. In 2001, such loans accounted for only 7.4 percent of all MBS issuance. They had increased to 42 percent by the time house prices peaked in 2006; of nonconforming MBS, Alt-A and subprime accounted for 79 percent.

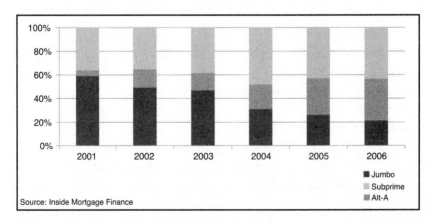

Figure 3.3   Nonconforming MBS issuance

In fact, the growth of MBS issuance was entirely due to the increase of Alt-A and subprime mortgages. Together they rose by $715 billion between 2001 and 2006, while total MBS issuance increased by $610 billion.

Figure 3.4 tracks the increase of subprime and Alt-A MBS issuance and the rise of home prices using the S&P Case-Shiller index (composite of 20 cities) between 2001 and 2006. They moved in locked steps: The expansion of mortgages to poor credit borrowers helped home price increases by bringing in marginal buyers and creating additional demand for housing ownership. Remarkably, both house prices and MBS issuance flatlined between 2005 and 2006. The rise of home prices stopped, while subprime Alt-A issuance tried to push ahead, but increasing at only 2.1 percent in 2006 from the previous year.

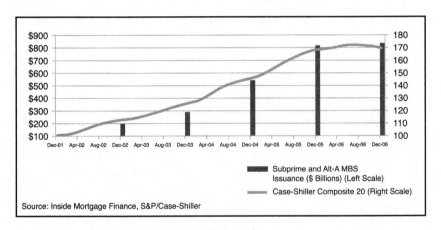

Figure 3.4   Subprime MBS and home prices

There is only so much artificiality that Wall Street and easy money can create!

Excess: Upside-Down Pyramid

The securitization of housing did not stop with mortgage-backed securities.

Like home mortgages, securitization also included other debts, such as commercial real estate bonds and corporate loans. These securitized loans are called asset-backed securities (ABSs).

The next step in the securitization chain is to bundle all these MBSs and ABSs into special-purpose companies called Collaterized Debt Obligations (CDOs). CDOs are essentially bonds that are backed by pools of other bonds, including MBSs. Each bond or share of a CDO represents a fraction of the underlying pool of assets. To attract a wide spectrum of investors with different risk appetites, CDOs are sliced and diced into tranches that have different risk and return characteristics. Investors in the lowest-rated tranche absorb the first losses until it is exhausted. The remaining losses are then allocated to the next-lowest-rated tranche, and so on. The highest-rated tranche does not incur a loss until all the tranches below it are wiped out. A six-pack structure has six tranches or levels of subordination. This is how the top tranche gets AAA ratings from rating agencies. In a typical CDO, a large percentage of the bonds receive the highest rating even though they were collaterized by MBSs that were in turn collaterized by subprime home loans.

CDOs may also own bonds issued by other CDOs, including those that have been repackaged from the lowest-rated MBSs. Like a pyramid, the ratings are exponentially removed from the real quality of the underlying assets at each higher layer of the derivatives of the CDO structure. This is where mortgage-backed securities get really complicated and confusion reigns over the risks of these structures. If a CDO owns bonds issued by other CDOs, it is called CDO-squared. A CDO-squared can be cash or synthetic. A cash CDO-squared is a CDO that owns other CDOs, which may be backed by a portfolio of bonds. A synthetic CDO does not own the actual MBS or the CDOs that own them. Instead, it holds a portfolio of credit default swaps (CDSs). Through CDSs, synthetic CDOs can gain exposure to the underlying reference bonds.

If all this sounds confusing and complicated, that's because it is. CDOs are notoriously hard to value, and market prices are difficult to obtain even in the best of times. As legend has it, it would take a Cray supercomputer 48 hours to construct the cash flows on the first three tranches of CDO, not to mention the next-lower-rated and riskiest tranches.[1] So, to cut through the complexities, traders rely on indices with names like ABX, CMBX, CDX, and LCDX to price the CDOs they trade, as opposed to the underlying values of the assets. These indices are constructed to reflect specific types and ratings of a basket of securities. For example, ABX consists of credit default swaps based on subprime mortgages, whereas CMBX are derived from commercial mortgage–backed securities. Each of these indices are further divided into subindices; for example, an ABX may contain 20 credit default swaps of subprime home loans whose reference obligations are AA-rated bonds. A committee on credit risks of the Bank for International Settlements noted in a report:

> The growing complexity of [CDO and CDS] products and the growing participation of a diverse set of...investors have increased the influence of credit rating agencies since the 2005 report. Some investors appear to have entered the [CDO and CDS] market despite lacking the capacity to independently evaluate the risks of [these] complex products. These investors appear to have done little independent risk analysis of [these] products beyond relying on the rating. While the lack of independent risk analysis and reliance on rating agencies was also discussed in the 2005 report, this seems to have become more entrenched since then.[2]

Trading in these "credit derivatives," as they are called, is unregulated. Traders and banks that serve as dealers do not always know exactly what is covered by a credit default swap contract. Dealers at banks trade e-mails throughout the day with bid and offer prices, and their customers have to wade through this maze of electronic messages to sort out the prevailing market conditions.[3] There are no public records that confirm the ability of the participants to live up to their obligations. Sellers of default swaps are not required by law to set aside reserves to support their potential CDS liabilities, and there are no industry standards; it is just a matter of negotiation between the parties. The famed George Soros noted, "It is a Damocles sword waiting to fall....To allow a market of that size to develop without regulatory supervision is really unacceptable." A chain reaction of failures in the swaps market could trigger the next global financial crisis, he added.[4]

CDOs allow mortgage lenders to transfer their risks to institutional and individual investors. However, synthetic CDOs do not own the underlying assets like the cash CDOs; through CDSs, they make bets on the rise and fall in the values of the portfolios of assets in the reference CDOs. In a credit default swap transaction, the seller sells credit protection on a reference portfolio and receives cash flows that portfolio generates, less financing costs paid to the swap counterparty. Thus, in theory, a CDS is supposed to be like an insurance policy against the risk of default.

In the real world, an insurance contract is between an insurance company and the insured. In Wall Street, a CDS is a contract between two parties that may have nothing to do with the underlying reference MBS portfolio. Similar to a bond futures contract and such derivatives, the buyers and sellers of CDSs merely bet on the future values of the underlying pool of securities. The buyers bet on the portfolio values to go down, driving up the insurance values of the CDS; the sellers bet the other way. Importantly, any two parties can issue a CDS on the same reference portfolio, except that these CDS contracts would have different terms to suit the requirements of the buyers and the sellers. Thus, a firm like Bear Stearns or AIG can have multiple contracts on the same reference portfolio with different buyers and sellers, with different terms for each of those contracts; it is like multiple bettors making bets of different odds on the same horse. Furthermore, the cost of the CDSs started out to be tiny (less than 1 percent of the notional value of the reference portfolios), just like the premium of an insurance contract—that is, until the bonds begin to be in trouble, at which time the premium soars, benefiting the buyers or hurting the sellers. For a buyer, the up-front cash is small for the potential profits. For a seller, the Aaa ratings on the bond portfolios give seeming assurance of safety; it's like free money. This was how AIG Financial Products, the very subsidiary of AIG that was responsible for all the profit growth and eventually the collapse of the giant insurer, expanded its business: by selling CDSs.

Herein was the potential and opportunity to create CDSs that have in aggregate notional values many times the value of the underlying portfolio of MBSs and other bonds—as well as the opportunity for generating huge profits for all parties in CDS transactions.

An analyst's description of the trading opportunities and the profit potential of CDSs is instructive:

The market is moving toward "on demand" credit risk, where an investor can specify a product's risk/return and the bank originates the "raw material" (bonds, ABS, etc.) and then *distorts* [emphasis added] the risk/return ratio of its portfolio and delivers a new product to its client.... In the medium term, regional and smaller banks will concentrate on sourcing risk (especially via loans), while brokerage houses and investment banks will focus on deal structuring. The distribution will be shared between various players, from large banks to insurance companies....[5]

Perhaps even the terms "alchemy" and "Ponzi scheme" are still inadequate to describe the CDO and CDS structures and what they spawned.

Given the lures of profits in these CDO structures, financial institutions of varying stripes issued enormous amounts of these securities until the debacle in 2008. By June 2006, Merrill had accumulated $41 billion in subprime CDOs and mortgage bonds, according to *Fortune* magazine.[6] Bear Stearns held nearly $40 billion in mortgage bonds that were essentially worthless.[7] Overall, global CDO issuance was estimated at $520 billion in 2006 and $481 billion in 2007 before coming to a virtual halt in 2008 (see Figure 3.5).

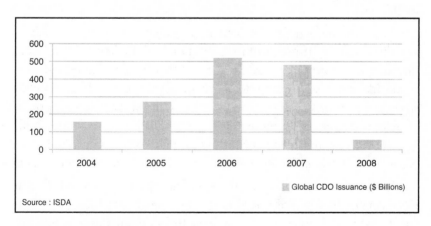

Figure 3.5   Global CDO issuance

The nexus between house prices and Wall Street trading was further increased by the leverages that were engineered into these securities, through the credit default swaps. As shown in Figure 3.6, at the high of the housing bubble in 2006, Celent Consulting estimated the value of outstanding CDOs to have reached $2 trillion, from a standing start 10 years earlier.[8] At that time, the notional value of the CDSs was $34 trillion, according to International Swap and Derivatives Association, Inc. (ISDA), the trade group of derivatives traders. By the end of 2007, the CDSs had climbed to about $62 trillion, more than the gross domestic product of the entire world, and 100 times more than the values in 2001. For perspective, the size of these obscure securities then was 4.4 times the $14.4 trillion U.S. stock market at its peak in October 2007, and it easily dwarfed the $7 trillion mortgage market, the very assets that supported these CDSs. The giant insurance company American International Group alone had $441 billion of these CDSs on mortgage-backed securities and other corporate bonds. As these securities declined in value and the CDSs rose in price, AIG, as a CDS seller, had to post more funds for collaterals. Like LTCM, AIG did not have the cash, although its core insurance operations were profitable; a failed AIG would have led to its counterparties in the CDS contracts, which often were other institutions like Goldman Sachs or Morgan Stanley, suffering financial meltdown.

Thus, the innocuous, down-home mortgages were cut up, sliced, and diced into instruments of risk and then built up layers upon layers into an edifice without regard for the fact that the foundation was tiny. It was like a colossal upside-down pyramid with its tiny base made of shaky poor credits of subprime borrowers and inflated home prices. Somehow it escaped the regulators that the upside-down pyramid built like a house of cards would unravel at the slightest stir of its foundation. No matter! It was an opportunity to make huge profits for Wall Street.

In this, the Street had the sanction of no less than the revered Alan Greenspan, chairman of the Federal Reserve Board. In a speech on risk transfer and policy implications at the Federal Reserve Bank of Chicago's Forty-First Annual Conference on Bank Structure, the chairman praised the benefits brought about by derivates.[9] He said at the beginning of the speech:

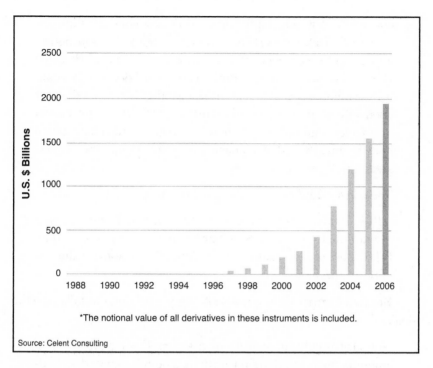

Figure 3.6   Estimated size of the global CDO market*

Perhaps the clearest evidence of the perceived benefits that derivatives have provided is their continued spectacular growth.... Derivatives have permitted the unbundling of financial risks.... Because risks can be unbundled, individual financial instruments now can be analyzed in terms of their common underlying risk factors, and risks can be managed on a portfolio basis.

Greenspan fully recognized that:

...the benefits of derivatives, both to individual institutions and to the financial system and the economy as a whole, could be diminished, and financial instability could result, if the risks associated with their use are not managed effectively. Of particular importance is the management of counterparty credit risks.... Two years ago I expressed particular concern about the implications of dealer concentration for risks in derivatives markets. Among the markets identified as appearing to be especially concentrated were the markets for U.S. dollar interest rate options. Those markets have become increasingly large and important as the U.S. markets for fixed-rate mortgage-backed securities (MBS) have grown and as an increasing share of those securities have come to be held by investors that manage the prepayment risks associated with those instruments.

The former Fed chairman also acknowledged:

...BIS [Bank for International Settlements] data showed that the notional value of U.S. dollar interest rate options sold by OTC derivatives dealers exceeded the notional value of options purchased.

But don't worry, he assured soothingly. The Fed has talked to the dealers!

Not surprisingly, an analysis of risks based solely on notional amounts turns out to be misleading. The interviews that Federal Reserve staff members conducted last year indicate that dealers run fairly well-balanced books in terms of sensitivities to changes in interest rates and especially to changes in interest rate volatility. The options that dealers sell tend to have terms that create less sensitivity to changes in interest rate volatility than the options that they buy. Thus, in order to limit the overall sensitivity of their options portfolios to changes in interest rate volatility, dealers must sell a larger notional value of options than they buy.

Because the terms of the options that they sell differ substantially from the terms of the options that they buy, dealers do assume significant basis risks, and their hedging strategies are dependent on options market liquidity when rates and volatilities are changing rapidly. In general, such risks are monitored and limited by various internal controls. If the options markets were to become illiquid, dealers could suffer significant losses; but their controls appear to be sufficiently tight that the losses seem quite unlikely to be large enough to jeopardize such large, diversified intermediaries.

Participants in the OTC derivatives markets typically manage their counterparty credit risks to dealers by transacting only with counterparties that are perceived to be highly creditworthy, by entering into legal agreements that provide for close-out netting of gains and losses, and with the exception of most exposures to the few AAA-rated dealers, by agreeing to collateralize net exposures above a threshold amount. All the major participants in the markets for U.S. dollar interest rate options markets that Federal Reserve staff interviewed follow these practices. The widespread use of collateral, in particular, usually is a powerful means of limiting counterparty credit losses.

However, when counterparties hold very large net positions in illiquid markets, as the hedge fund Long-Term Capital Management (LTCM) did in 1998, the effectiveness of collateral as a risk mitigant may be reduced significantly. In such circumstances, when the nondefaulting counterparties seek to close out their positions with a defaulting counterparty, those actions can cause market prices to move rapidly in directions that may amplify losses to levels significantly exceeding even very conservative collateral requirements. In contrast to LTCM, however, dealers typically limit the size of their net open positions in markets, even though their gross positions often *substantially exceed* the size of LTCM's. Thus, the collateralization of exposures to dealers is likely to be quite effective in limiting the counterparty risks from dealer concentration.

In the Fed, we trusted our money and our life savings!

Leveraging Household Assets

Not to be outdone by the big institutions in the pursuit of profits by leveraging, and faciliated by lenders from banks to credit card issuers, households took on unprecedented amounts of debt, unsecured or pledged with their homes. Since the start of the 2000 downturn, household debt jumped by twofold to $14.3 trillion at the end of 2007. While 73 percent of this amount was for mortgages, $2.5 trillion was for consumer credit, including revolving credit card debts.

Remarkably, despite the recession and the financial crisis, both home mortgages and consumer credit continued to rise, although by the end of 2008, both mortgages and consumer credit had leveled off somewhat.

To appreciate the amount of leveraging that these debt burdens entail, we need only to look at the acceleration of household debt as percentage to GDP, as shown in Figure 3.7. This ratio rose from 62 percent during the 1991–92 recession to 68 percent in 2000, or an increase of about 10 percent. By the end of 2007, the percentage of household debt had been catapulted to 100 percent of GDP, from which it changed little as 2008 ended because GDP had declined by an annual rate of 6.8 percent in the last quarter. (In Figure 3.7, the debt amounts exclude credit and trade liabilities and insurance premiums; together they account for about 4 percent of GDP.) In less than a decade, the leveraging of household debt had increased by a whopping 47 percent.

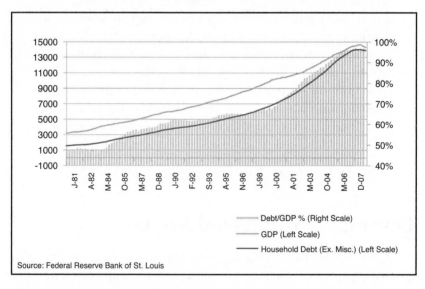

Figure 3.7   Household debt and GDP

Not only did household debt increase in relation to national income, but also in relation to household ability to take on additional debts. As shown in Figure 3.8, once the 2001 recession was over, household debt started to rise along with house prices and later on with equities. Starting at 16 percent of net worth and one time of disposable income in 1999, household debt rose to 22.9 percent of net worth by 2007 and then 24 percent in the first quarter of 2008, for a 49 percent increase; debt also rose to 1.41 times disposable income at the end of 2007, but it declined somewhat to 1.39 times by the first quarter of 2008.

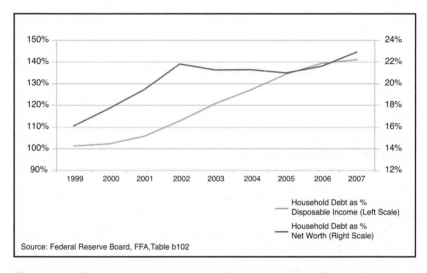

Figure 3.8 Household debt: percent of net worth and disposable income

Leveraging the Economy

As if it were not enough to stack on leverages on the mortgage-backed securities, the banks stepped up on the leveraging of their own balance sheets. Going into the crisis, financial debts taken on by financial institutions doubled from $8.1 trillion in 2000 to $16.2 trillion in 2007 (see Figure 3.9), keeping pace with the increase of mortgage securities from $4.9 trillion to $10.5 trillion. In the process, the debt-to-capital ratios of the ten largest bank holding companies in aggregate jumped to 21:1, from 14:1 in a space of 10 years. The investment banks juiced up their balance sheets even more with debt-to-capital ratios reaching 30 to 1.[10] These are the leverage ratios of hedge funds, not quite matching LTCM's strastophere, but at the most extreme end of the range for them.

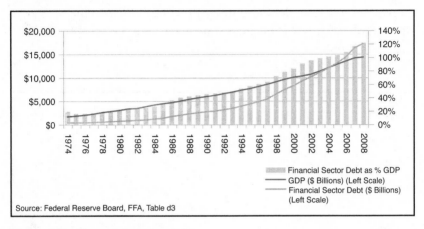

Figure 3.9   Financial sector debt

Federal indebtedness had leveled off in the mid-1990s and then decreased until 2002. By that time, federal budget defects from tax cuts and spending rose sharply, driving the federal government debt well ahead of GDP growth. Likewise, borrowings and debt levels of state and local governments tapered off in the mid-1990s, only to reaccelerate in 2000 even faster than growth in the federal government's debt (see Figure 3.10).

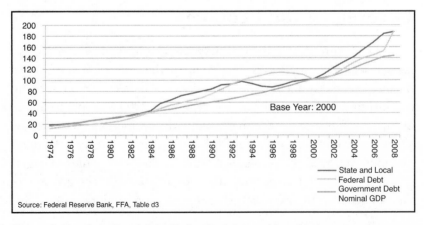

Figure 3.10   Growth of debt: federal, state, and local governments

As such, the growth of debt balances by the different sectors of the economy has accelerated since 2000 well in excess of the growth of GDP. Up until the early 1990s, debts in the public sector accounted for the excess borrowings in the economy, while borrowings by financial institutions lagged the growth of GDP. As the federal government began to reduce the budget deficits in the decade's later years, debt growth was taken up in the financial sector. Starting in 2000, the picture changed dramatically, with debt growth in all sectors outpacing the growth of the nominal GDP. Financial sector debt more than doubled between 2000 and 2008, while the nonfinancial sector debt grew 185 percent and the public sector debt increased by 187 percent.

Of course, these statistics are not at all surprising given the increases in the federal budget deficits, fnancial leveraging from mortgage issuance, and household accumulation of debt since the beginning of the decade. However, the figures underscore the fact that the entire economy has become much more leveraged. Unlike previously, it was the federal government that went on a spending binge and took on excessive debt as a result, while debt in the private sector grew at roughly the pace of nominal GDP. Leading to the crisis, all sectors of the economy were leveraged up with debt growing at a much faster rate than the growth of GDP. The debt binge raised the total U.S. debt to above the levels seen only during the Great Depression in 1929. This is illustrated in Figure 3.11.

Thus, the entire U.S. economy was leveraged—and the leveraging continues to increase. And no one sector in the U.S. economy has the money to lend to any other sector—except foreign governments!

Indeed, a substantial portion of the U.S. federal government's debt is owned by foreigners. As shown in Figure 3.12, as of March 2009, 48.6 percent of U.S. Treasury securities were in the hands of foreign entities and governments. China was the largest holder, with 11.4 percent; together with Russia, Brazil, and the oil-exporting countries, the total added up to 18.3 percent, or $1,224.9 billion. This stands in sharp contrast to Japan's placement of its government's debt.

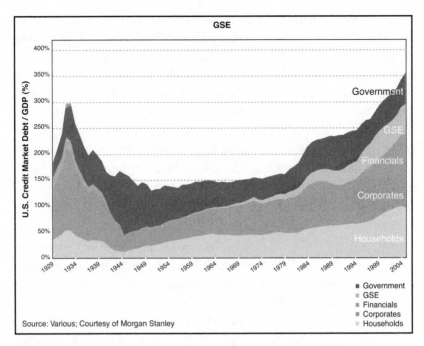

Figure 3.11   Total U.S. credit market debt as percent of GDP

Figure 3.12   Foreign holders of U.S. Treasury securities

As Japan began its two decades of economic malaise, its government debt rose steadily, starting with a relatively low base of 15.2 percent of GDP in 1990, according to IMF statistics. Ten years later, this ratio had quadrupled to 60.4 percent as Japan embarked on numerous fiscal programs to stimulate the economy. On the eve of the 2008 global crisis, the debt-to-GDP ratio further climbed to 80.4 percent.

However, most of this debt had been financed with internal funds; only about 7 percent was held by foreigners.[11] Another 9 percent of Japanese Government Bonds was held by the Bank of Japan, effectively funding the government debt by printing money. Japanese retirees also played a part, with both public and private pension funds holding 15.5 percent, thereby funding the government at vitually zero interest rates. Japanese households pitched in another 5.2 percent, while the banks held the largest amount at about 40 percent; the rest was in the hands of insurance companies. As such, presumably Japan had much greater flexibility than the United States to finance its debt, without undue reliance on foreign creditors.

Nevertheless, Japan had to deal with the acute embarassment caused by the lowering of its sovereign risk ratings by Moody's and Standard & Poor's. Several times, the agencies have cut ratings on yen-denominated Japanese Government Bonds from triple-A. At one point in 2002, Moody's rated Japan's sovereign risk at A2 and on a par with Israel, Greece, and South Africa and below Chile, Taiwan, and a host of such smaller countries. At the same time, Standard & Poor's rated the country's risk at Aa-, but, unlike Moody's, it spared the world's second-largest economy from being in the same lot with South Africa and below Bostwana. In arriving at its lower rating, Moody's argued that "Japan's general government indebtedness, however measured, will approach levels unprecedented in the postwar era in the developed world, and Japan will be entering uncharted territory."[12] How could that be? Japan was rated below an African country with half of its citizens living below the poverty line. In May 2009, the rating agency revised both Japan's local and foreign currency bond ratings, raised them to a unified Aa2, from Aa3. In making these changes, Moody's cited

> ...Japan's considerable strengths. These include Japan's large domestic savings, a strong home bias on the part of its domestic financial institutions and institutional investors, relatively low holdings of government debt by foreign investors, and Japan's $1 trillion of official foreign exchange holdings. Moody's believed the domestic market would absorb the record level of bond issuance that year to fund the government's economic stimulus program. However, the rating also

reflected the risks of Japan's high level of debt, which leaves the country's fiscal position vulnerable to shocks or imbalances that would cause a sharp rise in interest rates.[13]

A New Reality

The United States may face the same embarassment from rating agencies that had rated toxic subprime mortgage-backed securities at triple-A. As reported in the *Financial Times*, Moody's said in 2008 that "...10 years from now we would have to look very seriously at whether the U.S. is still a triple-A credit."[14] As preposterous as the notion that the sovereign risk of the United States of America, with its status as safe haven of choice and reserve currency of the world, is regarded less than the toxic CDOs backed by subprime credits of unqualified mortgage borrowers, it could happen, for the rating agencies have their own methodologies and logic.

Just as they have done to Japan, "a slap in the face" as noted by a Japanese commentator, the rating agencies will have in their favor the unprecedented leveraged financial conditions of the United States to support a rating change. Moody's has already proclaimed, "The U.S. is losing altitude in the Aaa range."[15] And Standard & Poor's lowered the UK's rating outlook to "negative" from "stable" in mid-2009. As we have discussed in this chapter, the excess and leveraging have occurred throughout the entire U.S. economy, in all sectors, and the United States is relying a good part on the largesse of some foreign countries, which are not exactly its most friendly allies, to continue funding a large part of its debt. In this connection, the rating agencies might be most reluctant to say that the United States has "...large domestic savings, a strong home bias on the part of its domestic financial institutions and institutional investors...." Or that "the domestic market will absorb the record level of bond issuance... to fund the government's economic stimulus program."

A new reality has dawned on the U.S. economy and stock market. We turn to this subject in the next chapter.

4

The New Economic Reality

As the stock market cheered the presumed newfound soundness of the nation's banks by rising to the highest levels since the lows in March; General Motors filed for bankruptcy in June 2009. Who would have thought; General Motors was recognized as the largest automobile company in the world only a year ago!

As recently as a couple of months earlier, its chief executive officer Rick Wagoner all but ruled out Chapter 11 protection while asserting the company could turn profitable again. He was promptly fired by the newly sworn-in president of the United States. The incoming new CEO Fritz Henderson smartly hinted that he could see how a bankruptcy could be possible for GM. Yet he was still mincing words, "If we need to pursue bankruptcy, we will make sure that we do it in an expeditious fashion. The exact strategies I'm not getting into today, but we'll be ready to go if that's required," he said.[1]

One cannot help but feel sympathy with the man.

Once the cornerstone of the U.S. economy, the Big Three automakers were now mere shadows of their former selves. While GM was still trying in vain to escape the inevitable, Chrysler, the third ranked of the Three, was already bankrupt and hoped to emerge as a division of the Italian company Fiat (which it did), whose cars had disappeared from American streets decades ago for, what else, poor quality. What's left of the U.S. automobile companies is a struggling Ford Motors, whose $31.5 billion debt had earned it one of the worst ratings by Moody's. The company is now trying to refashion itself "from a company focused mainly on trucks and SUVs to a company with a balanced product lineup that includes even more high-quality, fuel-efficient small cars, hybrids, and all-electric vehicles," according to Mark Fields, Ford's president of The Americas.[2] Ford should have done this years ago. At this stage, it will need to do a lot of things right.

Now the field of global automobile manufacturing is left to a handful of European companies producing high-priced cars, the efficient Japanese makers, and the Korean companies, which are nipping at their heels. However, even their future places in the industry can only be speculated upon, for the largest automobile market in the world may soon shift from the U.S. to China. The country is expected to see its domestic car production reach 10 million, and a wobbling increase of 10 percent from the prior year, in the midst of a global economic meltdown.

In the meantime, the United States was relying on the "cash-for-clunkers" program to stimulate the demand for automobiles in its market. As it turned out, the program, which cost $3 billion, mostly benefited foreign makers. Of the top ten models purchased under the program, eight were Japanese. Ford featured two models: Ford Focus and Escape, in fourth and tenth place.[3] Germany had launched a $7.5 billion "cash-for-clunkers" program, which the United States used as the model. German Federal Statistics Office estimated that the program generated a modest increase of 0.1 percent in private consumption; without it, consumption would have declined by 1 percent, and the economy would have contracted even more. However, the success of the program may rob the industry of sales in the coming years. A recent study by a respected consulting firm in the German car industry projected a fall of more than 20 percent in Germany's car sales in 2010 and as many as 90,000 jobs lost across the industry by the end of 2011.[4]

Being the volume leader and growth market, China will have a huge say in determining the kinds of cars that will be produced to satisfy the rising appetite of its 20- to 30-year-old citizens who consider cars as status symbols. Unfortunately, these will surely not be the kinds of automobiles the former Detroit Big Three companies used to produce: the gas-guzzling hulks of steel and chrome that are now piling up in the unsold car parking lots at the auto dealers, thousands of which are being shut down. Already the fastest-growing segment of the Chinese market is dominated by vehicles with less than 1.6 liter displacements, which are virtually nonexistent on American highways.

Increasingly, these cars are fueled not by gasoline but by electricity and hybrid engines.

In this technology, it is the Chinese companies that are gaining a growing edge. Although Volkswagen, Hyundai, Toyota, Honda, and Nissan remain the five top-selling names in China—albeit the first four are joint ventures with old local state-owned companies like Shanghai Automotive Industry Corp—some local companies are making their presence and ambition felt in the market. Among them are aggressive rising stars like Chery Automobile Co., Geely Automobile Holdings, and BYD Auto Co. The last one is a Shenzhen-based firm that has put batteries in one-fourth of the world's cell phones. If ever the U.S. Big Three, or what's left of them, are going to regain competitive footing, they have to overcome the head start and the market advantages that the Chinese have in the green technologies, as well as their favored positions in the world's fastest-growing small car market.

The former Big Three are little seen in the green technology space, whereas Nissan expects to unveil an affordable zero-emission electric car for sale in Japan and the United States in 2010. Other Japanese car makers and a Chinese company are lining up right behind in the race to sell electric cars in the United States, while the only American presence is a small sports car company that is said to have an electric car prototype ready in 2011.

That an American industry lost to foreign competition through a variety of unfortunate circumstances, changing economic climates, and self-inflicted wounds has become a familiar story over the past three or four decades. From textile and apparel to consumer electronics, computer manufacturing, and now car making, foreign companies have become dominant producing those things that had helped to create the American middle class. Millions of U.S. jobs have been eliminated as a result. Many of the workers who have lost their jobs in these industries eventually did find jobs in other occupations. But the jobs they found were in lower-paying positions, often working for the likes of McDonald's and Wal-Mart and other service industries that in no way offered the high wages that manufacturing workers had commanded—the kind of wages that had helped create America's middle class.

It was no coincidence that Japan rose to be a formidable economy on its ability to produce manufactured goods and sell them to Americans at low prices. This model has been repeated many times over, with South Korea, Taiwan, and other countries among the fast-growing economies nicknamed the Asian Tigers. Now China presents the biggest transformation of the twenty-first century. Some economists predict that in 30 years, China will surpass the United States as the largest economy in the world. This pattern of economic growth and dominance should not be unfamiliar to Americans: that of supplying to the world virtually everything that it is now importing. Now Americans go to Wal-Mart and other discount stores to buy everything from plastic toys to the most sophisticated electronic gadgets made in China and other countries. This explains why changes in U.S. personal income followed so closely changes in the overall manufacturing employment (see Figure 4.1). Workers in manufacturing support a host of other economic activities, from retail sales, to housing, health care, and state and local governments—not just the factories they toil in.

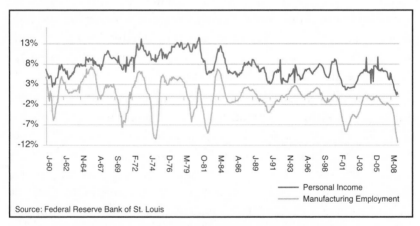

Figure 4.1   Manufacturing employment and personal income

The shrinking of the American automobile makers and the resulting massive layoffs of workers and closures of thousands of related businesses are only the latest signs that cast doubt on the future growth of the U.S. economy.

This can be explained with a simple analogy. The functioning of an economy, despite the myriads of complexities as well as the dynamics between the public and private sectors, is similar to a business in key respects. A company loses its viability, its future is undermined once its balance sheet is severely impaired, or its profitability declines and its earnings prospects are increasingly in doubt.

Businesses normally have debt, and few can function without it. Taking on debt allows a company to leverage its earnings; that is, to earn more than it could otherwise by using its own capital. The higher the debt load, the more leveraged it is, and the higher earnings growth rate expected. The more debt-leveraged a company is, the higher the earnings it can generate, but also the higher the interest charges. On the other hand, if earnings are lower than expected, the company may not be able to pay interest on the higher debt load and putting it at risks for defaulting on its loans. Thus, the more leveraged a company is, the more vulnerable it is to any shock that might be manageable otherwise.

As a business takes on more and more debt, its capital position is impaired unless it can generate higher earnings growth rates commensurate with the additional debt burden. If the future earnings streams become increasingly uncertain, investors would factor in additional discounts to the company's value. Expectations of reduced future earnings would eventually lead to lower stock prices. Negative earnings surprises invariably precipitate sell-offs of a company's stock; such sell-offs are often substantial and violent. By the same token, impaired balance sheets due to increasing debt loads, without commensurate increases in earnings, would negatively impact stock prices contemporaneously; it's a formula for stock price destruction.

In 2008, after years of increasing debts to leverage its economy while losing its manufacturing base to foreign competition, the U.S. economy faced a tattered balance sheet and worsening earnings power. The signs of this new reality were everywhere. But recognition of this reality, although visible for all to see and reminded periodically by government statistical releases, is hardly evident in the government communication to the American public or in the mass media. As to those who promote stocks to the investing public, they would rather ignore this new reality and focus on the news of the day, especially if that gave them an excuse to talk up the market.

Impaired Balance Sheet

Concerns have been raised in recent years of the rising federal budget deficits and national debt. However, the alarms were sounded as the economy just came off nearly a decade of strong growth with federal budget surpluses, equities rallying to new highs after the 2000 bear market and home prices soaring. Consumers were feeling the flush of rising wealth and were eager to spend, even if the newfound wealth was mostly on paper. Businesses benefited while bankers were mass feeding on the ever-expanding securitization and trading markets. So, why worry about budget deficits and national debt? "We'll grow out of it, and the good times will roll on," so went the belief.

"Frightful Storm"

What was not registered in our collective consciousness was that the good times were fed with money coming from debt—a lot of it—borrowed by households, financial institutions, and not least the federal and local governments. The collapse of house prices broke this circle. Consumers can't borrow anymore because lending standards have been tightened and the jobless rate is mounting. Banks can access private capital only because of government subsidies and the unspoken understanding that the government will not let the biggest institutions fail. That is why the large regional banks like Colonial BancGroup and Guaranty Financial were let go; they were not in the same league as the likes of Citigroup, to be bailed out with taxpayers' funds. That leaves the federal government as the last borrower of good standing, at least for the time being.

With the dollar as the world's reserve currency, the United States as a safe haven, and the government's power to print money and impose low interest rates on lenders whether they are U.S. citizens or foreign investors, the United States keeps piling on unprecedented amounts of deficit spending and debt. This is an "...economic problem that we must soon confront or else risk losing our primacy as the world's most powerful and dynamic economy," said the president of the Federal Reserve Bank of Dallas in the midst of the banking crisis in 2008.[5] He did not have a decade of economic prosperity to look back on, as it was in 2000, but instead has a tech bubble burst, a housing price collapse, and an insolvent banking system on the verge of bankruptcy without government intervention and, to top it off, record government debt.

"In the distance, I see a frightful storm brewing in the form of untethered government debt. I choose the words 'frightful storm' deliberately to avoid hyperbole. Unless we take steps to deal with it, the long-term fiscal situation of the federal government will be unimaginably more devastating to our economic prosperity than the subprime debacle and the recent debauching of credit markets that we are now working so hard to correct," the normally "taciturn" central banker continued.[6]

The federal debt has been rising, and there is nothing in sight in the foreseeable future that this orgy of debt accumulation is going to stop. At the end of the first quarter of 2009, the public debt was $6.8 trillion, while total outstanding debt (which includes debt held in different government agencies) was over $11 trillion; both of these amounts rise by more than $4 billion a day. And this leveraged condition is set to worsen in the years ahead. The federal budget deficit passed the $1 trillion mark early in the year; by mid-2009, the deficit forecast was revised by the Congressional Budget Office to be $1.58 trillion or 11 percent of GDP, the highest since World War II. For the next ten years, the deficits are projected to increase to some $9 trillion. However, this figure could climb to over $14 trillion, as estimated by The Concord Coalition, if adjustments are made for such items as likely continuation of major tax cuts beyond 2010.[7] Overall, projections by the IMF in its April 2009 *World Economic Outlook* report indicated the federal government's debt-to-GDP ratio would surpass 100 percent by 2014 from 59.9 percent at the end of 2008.

These numbers do not include the unfunded liabilities coming from Social Security benefits and the Medicare programs. These are the kinds of liabilities that had incapacitated the competitiveness of the Big Three Automobile companies and eventually drove them into near disappearance. For Social Security, the amount is about $14 trillion, the size of the U.S. GDP. The Medicare programs have unfunded liabilities of some $86 trillion.[8] The total sums up to $100 trillion, or seven times the size of the U.S. economy. In the meantime, the Social Security Administration reported in its 2009 annual report released in May that it expected the trust fund to go into deficit paying out more in benefits than it receives from payroll taxes by 2016; this is one year earlier than it reported last year. By 2037, the trust fund would be depleted, which is four years earlier than previously reported. At the same time, "Medicare's financial status is much worse.... [Its] financial difficulties come sooner—and are much more severe—than those confronting Social Security," the report said. The trust fund would be in deficit in 2009 and run out of money in 2017. By the year 2030, the outlays from both Social Security and Medicare are expected to rise to 12 percent of GDP, from 7 percent currently, partly as a result of the baby boomers' retirement. From then on, Medicare expenses will keep climbing. In 50 years, the combined outlays of both programs are projected to reach over 17 percent of GDP. To underscore the message, the report noted wryly, "As a point of comparison, in 2008 total federal receipts amounted to 17.3 percent of GDP." At least GM and Chrysler had the U.S. government to bail them out!

If we stack up all these numbers—the budget deficits, increases in the national debt, the unfunded liabilities in Social Security and Medicare, the prospects of further federal expansion of social programs like universal health care, and the existing debt burden in all sectors of the economy—the liabilities, the challenges, and the prospects of trouble lying ahead are so huge that the mind has difficulty absorbing the meaning. Against these huge figures, recent reportedly sharply rising savings rates in the household sector appear almost trivial.

Higher Savings?

Evidently, personal savings have shot up sharply since the beginning of 2009. Perhaps this signals a new trend in American consumer behavior? However, upon scrutiny, these statistics need to be viewed with caution. Figure 4.2 compares the savings rate as computed using the FFA method, and alternatively by the NIPA approach used by the Bureau of Economic Analysis of the Department of Commerce. The NIPA, or National Income and Production Accounts, calculate income and savings differently from the FFA. The FFA measures of income and savings are based on households' net acquisition of financial assets and net investments in tangible assets, minus net increases in liabilities. It is like netting out changes in the liabilities and assets of a company, and calling the difference income. The NIPA approach subtracts taxes and spending from income; the difference is savings. Income in NIPA includes wages and salaries, contributions to savings plans, life insurance premiums, and transfer payments from the government, such as Social Security. Spending on durable capital goods is treated in NIPA as an expenditure, not as income as in FFA.

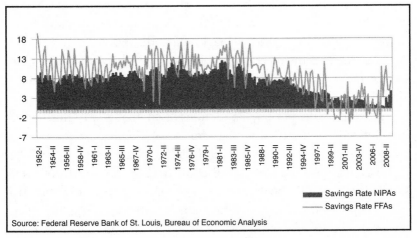

Source: Federal Reserve Bank of St. Louis, Bureau of Economic Analysis

Figure 4.2   Personal savings rate NIPA versus FFA

Although the methodologies are different, the patterns from the analysis are similar. Both show that the household savings rate in the United States has declined persistently and rapidly, from more than 10 percent in the early 1980s to virtually zero in the past few years. Both series also show a pick-up in the savings rate in the more recent few quarters. The NIPA series showed the savings rate rising from 0.4 percent at the end of 2007 to 4.3 percent at the end of the first quarter. The FFA data initially showed an improvement from 2.9 percent to 6.9 percent. However, revised figures showed the FFA savings rate was actually lower in the first quarter of 2009—only 3.5 percent—but had risen to 4.5 percent in the second.

The FFA data tends to be far more volatile than the NIPA series—by reason of the volatility of asset prices. FFA savings rates have also been mostly higher than reported in NIPA, because of the wealth effect of rising asset prices. This wealth effect has, of course, turned negative due to the 2008 crisis. Although the FFA rate suggests Americans may have returned to the more frugal time in the 1960s and 1970s, the NIPA indicates that the savings rate may have only returned to the norms seen during the 2001 recession; they still are far below the averages of the previous 40 years.

Furthermore, the increase in savings in NIPA in the first quarter of 2009 was $271.5 billion, even though personal income declined by $52 billion. Sixty-seven percent of that saving increase was accounted for by the reduction of taxes, $182.1 billion; the difference of $141 billion was due to reduced spending. It remains to be seen if the higher savings rate can be maintained once the effects of tax cuts and stimulus rebates wear off and the financial consequences of joblessness begin to have a deeper impact on household finances. In this regard, it is noteworthy that real median household income increased by a meager 0.7 percent a year from $41,258 in 1980 to $50,233 in 2007; this was disproportionately small compared to the growth of GDP. With little income growth, the average consumer had no alternative but to cut back on savings. As shown in Figure 4.9, later in this chapter, in the midst of this recession, which has lasted longer than any time since the 1929 Depression, consumer income has taken a drastic dive. How can consumers increase savings and spend at the same time to an extent sufficient to stimulate growth in the economy? One possible answer is that the savings rate will come back down as that of Japan following the collapse of the country's asset prices. In the five years until 1989, the savings rate in Japan averaged 12.9 percent. It has steadily declined in the subsequent ten years; by 2000, it was down to 5.7 percent.[9] American consumers face a dilemma, caught between mountains of debt and huge losses in real estate and equities, as well as stagnant or declining income. Where's the money to save?

At any rate, the recent increases in savings were not accompanied by reduction in the overall debt levels of the economy. As shown in Figure 4.3, household borrowings were reduced somewhat in the first quarter of 2009, possibly because of tightened lending standards. Financial institutions also substantially cut down on their borrowing for the first time, to the tune of $1.79 trillion, from a combination of responses to the government's mandates to strengthen their balance sheets, as well as in recognition of investor demand. All this reduction was, however, easily offset by increases in borrowings by the public sector.

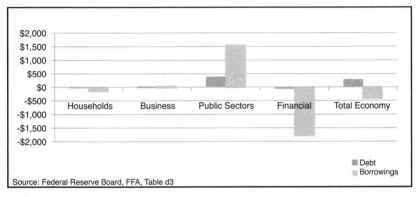

Figure 4.3 Changes in debt and borrowings by sector (first quarter 2009, $billions)

In the end, the overall indebtedness of the U.S. economy rose by $328 billion in the first quarter. As shown in Figure 4.4, the total debt level has increased since the end of 2007 by 5.9 percent, whereas its ratio to GDP has risen from 357 percent to 372.8 percent. Despite a year of economic contraction and tightened lending standards, which have contributed to a slight reduction in borrowings, household debt remains higher than at the end of 2007, although it has declined by a negligible 0.3 percent from the 2008 year-end level. Credit market debt in the financial sector has also remained above the 2007 level, increasing by 5 percent, despite borrowing reduction in the first quarter. However, any slackening in private sectors' indebtedness was more than made up by increases in federal, state, and local governments' debt.

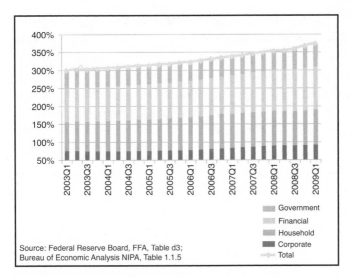

Figure 4.4   Debt keeps rising

Reliance on Foreign Lenders

As debt leveraging continues to increase across the economy, the expansion of federal deficits and national debt poses special worrisome concerns. Due to its overwhelming presence in the credit markets, increases in government borrowings choke off availability of private capital, as well as induce higher interest rates on treasury securities to attract funding. A rise in interest rates would increase funding costs to all sectors and reduce profitability of businesses. Furthermore, regarding the federal budget, deficits are forecasted to rise possibly to some $14 trillion in the next ten years, driving the national debt to even higher levels. It will take all the power that Treasury Secretary Timothy Geithner can muster to persuade China and other countries to buy U.S. Treasuries. As noted in the previous chapter, of the $3.3 trillion of Treasury securities held by foreign governments, or almost 50 percent of the public debt, at the end of March 2009, 37.5 percent came from China, Brazil, Russia, and the oil-exporting countries; China and Japan alone accounted for 45 percent of the total. In comparison, over 90 percent of Japan's national debt is funded internally.

China has already sent signals in public of its discontent to the U.S. government on the financial crisis, which it blames entirely on the Americans. It has threatened to reduce dollar holdings and urged a shift to another mechanism, such as the International Monetary Fund's Special Drawing Rights to supplement or replace the dollar as the world reserve currency. "As a major reserve currency-issuing country in the world, the U.S. should balance and properly handle the impact of the dollar's supply," said Chinese vice premier Wang Qishan in a meeting in July with Secretary of the Treasury Timothy Geithner.[10] Russia and India said the global financial crisis highlights the dollar's flaws and called for a debate. In trade settlements, merchants are demanding the Chinese Yuan in place of the dollar in China's border zones with Vietnam, and the program is being expanded to its largest financial centers, including Shanghai, Guangzhou, and Hong Kong. The Yuan settlement is also being applied to export and import transactions with Malaysia, Indonesia, Brazil, and Russia, all of which seek to reduce the dollar's role as the linchpin of global commerce and finance.[11] France has also joined the chorus for a diminished role for the dollar as the world's reserve currency. French President Nicholas Sarkozy did not mince his words, "The political and economic reality of a multipolar world will have to find sooner or later a translation on the monetary level. A multipolar world can't count upon one currency only."[12]

It is like the Damocles sword hanging over the debt issue, the subject of whether foreigners—and China in particular—will continue to buy U.S. Treasury securities to fund the U.S. federal debt and whether and how long the U.S. dollar remains the world's reserve currency. For now, the horsehair thread is still holding. China is continuing to buy U.S. Treasuries, although in some months, they were reported to be net sellers sending stocks tumbling, and the debate flared up. However, according to data from the U.S. Department of the Treasury (as shown in Figure 4.5), foreigners may have recently shunned new investments and sold off agency securities that are so important to the housing market.

But the debate also underscores the precariousness of the prospect of the U.S. economy. As long as foreigners continue to buy U.S. Treasuries, the United States can continue to rely on debt leveraging to stimulate growth. But debt-driven economic growth can only go so far, as we have seen from the below-trend growth after the 2001 recession. In the aftermath of the 2008 crisis, the overall debt burden has increased at rates faster than GDP growth, without a slack in any sector to supply funds to the others as experienced in the 1980s and

1990s. Worse, the federal government is taking a command role in the economy, and one can hardly expect the government to be an efficient enterprise.

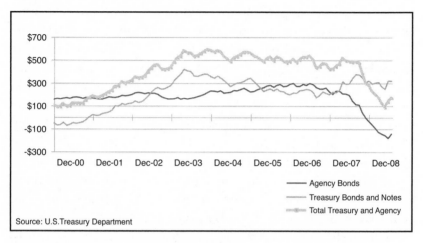

Figure 4.5   Foreign purchases of long-term U.S. Treasury and agency securities ($ billions—trailing 12 months)

Long Term Capital Management went bust because, toward its end, it could not get funding. If the U.S. economy experiences slower growth as is expected with all this debt burden and uncertainty, its attractiveness as an investment will dim in the eyes of foreigners. When such assessment comes to bear, it will dampen their appetite for U.S. investments. Some countries have already stopped purchases of non-Treasury securities, as noted in Figure 4.5. Once they stop buying U.S. Treasuries, as the banks had done to LTCM, the unraveling will know nowhere to stop. It works like a vicious circle, difficult to predict where it will begin; it can start anywhere. But once it starts, subsequent events tend to reinforce one another, with fear as the catalyst.

Lower Economic Growth

As in the past, economic recovery is expected after this recession. Even Japan has enjoyed economic growth, not a recession like the United States, in the aftermath of its stock and real estate bubble bursts as well as subsequent growth spurts. The question is about the growth trend afterward. Figure 4.6 shows the trends in U.S. GDP growth rates since 1930 and three- and five-year rolling averages.

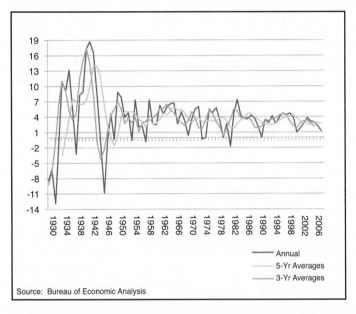

Figure 4.6   GDP growth rates: annual, three-year, and five-year rolling averages

The 1929 depression and its aftermath, as well as World War II, wreaked havoc on the economy, with periods of extremely high growth and sharp contraction. In post-war years, growth steadied at an average of 3.9 percent between 1950 and 1979, even including the stagflation period of the 1970s. After the 1981–82 recession, the United States experienced stimulating economic policies as inflation and interest rates declined sharply, amid a new regime of huge tax cuts as well as federal budget deficit spending. Yet, the ensuing growth spurt was not enough to prevent the decade's growth rate to decline to 3.1 percent. In the 1990s, favorable economic conditions still prevailed with the federal budget deficit turning to surplus, the fruits of the so-called peace dividends, the collapse of the Communist world, and perhaps most important, the advance of the personal computer and Internet technologies. Yet the average growth rate of the decade still remained at 3.1 percent.

Below Trend Line Growth Rate

A significant feature of the economic recovery after the 2001 recession was that the pick-up in economic activity after the economy had bottomed out fell significantly short of similar periods in past recoveries. During 2002–04, the GDP grew at an average of 2.6 percent, significantly lower than the 3.3 percent and 5.3 percent rates of the 1992–94 and 1983–85 periods, respectively. Overall, the average growth rate between 2002 and 2007 was 2.6 percent, which was decidedly lower than prior periods. Remember that this lower growth occurred at a time of high debt leveraging in all parts of the economy. Also, there were large tax cuts and huge deficit spending, as well as accommodative monetary policy and easy credit. In fact, the Fed had begun to reduce interest rates as soon as there were signs of economic weakness, and it kept on cutting well past the time when the recession was over, which was officially dated to be November 2001.

In the 2008 crisis, the Federal Reserve repeatedly promoted an optimistic prospect of economic recovery. This upbeat attitude was served up to the public by top government officials. And optimistic scenarios were used in the so-called stress tests to assess the banking system's viability.

However, there are more sobering views suggesting a grimmer outlook. The Federal Reserve itself has had to revise its forecasts downward, predicting a larger contraction for 2009 than previously indicated. It has also reduced its forecasts of GDP growth for 2010 and 2011. Even these tamer forecasts were still too high for some. The International Monetary Fund in its April 2009 World Economic Outlook expected the U.S. economy to contract by 2.8 percent in 2009, larger than the Fed's projections of a contraction between 0.5 to 1.3 percent, which were later increased to 1.3 to 2 percent. For 2010, the Fed has projected growth between 2 and 3 percent, compared to a forecast of 2 percent by Blue Chip Economic Indicators, which would be a weaker recovery than usual. The IMF saw zero growth. For 2011, the Fed foresees a growth rate of 3.5 to 4.8 percent. The highest annual GDP growth recorded after the 2000–2001 recession was 3.6 percent in 2004, amid soaring house prices, and the recession itself was confined mostly in the tech industries. Nouriel Roubini, who earlier than most people had predicted the coming of this crisis, projected that the economy would contract at 3.7 percent for 2009.[13] For the years beyond, he predicted "below-par and below trend recovery where growth will average about 1% in the next couple of years when potential is probably closer to 2.75%."[14]

For our purpose, the growth figures in any short-term period are not the issue. The economy is bound to show periods of growth thanks to the massive doses of fiscal and monetary stimulus—and more are in the making. The "cash-for-clunkers" giveaway to promote consumption and aid the car industry, as well as the promise of the Fed chairman to keep interest rates near zero for an "extended period," are only the more visible parts of the artificial stimulation of the economy. Thanks to these booster shots, the economy should show some growth spurts—enough to give stock market pundits something to claim a new bull market!

Of greater importance are both the overall trend of the economy and the sustainability of the growth trend. And it clearly is on a lower growth path now that the leveraging of the economy is restricted. As Bill Gross of PIMCO said, "...an economic growth rate that staggers forward at a new normal closer to 2 as opposed to 3½%. There's no magic in that number, and no model to back it up, just a lot of common-sense that says this is how people and economic societies behave when stressed and stretched to a near breaking point."[15]

Like a car traveling at a constant speed, for the economy to accelerate, its engine would need to be revved up to a higher speed. The problem is that the engine has already been pushed to the limit, and now the car is headed into hilly terrain. The economy's momentum actually reversed during the recession while leveraging continued. If the engine of growth—which is leveraging, through deficit spending, borrowing, and easy monetary policy—slows, the economy is bound to slip backward. An editorial in *The Wall Street Journal* observed that the Fed has been running at 200 miles an hour, and suggested that the central bank slow down to 160 miles an hour. The Fed of Ben Bernanke may not have any choice other than keeping the gas pedal down. His situation is not unlike that of former Fed Chairmen Arthur Burns and G. William Miller of the 1970s, who persisted in an accommodative monetary policy in the face of rising inflation—with the same unfortunate results!

Rising Unemployment and Its Lingering Effects

Among official circles, the cheerleading (or is it the refusal to recognize the dire state of the economic outlook?) continues. In the
stress tests for the banks, the underlying statistics for the worst-case
scenario called for the unemployment rate to top out at 10 percent.
At the same time, the International Monetary Fund (IMF) has projected the rate to average 10.1 percent in 2010. But even this forecast
is likely to be exceeded. For June 2009, the Bureau of Labor Statistics
reported the unemployment rate rise to 9.5 percent, adding 7.2 million people to the unemployment ranks since the recession started in
December 2007. Since then, 6.5 million jobs have been lost, and the
unemployed has swelled to 14.7 million people. Typically, unemployment continues to rise even after a recession has ended. In the 2001
recession, which was short and shallow and lasted for only 8 months,
job losses continued for 19 months until August 2003, while the
unemployment rate rose for an additional 1 percent to peak in June at
6.3 percent. It is hardly possible to see how it would be different this
time given the severity of the economic contraction. That's why many
economists today predict the unemployment rate could easily pass
the 10 percent mark and may even surpass the worst level recorded in
1982 at 10.8 percent.

An important question is, can the jobless find work when the
economy recovers and thereby drive the unemployment rate to
return to a level approximate that of full employment? To workers
formerly in the automobile industry, the outlook is almost hopeless.
"The days of walking out of one factory and walking into another one
down the street are over," said Jim O'Connor of Pekin, Illinois, a former president of United Auto Workers Local 974. "The unions don't
have any leverage anymore at the bargaining table. So these young
people (today) aren't only out of work, you know. They weren't making a living wage when they lost their job," he said.[16]

Many of those unemployed have already been discouraged from
looking for a job; they are not even counted as part of the unemployed. At the end of the first quarter 2009, their ranks had risen to
2.1 million; no doubt this figure has increased since then. If they were
counted in the labor statistics, the unemployment rate would have
already passed the 10.8 percent in June. Adding the part-time workers

to the unemployed would bring the rate to 17 percent. At any rate, the duration of unemployment had already lengthened, well surpassing the post-1929 worst record in 1982 (see Figure 4.7). As the duration of unemployment lengthens, the unemployed will likely give up looking for work, thus reducing the labor force and artificially projecting a more rosy employment situation, when the truth is actually worse.

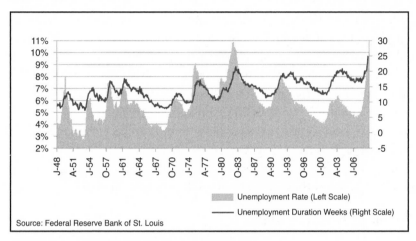

Figure 4.7   Unemployment duration and rate

At the same time, even employed workers have seen their work weeks shortened to new records. The trend of fewer weekly hours worked has been in place for some time. According to the Bureau of Labor Statistics, by 1999, average weekly hours worked was reduced by 10.9 percent since 1964, from 38.7 hours to 34.5.[17] In June 2009, the average weekly hours worked was recorded at 33 hours, a reduction of 5 percent in 10 years. Americans are now working no harder than Europeans, although not by choice! When economic growth picks up, it is likely that full-time employment growth will lag behind increases in hours worked by employed workers.

Rising unemployment also casts doubt on the strength of economic growth after the initial recovery because of its impact on the finances of state governments, which were already in dire conditions. "States will lose sales tax fairly early in the cycle because people start cutting back in purchasing things. But the big loss, of course, is going

to be in income tax revenues, and that's pretty aligned with unemployment," the executive director of National Governors Association
explained.[18] At least 48 states are facing budget shortfalls for the 2010
fiscal year, and the majority of them are expected to have shortfalls in
2011 and beyond.[19] Through 2011, the aggregate deficits of state
budgets will likely exceed $350 billion.[20] This is why, as the governor of
Indiana put it, "State government finances are a wreck.... Washington,
as long as our Chinese lenders enable it, can practice denial a bit
longer. But for states, the real world is about to arrive."[21] California is
only a special case because its deficit is the largest and it has resorted
to making payments with IOUs—which, of course, is only to delay the
time of default. Although some money was made available to the states
from the federal bailout of $787 billion, when the program expires
after two years, state governments may have to face the anticipated
budget shortfalls by themselves. In the meantime, across the country,
state governments have selectively shut down their operations one day
at a time among other cutbacks in services to save money.[22]

Stagnant Housing Market

The construction trade does not offer much near-term relief
either, for employment or economic recovery. Prior to the release of
housing starts for April, hopes rose that the new figures would signal
a return to stability in the housing market. "Builders probably broke
ground on more houses in April..., adding to signs the recession was
abating, economists said before reports this week," Bloomberg
reported.[23] "An easing in the housing slump, now in its fourth year, is
an essential element of most forecasts for an economic recovery later
this year," it continued. As it turned out, the U.S. Department of
Commerce actually reported a record drop to 458 thousand units,
12.8 percent below the March figure and 54.2 percent lower than a
year ago. Although some analysts singled out a small rise in single-
family construction for encouragement, the reality is that "Home
building conditions remain weak," Paul Dales, U.S. economist for
Capital Economics, said in a note to clients. "The excess supply of
new homes for sale is still high, and heavy discounts on foreclosed
properties have made new homes less appealing. Any rebound in
starts will be modest."[24] Indeed, as shown in Figure 4.8, starts and
permits have been bouncing around near the bottom.

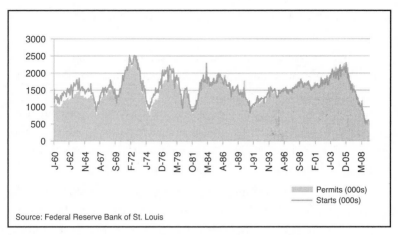

Figure 4.8   Housing starts and permits as of July 2009

Furthermore, Fed Chairman Bernanke had expected home prices to begin bottoming out. "So as I look at the housing market...we are finally beginning to see the seeds of a bottoming,"[25] he said. However, the decline of home prices in 2009 first quarter turned out to be much more precipitous. When the S&P/Case-Shiller index for March was released, it showed home prices dropping by 18.7 percent from a year ago, significantly worse than the stress tests' assumption of a fall of at worst 14 percent for all of 2009. It was also the fastest decline in annual rate ever. "We see no evidence that a recovery in home prices has begun," said David M. Blitzer, chairman of the S&P index committee.[26] Adding to the uncertainty, the S&P/Case-Shiller index did show a national increase of 2.9 percent in the second quarter of 2009, although it recorded a decline of 14.9 percent from a year ago, following a 19.1 percent fall in the first quarter. At the same time, the Federal Housing Finance Agency reported that home prices fell by 0.7 percent in the second quarter, a larger decline than the 0.5 percent in the first. The housing agency tracks house prices from sales price information from Fannie Mae- and Freddie Mac-acquired mortgages, whereas the S&P/Case-Shiller index measures the average changes in market prices of similar homes in a given market. In June 2009, new home sales rose at a seasonally adjusted rate of 11 percent in June, although nonseasonally adjusted sales figures were down 4 percent from May. But the median sales price of $206,200 was down

12 percent from $234,300 a year earlier, and down nearly 6 percent from $219,000 in May.

Furthermore, the sales increases belied a troubled market reality. In June, the trade publication *Inside Mortgage Finance* sponsored a survey of 1,500 real estate agents.[27] It found that 64 percent of home sales were either foreclosures or bank sales taking losses on foreclosed properties. One-quarter of the sales were due to some kind of financial or personal crisis. Only 11 percent of the total was unforced or optional, bearing the semblance of a normal market.

On top of it all, home foreclosures accelerated, not slowed down. In April 2009, home foreclosures jumped 32 percent higher than a year ago, the highest monthly foreclosure rate since the peak of home prices. This came as a surprise even to observers closest to the scene. "It's the volume that's surprising," said Rick Sharga, senior vice president for marketing of RealtyTrac, the firm that collected the data. "We've never seen two consecutive months like this," he said.[28]

On the heels of 340,000 foreclosures in March, April's record foreclosure rate showed the poor condition in the mortgage market where the rate of default failed to abate. In May, the foreclosure rate dipped a bit; it then rose 33 percent in June, as compared to 12 months ago. Despite $50 billion in subsidies handed out to the lending industry as part of the stimulus program, 1.5 million homes received foreclosure filings in the first six months of the year. Additionally, borrowers who were late making monthly payments were being pressured more vigorously by lenders after foreclosures were temporarily suspended by Fannie Mae and Freddie Mac, and other lenders. "All of these loans are now being processed pretty rapidly by the servers," Mr. Sharga said.[29] Industry analysts predicted 3.1 million homes will receive foreclosure notices in 2009.[30] In July, foreclosure filings again were up by 7 percent from June and 32 percent from a year ago. More disturbingly, while the default rate by subprime borrowers was stabilizing, it rose by 5.8 percent among prime mortgage borrowers. Overall, loans to prime borrowers accounted for 58 percent of foreclosure filings, up from 44 percent the previous year. Increasingly, foreclosures were being driven by rising unemployment, falling income, and declining home prices.

Hopes of home price recovery aside, after the 1990–91 recession, which lasted for only eight months, home prices stagnated for several years. When the recession ended in March 1991, the quarterly GDP grew at an average annual rate of 3.0 percent for the next five years. However, the S&P/Case-Shiller index rose at an average of 1.6 percent, below the inflation rate during that period. In this cycle, debt leveraging had driven up home prices; however, the lending spigot has been virtually shut off by mortgage lenders, except to the most qualified. Therefore, it is hardly realistic to expect home prices to pick up anytime soon and then have a sustainable recovery in the next few years. On this subject, Robert Shiller, the originator of the Case-Shiller index, noted on the eve of the report of improved home prices in the second quarter, "It's clearly not over yet. It's not obvious that people are really ready to spend again. That may take years to rekindle that normalcy.... We'll have a recovery, and it will be exceptionally weak for years to come." [31]

Consumer Spending

Consumer spending accounts for about 70 percent of the U.S. economy, compared to Japan's almost 60 percent. For the recovery to be sustained and robust, consumers have to pick up the slack if housing is sluggish as expected. On this front, the prospects are not encouraging. Along with rising joblessness and high debt burden, consumer spending will be dampened by the decline in household wealth, a result of the decline of home prices and the stock market. This is the wealth effect in reverse. In prosperous times, with their properties and investments rising in value, consumers would feel confident in their financial conditions and tend to spend more. Additionally, they would collect income from their assets, such as dividends and capital gains.

This recession has wreaked havoc on consumers' wealth. From the peak in 2007, household assets have declined in value by $12.2 trillion, or 19.5 percent in the first quarter of 2009, according to the Flow of Funds accounts from the Federal Reserve Board. Seventy-five percent of this loss was from financial assets, while the decline of home prices mostly accounted for the balance. Additionally, income from fixed income securities, which account for a large part of retirees' financial assets, has declined substantially as interest rates have tumbled. As a result, personal income receipts from assets have declined since the beginning of 2009. Figure 4.9 shows how changes in income derived from assets have affected the overall personal income in this recession as well as during 2000–2002. The drop-off in investment returns and the overall personal income have led to pre-cipitous declines in consumer spending since late 2008 and are still continuing. In fact, as shown in Figure 4.10, consumption expendi-tures have fallen off the cliffs since early 2009, declining at double-digit rates.

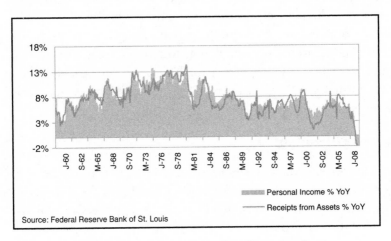

Figure 4.9   Personal income and receipts from assets

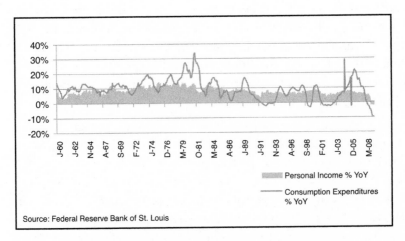

Figure 4.10   Personal income and consumption expenditures

If, in fact, deleveraging picks up with consumers trying to pay off debt and save more, the effects on consumption expenditures can only be expected to be more negative. With the savings rate having backed up to around 4 percent, a return to a 5–7 percent savings rate, which was normal in the 1980s, can hardly help to sustain a robust recovery in consumer spending in the midst of debt reduction and tightened lending standards. Some observers think a 10 percent savings rate would bear troublesome consequences for the economy.

Lower World Growth

A remarkable aspect of Japan's 20-year slumber was that in the years following the peak of the Nikkei in 1989, the world economy advanced at a healthy rate. Even the United States experienced growth on average in excess of 3 percent in the five years following the 1991 recession.

In contrast, as the United States sunk into a deep recession starting in December 2007, the world economy also slipped into severe contraction. In the first quarter of 2009, the United States reported a 6.1 percent decline in GDP. Three of its largest trading partners descended into even steeper declines. Mexico's first-quarter growth decreased by 21.5 percent, while Japan's GDP contracted at a 15.2 percent annual rate, and Germany reported an annualized rate of 14.4 percent loss, the worst decline the country had experienced since 1970.

At these rates of contraction, the global economy should contract in 2009 at a faster rate than the 1.3 percent projected in the International Monetary Fund's April 2009 World Economic Outlook. Even at that rate, it still would be the deepest recession post-World War II. And "the downturn is truly global: Output per capita is projected to decline in countries representing three-quarters of the global economy," the report noted. For 2010, the recovery was expected to be 1.9 percent (later revised to 2.4 percent); this still would be sluggish compared to past recoveries. Indeed in June, the World Bank updated its projections for the world economy to contract 2.9 percent in 2009, compared to its previous forecast for a 1.7 percent contraction—as banks continued to get their balance sheets back into shape from leveraging.[32] "Unemployment is on the rise, and poverty is set to increase in developing economies, bringing with it a substantial deterioration in conditions for the world's poor," the Bank noted.[33]

In this connection, one is reminded of the contraction of world trade in the 1929 depression, which historians blamed for the worsening of the economic conditions. The World Trade Organization now projected for world trade to contract by 9 percent in 2009, "the biggest contraction since World War II."[34] World trade growth has slowed since 2006, when world trade volume expanded by 8.5 percent. The growth rate, however, slowed down to 6 percent in 2007. Sharp deterioration of world trade became evident in the second half of 2008, although for the year total trade expanded by 2 percent. The developed countries, where export volume is expected to decline by 10 percent, were to be the most severely hit. The authors of the report further bleakly commented, "For the last 30 years, trade has been an ever-increasing part of economic activity, with trade growth often outpacing gains in output. Production for many products is sourced around the world, so there is a multiplier effect—as demand falls sharply overall, trade will fall even further.... As a consequence, many thousands of trade-related jobs are being lost."[35]

The outlook of depressed world economic growth and trade collapse cannot bode well for the U.S. economy. Furthermore, WTO's forecasted trade contraction was based on assumptions that did not include a possible rise in protectionism. Trade actions viewed as protectionist by the subject nations can take many forms, from such measures as a ban of U.S. pork and other import restrictions based on health concerns by Russia, China, and other countries; or clauses regarding labor rights in bilateral trade pacts involving emerging market countries, which typically have weak labor laws. If protectionist sentiments intrude into trade policies and negotiations, especially if the dollar is to depreciate precipitously, by design or capital flow imbalances, retaliatory trade actions may deepen the contraction of world trade to the detriment of economic recovery both in the United States and abroad. Indeed, the Organization for Economic Cooperation and Development reported continuing deterioration of the value of trade in the 30 OECD countries, extending the trend since the second half of 2008 (see Figure 4.11). For the first quarter of 2009, the OECD report showed declines of 13.4 percent in exports from OECD countries, and 15.2 percent in imports.[36] Since then, despite some significant pick-up in world trade volume, the overall trends "remain dismal" as reported by *The Wall Street Journal*.[37] Exports from Germany and Japan were down more than 30 percent during the first five months of 2009, while officials at the busy Port of Long Beach in California "don't expect 'any steady improvement' in volume until next year."[38]

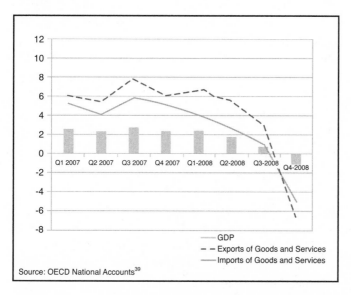

Figure 4.11   Real GDP and trade growth of OECD countries, 2007–2008

Additionally, while the United States was beginning to worry about the return of inflation, drops in prices into negative territory were beginning to show up in some industrialized economies. For example, Germany's consumer price index declined by 0.6 percent on annual rate in July 2009. This was the second month that this index of inflation dipped into negative territory. In June, it had declined by –0.1 percent. At the same time, the Harmonized Index of Consumer Prices (HICP), used by the European Central Bank as an indicator of price stability, fell by 0.6 percent year-on-year in July, although it was unchanged from June.[40]

A Future Unlike the Past

In past recessions, the U.S. economy was able to bounce back quickly; there was no prolonging of slow growth periods. A combination of monetary easing and fiscal spending were sufficient to do the job of bringing the economy back to life, giving vivid meaning to the phraseology "V-shaped recovery" (see Figure 4.12). Japan also experienced such economic rebounds even during its prolonged economic malaise. John Makin, an economist at American Enterprise Institute, recounted the Japanese experience with "...increased federal spending by...3 percent of [GDP], cut short-term interest rates to below one-half of 1 percent, and flooded the economy with liquidity so that long-term interest rates were held below 3 percent while the [currency] weakened by 30 percent...." If these policies were applied in America, "U.S. growth and employment would have boomed, and inflation would have jumped as the economy overheated." They did in Japan, where "[t]he payoff was a sharp, brief surge in growth to an annualized rate of 12.2 percent during the first quarter of 1996. Meanwhile, Japan's stock market, hailed by American brokerage houses as the next major bull market, rose by more than a third, from 15,000 to a peak of 22,500 in June, before dropping back below 21,000 this fall." However, "these are precisely the steps that Japanese policy makers have taken since the summer of 1995, with little *lasting* positive impact on the Japanese economy," Makin observed.[41]

To combat the 2008 recession, the United States has taken similar measures but with a greater sense of urgency. The U.S. stock market has responded as favorably, expecting a growth spurt leading to a sustainable recovery like in the aftermath of past recessions.

Let's hope it will be so.

In this regard, it is instructive to recall the words on the danger of deflation of the then-Federal Reserve Board governor Ben Bernanke following the 2001 recession:

> Over the years, the U.S. economy has shown a remarkable ability to absorb shocks of all kinds, to recover, and to continue to grow. Flexible and efficient markets for labor and capital, an entrepreneurial tradition, and a general willingness to tolerate and even embrace technological and economic change all contribute to this resiliency. *A particularly*

important protective factor in the current environment is the strength of our financial system: Despite the adverse shocks of the past year, our banking system remains healthy and well regulated, and firm and household balance sheets are for the most part in good shape. [Italics added.]

The second bulwark against deflation in the United States, and the one that will be the focus of my remarks today, is the Federal Reserve System itself. The Congress has given the Fed the responsibility of preserving price stability (among other objectives), which most definitely implies avoiding deflation as well as inflation. I am confident that the Fed would take whatever means necessary to prevent significant deflation in the United States and, moreover, that the U.S. central bank, in cooperation with other parts of the government as needed, has sufficient policy instruments to ensure that any deflation that might occur would be both mild and brief.[42]

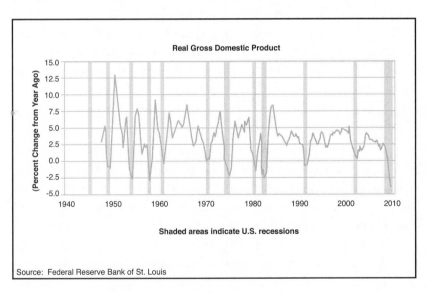

Figure 4.12   A sustainable V-shaped recovery?

Now that the Fed chairman's "protective factor" is damaged, he has vowed to keep interest rates low for an "extended period." Will Bernanke succeed for everyone's sake in his lonely combat against the twin evils of inflation and deflation? Or will he succumb to following the footsteps of his predecessors in the face of the economy's unprecedented debt burden and allow inflation to haunt the economy as it did in the 1970s? As Bloomberg has noted in "Leverage Rising on Wall Street at Fastest Pace Since '07 Freeze," the continuing near-zero percent interest policy is already bringing back leveraged buying of high-risk, low-quality securities financed by—who else?—banks.[43] Or will Bernanke pay heed to foreign creditors' demand to protect the dollar's value and preserve its primacy as the world's reserve currency lest it fall into an unstoppable downward spiral, which has been the fate of all currencies that followed the path of inflationary growth on the back of runaway borrowings?

These are uncharted waters. The economy is vulnerable to pressure points from many directions, as we have discussed. Past records in response to crises of lesser complexities offer little confidence in any prediction, much less a favorable outcome for the long term. The Fed chairman's responsibility is large and his burden heavy. But investors need not put their life savings at risk on the resolution or "call the bluff" and find out what will happen. There's no percentage in it. As demonstrated time and again in history, crises do not come with loud warnings. Even if they do, they will surely be ignored, just as the real estate bubble and its financial consequences had been largely brushed aside by the stock market until the eleventh hour when Lehman Brothers went bankrupt. By then, there was only panic and forced selling.

So, what can investors do? We need to have an investment posture that helps to protect our financial futures from not only the vagaries of the stock market but also from potential policy shocks that have caused equities to lurch alternately from euphoria to panic. The next chapter discusses the potential effects of the new economic reality on the stock market in the longer run. The subsequent two chapters discuss the investment approaches helping investors to navigate through these uncharted waters and preserve your capital, as well as position your portfolios to continue saving and building wealth while managing the risks of losses.

5

Bulls and Bears: The Long Cycles

Rising equity markets make investing simple. Just buy it! "A rising tide lifts all boats."

The 1980s and 1990s were such market periods. After more than a decade of upside-down moves in the 1960s and 1970s, the U.S. stock market finally bottomed out in August 1982 and began a long climb for almost 20 years. Although the rally was punctuated sometimes by dramatic losses, the market soon recovered and resumed the uptrend. Thus, from young people who had just started their careers to those approaching retirement, a generation of investors experienced little in the ways of truly volatile markets—that is, until 2000.

Volatility Is the Norm

Volatility, with sharp moves up and down, was the norm, not the exception, in the history of the U.S. stock market. Furthermore, prolonged periods of up and down moves lasting almost two decades were predominant after market peaks, ending with losses or little gains.

Figure 5.1 recaps the movements of the Dow Jones Industrial Average (DJIA) since 1915. Making its debut on May 26, 1896 with 12 industrial companies, the Dow spent the next two decades with up and down movements but yielded no gain. Then, the following 92 years saw three distinct cycles; each started with a low mark to begin an up year, followed by new highs to start a new bull market with subsequent new higher highs. The first period began in 1915 and ended in 1949, lasting for 34 years and having an annualized return in price of 3.7 percent. The second period lasted for 32 years, between 1950 and 1982, generating an annualized return of 4.4 percent. The current period began in 1983, having passed 25+ years, and is still continuing.

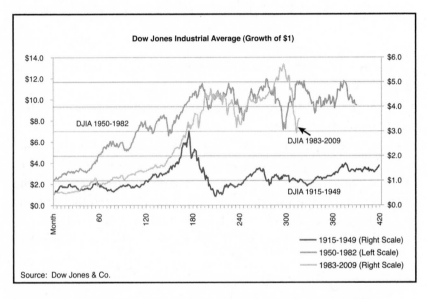

Figure 5.1   Three long-term cycles: DJIA between 1915 and 2009

Slumber Parties: Long and Sustained

Characteristically, in each of the three cycles, the Dow went through more than a decade of continuous uptrend. When a new peak was reached, a severe downturn characteristic of a bear market followed. The years subsequent to the peaks were punctuated with up and down movements but in the end produced only losses.

In each of the first two periods, the DJIA rallied for about a decade and a half, with only short-lived interruptions in between. When the new peaks were reached in 1929 and 1966, respectively, the Dow's movements for the next two decades were noted for their sharp gyrations, with periods of strong gains followed by substantial losses; cumulatively, only losses occurred at the end. After the crash in 1929, the Dow made a six-year high in 1937; it then dropped off sharply, losing 47 percent in about a year, by March 1938. It returned to this March low four years later. By the time this cycle ended in 1949, it was below the interim high in 1937.

In the years between 1950 and 1982, the Dow staged a strong 16-year uptrend until 1966, with corrections in between lasting for no more than a few months. Following the cycle peak in early 1966, the Dow dropped 22 percent in October. But the cycle's final lows were not reached until December 1974, for a loss of 42 percent since the 1966 high. In between, it went up and then down, testing the previous high points and then making new lows, frustrating both the bears and the bulls in the process. By the time the cycle ended in July 1982, the Dow had returned to the low marks in October 1966.

As shown in Figure 5.1, an investor investing $1 at the beginning of 1915 would see his investment valued at $3.67 at the end of 1949. This represented a compounded annual return of 3.7 percent for 35 years; it was a loss of 47.3 percent for a 20-year holding since the peak in August 1929. In the second period, the $1 investment in 1950 would reach the peak in about 16 years. It would then follow a roller-coaster performance with higher tops and substantial reversals for the remainder of the period. Holding on the Dow as an investment after the peak in 1966 would result in a loss of 16.5 percent by July 1982.

In the third period starting in August 1982, the market kept rising for almost 20 years and then was cut short by the tech stocks' bubble burst in 2000. Since then, the market volatility has surpassed any comparable periods in the past. By early 2009, the Dow had come back down to where it was 12 years earlier, wiping out more than a decade of gains. Between January 2000 and March 2009, the Dow lost a cumulative 44 percent; the drop was larger than the comparable period in the previous cycle.

Thus, within the entire period of 112 years, between 1896 and 2009, the Dow index treaded water the majority of the time—about 65 years. For holders of stocks as long-term investments, perhaps as a generational legacy, the annualized return of the DJIA was 5.4 percent for the 112 years. As of June 2009, the annualized return for the current cycle was 8.3 percent, or twice as much as the previous two periods. Will the current bear market run its due course to correct this cycle's anomaly? Or is it the comeback of the "New New Thing" of Netscape and Internet days when stock prices just climbed on expectations of never-ending unreality?

Staying in the stock market after the cycle highs in these three periods has not been a rewarding experience, regardless of one's patience or investment objectives. And the stock market has undeniably been in the middle of an upside-down market cycle. The only uncertainty is the contours of the gyrations and how long this period of volatility will last—10 more years, as some market observers have suggested, undoubtedly conscious of the historical cycles? Or 20 years like the Japanese experience, which started its two lost decades in a much better shape as an economy than the United States in 2008. Will the market continue to have recoveries lasting as long as those following the bottoms in 1932 and 1966, only to collapse later? Or will it maintain a holding pattern like the Nikkei after the lows in 1992? In the final analysis, whichever way it goes doesn't really matter. An investment that is directionless, with only some chance of winning but even higher odds of losing, is a lost opportunity and a dangerous trap for the unwary. It's even more so for those who need dependable cash flows and income—those who save and invest instead of trading in and out on the basis of every piece of news and exhortations.

Bull Traps and False Bottoms

Even in prolonged bear market cycles, there were still periods of substantial rising stock prices. Consider the 16 years between 1966 and 1982 (see Figure 5.2). The Dow reached this cycle's peak in February 1966, and then it declined. Yet there were several periods during this time that the Dow logged significant gains. Between October 1966 and November 1968, the Dow went up by 32 percent. The Dow also rose by 66 percent between the lows of May 1970 to the highs of January 1973. The gain between December 6, 1974 and March 24, 1976 was even more spectacular: 74 percent. Month by month, the Dow marched forward with small pauses in between. However, as the bear market conditions reasserted themselves, each of these bull runs was followed by precipitous declines; the market lows in October 1966 were surpassed by the lows in May 1970. The rise that ended in January 1973 was followed by a decline of a whopping 45 percent, and it lasted for 23 months.

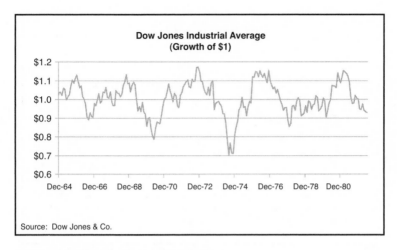

Figure 5.2   Stocks during stagflation

Overall, the Dow staged numerous strong rallies during those 16 years only to return to the levels of the 1966 bottom—an almost two-decade span of unrewarded patience for savers and long-term investors. An investor who entered at the market bottom in October 1966 would see no gain by July 1982 but a lot of euphoria and agony in between.

In the 1929 crash, seemingly the Dow went down in a straight line (see Figure 5.3). Nevertheless, it had a rally of 32 percent between November 13 and December 10, 1929. Overall, the years between 1929 and 1949 were a long period of market consolidation with gains and losses, sometimes large. After bottoming in June 1932, the Dow went on rallying until February 1937. By that time, it had only reached about halfway from the 1929 peak, but it was 4.4 times the value at the bottom in June 1932. That was an impressive return of 37 percent a year. Alas, in the next 12 years, the index was stagnant, despite some impressive gains in between. Overall, the Dow did not return to its 1929 high until 25 years later!

Fast forward to the 2000 bear market. The rally since the market bottom in 2002 was followed by another incline in 2003 back down to almost the 2002 low. Subsequently, fueled by leveraging with subprime mortgages and credit default swaps (CDSs), the gains painstakingly accumulated in the four years between 2003 and 2007 were wiped out in just a year.

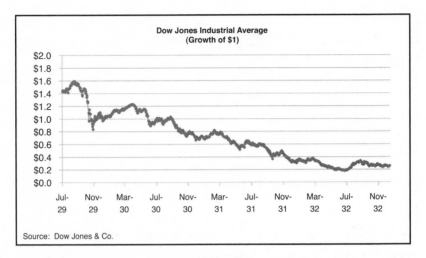

Figure 5.3   Stocks in the Depression

During the 2007–2009 crash, the Dow had so far behaved in a similar fashion. After hitting a low of 7,882 on October 10, 2008 amid the banking panic, the Dow bounced 22 percent on November 4. This see-saw pattern continued in the following months, with gains and losses reaching 20 percent or more in each move up or down. The Dow then tumbled to a new low on March 9, 2009 after the new president of the United States had his economic stimulus package passed by the Congress; between January 6 and March 9, the Dow lost 27 percent in two months of trading.

Another bounce followed the March 9 low, with a gain of 33 percent in June. That wasn't a bad move, but it was not an unusual bounce after a big sell-off.

Looking to the Future

This move is unlikely to represent the beginning of an extended new bull market lasting for years unless all the debt, the dislocations in the economy, evaporate into thin air.

Starting for the Future

A look back in the rearview mirror of history reveals that the 1983–1999 period was the most exceptional in the record of the U.S. stock market. In the entire 16-year duration of the uptrend, there was only one year that the market recorded a loss. That year was 1990, and the loss was puny—merely –3.1 percent—sandwiched between two years of spectacular gains, each exceeding 30 percent. If anything, that year was an opportunity not seen again in many years to participate in the market or to build up a larger position. Overall, for the 1983–1999 period, the Dow gained on average 16 percent annually. This was a spectacular performance compared to comparable periods in the past—that is, 1918–1929 and 1950–1965.

In retrospect, that kind of return could not be sustainable, and it was not. Fundamentally, the stock market in the 1980s and 1990s benefited from a combination of factors unlikely to be repeated. Starting with depressed prices for a decade, the equity market got a lift from a renewed sense of confidence in the Federal Reserve as an inflation fighter in 1979 when Paul Volker took over as chairman. By targeting money supply (the so-called M1, which consisted of currency in circulation and short-term deposit accounts), the Fed engineered successive interest rate hikes. In the process, it succeeded in bringing the inflation rate down from a record high of almost 15 percent in 1980. As inflation tumbled, the Fed was able to reduce interest rates (see Figure 5.4). The effective Fed funds rate reached 21 percent in December 1980, but it rapidly dropped from then on. Nevertheless, the stock market did not begin its rally (in August 1982) until almost the very end of the 1981–82 recession. Once ended, the economy grew at a rapid rate, reaching as high as 7.2 percent in 1984. At the same time, the economy benefited from huge tax cuts, but the federal government's debt still expanded at a rate below the growth of the nominal GDP. (See Figure 3.8 in Chapter 3, "The Root Causes: Leveraging and Excess.") The federal budget deficits also increased with the tax cuts, but they peaked at around 6 percent in 1983 and then declined in subsequent years. Concurrently, the financial sector by and large had strong balance sheets with debts growing well below nominal GDP growth. Mostly, everything was going right for the economy. A strategist recalling the economic background of the 1982 start of the bull market ruefully observed, "Unfortunately, unlike 1982, no such springboard for outsized market returns today.... Few would argue that excessive negative sentiment can be a powerful force for market rallies in the short term. But ultimately, fundamentals make the difference between a range-bound market and the start of a sustainable bull phase."[1]

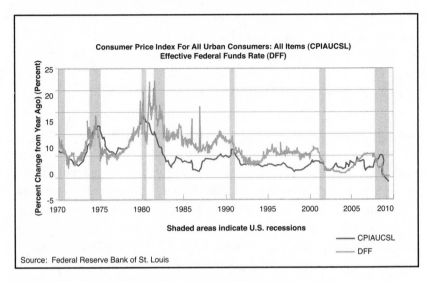

Figure 5.4   Consumer price index and Fed funds rate

When the 1990s came, the economy's balance sheet remained relatively healthy, with a reduction in both federal budget deficits (which eventually turned into a surplus) and in government debt (see Figure 3.10, Chapter 3), and with the trade deficits staying modest until the latter half of the decade (see Figure 1.6 in Chapter 1, "Black Swan Octobers"). Overall, the economy's debt grew roughly at the same rate as the nominal GDP. But all of that was more or less just a tailwind—albeit very strong—that pushed the stock market higher and higher, for the real drivers of the market's stupendous gains were the advance of the personal computer, Internet technologies, and the entire tech sector. The Internet mania seemed it would never stop. In the five years ending in 1999, the Dow tripled in price, even exceeding its appreciation in the same period that ended in August 1929.

As in 1929, it all came to a screeching halt with the tech bubble burst in 2000, and then again with the 2008 crash. From 2008 to mid-2009, the market went through a difficult and painful recognition of the excess leveraging and risk-taking in the entire U.S. economy, which we have discussed in the previous chapters. With both private and public sectors' debt remaining elevated at unprecedented and historic levels, with them projected to continue to rise, as well as with the prospect of lower economic growth, this adjustment will prove to be difficult and uneven. Already Fed Governor Janet Yellen warned that more volatility could lie ahead for the U.S. and world economies now that "...the Great Moderation is behind us, so we must be prepared for substantial shocks."[2] Even the Fed chairman acknowledged in testimony to the House of Representatives' budget committee that after a recovery gets under way, growth would likely remain below its potential for a while. "We now are on a process of slow and gradual repair, both in the financial system and the economy," he said.[3]

The bond market was jittery in 2009 as the stock market rallied, with the rates of economic deterioration decelerating—that is, the economy was not getting better, but the pace of worsening was not accelerating. Figures 5.5 and 5.6 show the reaction of long-term interest rates to the movements of the stock market. As stocks tumbled in 2008, the Fed stepped up the reduction of Fed funds rates, and longer-term rates declined correspondingly. The stock rally since March 2009, however, has brought 20- and 30-year Treasury rates back up to the pre-crisis levels, at the peak of the Fed tightening cycle in March 2007. The yield curve also turned positive with the 2- versus 30-year spreads widening from negative to flat early in 2007 and then to 362 basis points in June 2009. However, as the stock market pulled back from the rally in June, interest rates also retreated, and the yield curve flattened with long-term Treasury rates declined.

The widening of the spread and the spike in long-term rates were a reversal for the Fed's effort to revive the economy. In November, the Fed had announced a program to purchase agency mortgage-backed securities. In March, it expanded the program to the tune of $1.25 trillion, as well as started to buy $300 billion of long-term Treasury bonds. When yields were backed up, Fed officials expressed concerns that the bond market's reaction may reflect investors' fear of the consequences of the massive fiscal and monetary stimulus. And indeed, the movements retraced above only confirmed the dilemma the Fed was facing: Namely, a pick-up in stock market and economic activity would lead to higher interest rates, which in turn would undermine continuation of growth of the economy.

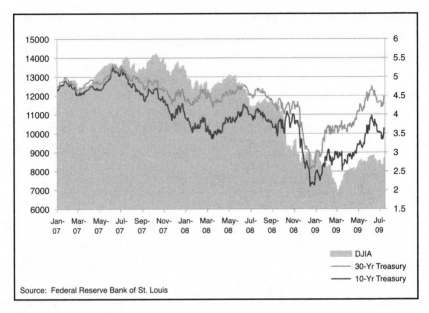

Figure 5.5   Long-term interest rates and stock prices

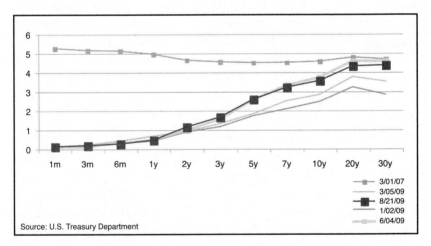

Figure 5.6   Yield curve shifts

The bond market fear is particularly worrisome when the economy is still reeling in the recession and rising unemployment. By mid-2009, the unemployment rate had shot up to 9.5 percent and was well on the path of rivaling or exceeding the unemployment rate in 1983.

However, back in the early 1980s, the economy had the benefit of the beginning of a monetary easing regime starting from 18 percent and a relatively benign federal budget situation.

At mid-2009, interest rates were at the lowest points in 30 years. When the Fed announced the Treasury bond program in March 2009, yields on Treasuries reacted immediately, dropping by 10 basis points in one day. So far, the Fed has expended $450 billion in the purchase program and still had $800 billion in its coffers to spend until the end of the year. But the effect of the Fed purchase has proved to be transient and short lived.

Rising unemployment and higher interest rates also have had a deleterious effect on the recovery of the housing market, which was ground zero of the current crisis. Although the Fed chairman said he believed house prices were returning to stability, indicators of the health of the housing industry have painted a far gloomier prospect. Foreclosures have risen, and not only among the subprime mortgage holders—they have spread to prime mortgages as well. As unemployment keeps rising, mortgage delinquencies among more credit-worthy borrowers are expected to increase, too, and they have. Also, mortgage refinancing activities came to a virtual halt with rates climbing in mid-2009; then they resumed as rates eased off in the following months.

The upward moves of interest rates further complicate, and likely undermine, the cornerstone of the government stimulus programs by running up huge budget deficits and expanding the Fed balance sheet. This, in turn, will have consequences on the U.S. ability to borrow from abroad. China has already indicated its concerns over the U.S. fiscal management and warned the United States of actions it could take to reduce its purchase and holdings of U.S. Treasury securities. For sure, China depends on exports to the United States for its economic growth, and the United States is the only market large and deep enough to invest its resulting surplus. Also, any action to diversify its foreign currency holdings away from the U.S. dollar will surely take time. However, the skepticism and doubt about the soundness of the U.S. financial system and economy have decidedly surfaced in China, and the country has taken steps to rely less on the dollar— although these steps are still small and peripheral, such as designating the Yuan for trade settlements with some of its neighboring countries.

Even Germany's Chancellor Merkel expressed concerns that central banks may have gone too far in trying to fight the global financial crisis. "I view with great skepticism the powers that the Fed has, for example, and how, in the European area, the Bank of England has developed its own little lines," she said. The ECB "also bowed somewhat to international pressure" with its decision to buy bonds, she added. "We must together return to an independent central bank policy and to a policy of good sense," Merkel said. "Otherwise, in 10 years, we will again be standing at exactly this point."[4]

The dollar has already heeded these warnings. Reversing the weak trend since 2002, the dollar strengthened against the euro and other foreign currencies as the financial crisis intensified in mid-2008 and global investors sought safe haven by flocking to the dollar. As a creditor currency, the Japanese yen also enjoyed renewed strength and rose against both the dollar and the euro.

However, these risk-aversion trades have been reversed with the passing of the worst of the banking crisis by March 2009. As shown in Figure 5.7, the yen and the euro had regained much of their lost ground amid the call by the Governor of the People's Bank of China, Zhou Xiaochuan, whom the secretary of the Treasury praised as "a very thoughtful, very careful, distinguished central banker,"[5] for a new international currency unit to replace the mismanaged dollar. The reason is that "[a] super-sovereign reserve currency not only eliminates the inherent risks of credit-based sovereign currency, but also makes it possible to manage global liquidity," Zhou wrote in a paper titled "Reform the International Monetary System."[6] "This will significantly reduce the risks of a future crisis and enhance crisis management capability," he continued. The remarks from Governor Zhou came on the heels of the chastisement a few days earlier from China's Premier Wen Jiabao. "We have lent huge amounts of money to the U.S. [and] we are concerned about the safety of our assets," he said.[7]

So, this is where we are, starting on the next journey to the future, beset by a highly leveraged debt burden with a worsening outlook, subpar economic growth, and grim prospects of retaining our jobs and preserving our life savings and assets; hampered on all sides by the exigencies of market forces; and dependent on the kindness or complacencies of foreign governments of questionable dependability. But the stock market has embarked on a rally, oblivious to all of what has ailed the economy. It has done so many times before, advancing on a momentum of its own, only to reverse course at the most unexpected moments, again hurting the unwary investors who rely on Wall Street experts to preserve their life savings.

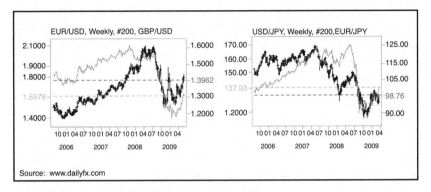

Figure 5.7   The dollar versus the euro and the yen

Looking into the Future

Predicting the future is a hazardous business, besieged with mistaken signs and distorted rearview mirrors, made foggier with the passage of time and emotion. But the more confusing the outlook, the clearer one thing is: The investing game is becoming less favorable, the odds are increasing, and winning is questionable and much less assured, as it used to be in the 1980s and 1990s.

It is with this sense of dread that we peer into the future, not necessarily to draw a map but to discern the contours of a vague outline. Our purpose is rooted in the view that unless the weather is fine, the journey would not be worth taken for savers and investors who rely on their nest eggs for retirement income and support.

It is tempting to start our review with the 2000 bear market. A lot of losses had been taken, and many of those who spread the mania were long gone. Perhaps the excesses had been wrung out of the system. Alas, that market debacle was confined mostly in the tech stock sector; unlike the 2008 crash, it was not a systemic breakdown. That was why the NASDAQ had taken an 80 percent loss, while the Dow Jones' loss had been "only" half as much. In retrospect, it took only an adjustment of the lofty valuation of tech stocks for the market to come back to its always-delicate balance. Important to remember also, at its recovery peak in 2007, the NASDAQ reached only half of its all-time high in 2000! And in 2008, it only returned to its lows in 2002, not breaking new ground, unlike such broad market indices as the Dow and the S&P 500, which this time bore the brunt of the systemic collapse.

Going into the 2008 crisis, the economy was further weakened and bereft with even greater imbalances than in 2000, with worsening outlook in the future years, by rising federal budget deficits and unprecedented leveraged balance sheets in all sectors of the economy. Whatever adjustments had been achieved by the burst of the tech bubble were undone, while new excesses were accumulated in the economy, not in one sector but throughout the system, from housing and banking to households and the federal, state, and local governments. The economy will need fundamental adjustments to right itself, but until then, the equity market will have only exhortations of the moment to support its rallies.

DJIA and the Nikkei 225

Let's start with the market peak in October 2007 and put it next to the Nikkei 225 index at its high in December 1989. After all, those data points were the two indices' historic highs, arrived on the back of waves of real estate speculation, which similarly took down the two indices once their respective bubbles popped (see Figure 5.8). In the chart, the Nikkei has endured two decades of slumber while the Dow just began its own. Nevertheless, the crash of the Dow since October 2007 looked eerily similar to the collapse of the Nikkei after the 1989 peak. And so far, the bounce in the Dow has been of a similar magnitude.

It is easy enough to dismiss this graphic similarity as merely an artifact or coincidence—that is, except for the circumstances of look-alike punctured real estate bubbles and similar policy responses, as discussed in the previous chapters. Furthermore, although Japan's two lost decades are impossible to imagine, they are real, and the United States is starting this uncertain journey in much worse shape.

Clearly, the Federal Reserve is aware of the risks. Fed Chairman Bernanke is a learned scholar of the deflation risks in Japan after its real estate crash and the collapse of its stock market. That's why the

Fed has flooded the system with money. It also understands that it's the money it doesn't have. The Fed merely hopes that the economy will right itself before it executes its "exit strategy." This exit strategy refers to a Fed plan whereby it will raise interest rates and possibly drain some of the liquidity it has injected into the system in its $1.75 trillion purchase program of mortgage-backed securities and bonds. "The time will come when the economy will be growing, the housing market will be recovering, that support will no longer be needed. And we will, of course, at that point taper off that support," Chairman Bernanke told a group of community bankers in Phoenix, Arizona in May.[8] We will grow out of this!

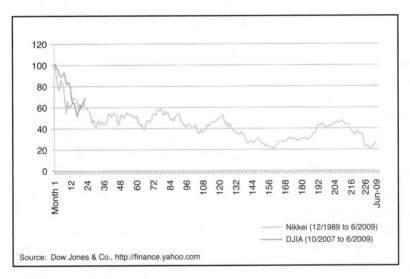

Figure 5.8   Nikkei's lost decades and the Dow

Monetary Policy and Inflation

According to a Bloomberg survey, the market expected the Fed funds rate to be raised to 1 percent by the third quarter of 2010. At the same time, the Federal Open Market Committee has a long-run forecast for price increases of 1.7 to 2 percent. If and when these forecasts materialize, the Fed funds rate will be about 1 percent below the inflation rate—that is, if the Fed funds rate is raised to 1 percent.

If the Fed followed through with this plan, it would be a delicate balancing act. As an economist observed, "It will be years before they can start selling, if ever [referring to the securities bought in the bond purchase program].... Can they raise interest rates with an expanded balance sheet? The answer is yes. Can they do it in a tidy way? The answer is, we don't know."[9] It is also a dilemma that the Fed had faced in the 1970s. As it turned out, the Fed had kept interest rates lagging behind inflation during that time, fearing that a tight monetary policy would choke off economic growth otherwise.

In the current crisis, the Fed faces more challenging circumstances created by its bloated balance sheet and unprecedented and rising debt levels in all sectors of the economy, as well as the severely weakened state of the economy. Furthermore, the federal budget deficits are set to approach 10 percent of GDP for years to come, as compared to 4 percent or so in the 1970s. As a result, premature application of the "exit strategy" with measures to drain liquidity from the system, including selling the purchased securities and increases of interest rates, could set off a chain reaction that would undermine economic growth, as well as possibly and more critically create renewed balance sheet distress for the entire economy. The current Fed chairman has made quite clear his concerns regarding these issues in various speeches. For example, in a speech in 2002 when he was still a Fed governor, he talked about an acceptable inflation range of 1 to 3 percent. "Second, the Fed should take most seriously—as of course it does—its responsibility to ensure financial stability in the economy.... Third,...when inflation is already low and the fundamentals of the economy suddenly deteriorate, the central bank should act more preemptively and more aggressively than usual in cutting rates," the Fed chairman continued.[10] The chairman has lived up to his words in dealing with the 2008 crisis. Given the distressed state of the economy, the Fed is likely to refrain from tightening monetary policy until well past the time any reflationary fears have resurfaced. In fact, that was the stance it adopted after the 2001 recession out of concerns for remaining deflationary risks. There is, thus, a clear and material risk that an accommodating monetary stance will prevail for a prolonged number of years like in the 1970s for the economy to have time to cure its balance sheet excesses.

DJIA: Stagflation and the 2008 Crisis

What would the stock market look like if such reflationary monetary policies were put in place, in the face of rising federal deficits and debt levels? It would be most unlikely that the Fed would telegraph to the world an intention of inflationary policies. The dollar would collapse, long-term interest rates would soar, costs of debt servicing would become unmanageable, and the economy would be severely undermined. Rather, as Chairman Bernanke said on more than one occasion, "The (Fed) believes that a highly accommodative stance of monetary policy will be appropriate for an extended period."[11] The Fed would probably allow benchmark interest rates to lag behind inflation like in the 1970s (see Figure 5.9).

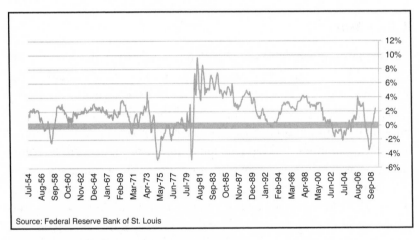

Source: Federal Reserve Bank of St. Louis

Figure 5.9   Real effective Fed funds rates

The stock market would not likely react well to such a development. It is thus instructive to look with a sharper focus at how stock prices evolved over the period between 1966 and 1982 (see Figure 5.10). It is no coincidence that the post-1966 market malaise lasted as long it did, given the conduct of monetary policies.

But it is noticeable that the contours of equity price movements during that period were hardly more desirable than the Nikkei's 20-year slumber. Most importantly, in both cases, the market malaise lasted longer than any investor's patience can tolerate. And in the end, stocks were poor investments either way.

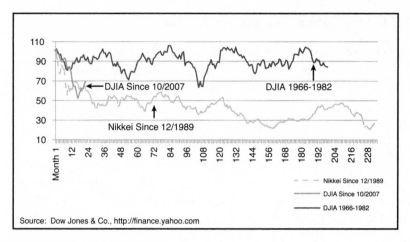

Figure 5.10   Lost decades?

A Bull Market?

It is not impossible to imagine that the rally from the March 2009 lows could turn into a multiyear extension, like the advances in the aftermath of previous crashes. The Federal Reserve can keep money cheap for far longer than expected, and the federal government can offer up one after another cash-for-clunkers programs. It is the power of printing money and deficit spending. Although current equity valuation is hardly a bargain with price-to-earning multiples in the middle of the historical range, stocks are bought often for no other reason than because prices are expected to go higher. We saw this phenomenon in Japan in the several years before the 1989 peak. We saw it again prior to the tech bubble burst in 2000. The multiyear market advance before the collapse in 2008 was built on a pyramid scheme of easy credit and inflated house prices. Before the collapse of Lehman Brothers and its abandonment by the Treasury and the Federal Reserve in September 2008, the stock market was almost oblivious to the subprime debacle and the coming banking collapse. The price decline, up to then, seemed to be a mere correction of the previous five years of nonstop rally. But when the recognition came, everyone in the crowd tried to exit by the narrow door.

The imperative that governs the stock market has always been higher and higher prices until proven otherwise. In the current cycle, the Fed seems more than willing to offer a ready, helping hand by keeping the Fed funds rate near zero and monetizing purchase of long-term bonds for an "extended period." And for now, the Fed can find comfort for its accommodative stance from the inflation front— or is it deflation?

In fact, year after year, the producer price index has been dropping since the previous year at annualized rates in the double digits, and the decline has accelerated in recent months. In July 2009, the drop was 16 percent, unseen since the 1930s depression. Clearly, businesses have found it difficult to pass on to consumers increases in their costs of production. The consumer price index has also been decreasing, albeit the decline has been attributed to food and energy. The Fed has thus enough justification for keeping interest rates at near zero. Until these price inflation indicators show up as a sustained upswing, bond vigilantes will not have much of a reason to push long-term rates higher, dire warnings of exploding debt notwithstanding— at least until China and other foreign creditors complain again or reduce their purchases of Treasury securities loudly enough for everyone to notice. Then the dollar may head into a precipitous decline, serving as an excuse and warning to sell equities.

Another Crisis, Another Bailout

However, another crash of the equity market and its depressive impact on the economy may not be easily reversed this time by lowering interests, with quantitative easing, or by federal government stimulus programs. Interest rates will have been too low to be reduced for effects and the Fed balance sheet already stressed out. The government will find that its budget deficits and record debt load make it difficult if not impossible, in the context of opposition politics in the Congress, to get a trillion dollars here, another there for bailout and stimulus spending. The banks, which reported profits on the back of subsidized capital provided by taxpayers while retaining toxic assets on their balance sheets, may find their financial strength inadequate to absorb new write-offs and loan defaults. Meanwhile, households are hardly in a position to take another hit, after losing trillions of dollars in equities and real estate, amid rising job losses and low savings rates.

Then again, how long can an economy grow on unsustainable debt and reliance on foreigners' largess to fund its relentless spending? How many fabricated booms and busts can a country absorb before its paper money loses its international standing and its social fabric is torn apart?

When the next crisis comes, there might not be money anywhere to bail out the banks, the homeowners, the consumers, or the governments—except for the Federal Reserve to crank up the printing press at full speed. But the global markets have a way to express their displeasure, through soaring interest rates, the dollar's collapse, and sell-offs of stock prices.

Until then, stock prices can keep rising even in the face of bad news, as long as the news is not worse than expected. Optimism and hopes are eternal in the equity market.

The danger is, savers and long-term investors might be attracted to this Wall Street's version of reality show, only to be disappointed later when it turns out that everything was staged, and their life savings are once more incinerated.

It does not need to be that way.

In the following chapters, we will discuss a framework and strategies to help long-term savers grow savings and build wealth in the long term, and avoid the vagaries and false promises of the stock market, while positioned to take advantage of opportunities in stocks (yes!) and global markets to enhance returns and earn profits. In the next chapter, we will review the paradigms of investment beliefs as they are currently practiced and how far off they are from reality.

6

Investment Paradigms: Beliefs and Reality

The stock market began the 1980s, with its long historic climb lasting for almost 20 years. As the rally gained speed with little pause, investors clamored to get into the game. According to data from the Federal Reserve Flows of Funds statistics (FFA), as percentage of household financial assets, directly held equities had reached 28.4 percent by 1999. Including indirectly held stocks in defined contribution and defined benefit plans, household ownership exposure to stocks had climbed to 50.1 percent. That was just in time to hit the wall of the bear market in early 2000.

The ensuing destruction of wealth by the bear markets in 2000 and 2008 went beyond the losses indicated by the percentage declines of the major indices. At the end of 2008, the DJIA had declined to the level approximately prevailing at the end of 1999. Does that mean investors' wealth came back to where it was in 1999? No. Equities held by households at the end of 2008 was 29.5 percent less than in 1999; the loss of $5 trillion in those 10 years wiped out not only the investment gains, but also the additional capital that had been put into the market during that time. By any measure, household allocations to equities had also been substantially cut to much less than what they were at the end of 1999. As a percentage of financial assets, equities accounted for 29.7 percent at the end of 2008, or 40 percent less than in 1999. In terms of total assets, equities dropped to only 18.5 percent, which was a 47 percent reduction from the 1999 allocation of 35.2 percent.

The stock market staged a rally from its low in March 2009. However, as indicated by major indices like the DJIA or S&P, the rally recaptured only a portion of the losses since the October 2007 peak. For either index, the losses were still 40 percent from the peak.

Importantly, the index values were pretty much the same as when the worst of the banking crisis hit the market in October 2008. This rally does not appear to be much different from the bounces in the past, which are characteristic of the market when it has gotten beyond the panic of fears. Despite this, many investors wonder if they should get back into the market, especially in view of such presumed certainties as a strategist's loudly proclaimed "inexorable continuation of the equity rally."[1] Another market sage of the Internet age, who had never predicted a down year, pronounced: "We do think the new bull market has begun."[2] Or should investors take advantage of this rally and sell at least parts of their stock holdings? Come to think of it, how much stock should investors have in their portfolios? Should they invest in stocks at all?

To answer these questions, investors have little to rely on, other than the myths and old beliefs spouted from two decades of rising stock prices. Reeling with the losses and the highly uncertain prospects of economic recovery, as well as the potential of future equity returns, investors worry about the possibility of more losses if they re-enter the market too early. But the emotional and practical desires to recoup at least some of the losses and the urgings of the promoters of the only game in town can be difficult to ignore. Many investors also face the prospect of *having* to sell their investments, in whole or in part, to fund their retirement, pay for college education, or for some other major expenditures. Above all, they are worried about issues that, lulled by years of rising markets, current investment practices have paid scant attention to:

- **Capital preservation**—How do you preserve capital in volatile markets where rising and declining stock prices intertwine in high frequency? Or in a lasting market downturn?

- **Liquidity needs**—How do you have sufficient liquidity to meet periodic spending needs and other obligations? How do you avoid selling stocks in a declining market to meet living expenses and other commitments?

- **Risk management**—How do you manage investment risks to avoid destructive losses?

- **Nontraditional investments**—Investors have been bombarded with recommendations to invest in such investments as commodities with little guidelines. How suitable are such risky assets to a retirement or savings plan that cannot afford devastating losses like those experienced in 2008 by commodity funds?

We will return to these issues in the following chapters. For now, let's focus on those aspects of investment paradigms that have rendered investors defenseless in both the 2000 bear market and the 2008 debacle.

Stocks as Protection Against Inflation

Inflation is a curse against money. It erodes your purchasing power while reducing your wealth and income by way of more government tax deductions (as your tax bracket moves up due to inflation). So, to provide protection against the corrosive impact of inflation, financial experts advise investors to invest in stocks. And the record of stocks as an inflation fighter was impressive during the long 16 years between 1983 and 1999 with the market continuously going up, as we have seen. However, if the curtain of history is raised further back to the start of the Dow, the inflation-adjusted record of stocks is even less impressive than the nominal returns we have seen in previous chapters. Figure 6.1 is a graphic presentation of the returns of the Dow after inflation starting in 1897. Note that the chart is drawn on logarithmic scale to account for proportional changes. There in the graph are three distinct cycles of stocks rising faster than inflation (up) and three distinct cycles of stocks lagging (down). The six up and down cycles came in sequence, one after the other. The first up cycle in the 1920s lasted about 10 years; the next two up cycles lasted about 20 years. However, the three down cycles lasted approximately 20 years. The current cycle shown to have started in 2000 is pointing down. Will the Dow repeat the previous cycles to fall behind inflation for the next 10 years or longer? Obviously, the chart is graphically suggestive that the outlook of inflation-adjusted equity returns is precipitously downward. It is also consistent with the analysis in the previous chapters of the economy and its outlook.

One thing, however, is quite clear: For all of these reasons, the outlook for stocks as an inflation fighter does not look promising!

Should investors treat stocks with greater caution and more skepticism than in the past?

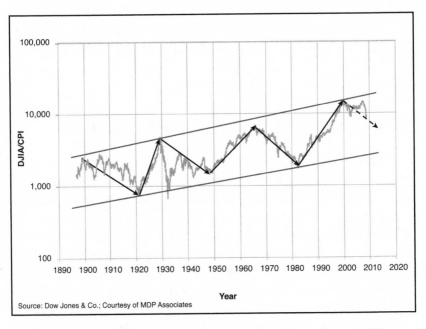

Figure 6.1   Inflation-adjusted returns of the Dow Jones Industrial Average (log scale)

But why should we think of stocks as a good investment in inflationary time? Hasn't anyone heard of the "Goldilocks" economy: It's best for stocks when it's not too hot and not too cold? Even then, you would need a strong economy that grows at a healthy rate for stocks to go up like in the mid-1990s! Stocks certainly were not doing too well during the inflationary time and easy monetary policy of the 1970s. When inflation gets a bit too high for comfort, the Federal Reserve will have to raise interest rates, even if reluctantly and insufficiently. As to the adverbs in the previous sentence, the Fed chairman has already made clear that it is the monetary posture he intends to take—he will keep money easy for an extended period of time. Holders of maturing debts—and we have a huge mountain of them here, such as the U.S. government, businesses, and consumers with revolving credit cards and reset mortgages, will have a chance to find out how the Fed's "exit strategy" will help them obtain financing at a cost that will allow them to go about their business as usual. Or perhaps they will find out that borrowing costs become so prohibitively expensive that it may be better to shut down their businesses. In this event, it is instructive to remember that the banks are not as generous with lending as they used to be. Then again, maybe China will step in to bail us out, because they always have, right? So, instead of Uncle Sam, now we go to Uncle Chin for help? Just remember that as generous (or misguided, as some say) as Uncle Sam was with the financial bailout, he did say NO on at least one occasion with Lehman Brothers, and all hell broke loose.

Averaging Out the Losses

In rising markets, investing is simple. However, what if investors fear that stock prices will go down after they have bought the stocks? The standard answer provided by Wall Street advisors is dollar cost averaging: Buy a bit today, and buy more later. It is a common refrain from Wall Street to lure investors when the market conditions look iffy. It is another version of "hold on, the market will come back rising again!"

In its benign version for long-term savers in 401(k) plans, dollar cost averaging can be useful. But as an equity investment strategy, it is difficult to apply. Anyway, the strategy depends on the market going up!

In this strategy, an investor sets out a plan to invest a certain amount in stocks with periodic regularity. Thus, the investor may set aside, say, $100 (or multiples thereof) to invest in the stock market every month, regardless of his expectations or feelings about the market, or whether the market is going up or down. Contributors to 401(k) plans are regular practitioners of this strategy, although they might change the contribution amounts allocated to stocks now and then with the market's changing fortunes. However, the required discipline may make it difficult for others whose cash flows, income, and available savings are uncertain or irregular.

The chart in Figure 6.2 shows the growth of a $100 investment that was put into the market in 1989 and the monthly returns of the Dow in the past 20 years between January 1989 and December 2008. This $100 investment would have grown to $430. Thus, if an investor invested $24,000 in one lump sum in 1989, this amount would have reached $97,200 at the end of the 20-year period. Suppose the investor instead invested only $100 at the beginning of each month, starting with January 1989. The total investment would still be $24,000, but it would be spread over 240 months. Table 6.1 shows the results of the two strategies—lump sum and dollar averaging—over four time periods over the past 20 years.

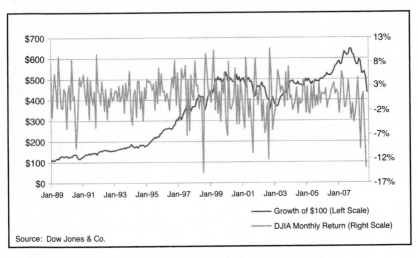

Figure 6.2   DJIA: monthly returns and investment growth

Note that after the first month's investment of $100, there's a balance of $23,900 that could be put into a short-term investment like a one-month CD. Likewise, the balances of $23,800 and $23,700 in the second and third month would be similarly invested. The interest income on these initial investments (assumed at the rate of 3 percent a year), as well as the following months for the rest of the 240-month period, would be added to the returns of the dollar averaging strategy.

	1989-2008 20-Year	1994-2008 15-Year	1999-2008 10-Year	2004-2008 5-Year
Investment Strategy	$ 24,000	$ 18,000	$ 12,000	$ 6,000
A-Lump Sum End-of-Period Value	$ 97,130	$ 42,081	$ 11,471	$ 5,037
b1-Dollar Cost Averaging	37,846	19,798	10,063	4,679
b2-Interest Income	7,170	4,028	1,785	443
B(b1+b2) - Dollar Cost Averaging End-of-Period Value	$ 45,016	$ 23,826	$ 11,848	$ 5,122

Source: Dow Jones & Co.

Table 6.1   Lump sum versus dollar cost averaging

As shown in the table, for the entire 20-year period, the lump sum strategy returned more than twice as much as dollar cost averaging. When the market was dominated by rising prices, such as in the 15- and 20-year periods, both strategies made significant gains, although profits from the lump sum strategy would be far greater than returns from dollar averaging. The 5- and 10-year periods (last two columns) coincided with variable markets. In the 1999–2008 period, the market's rise was interrupted by the tech bubble burst and the 2008 financial crisis; in between, the market rallied strongly between 2003 and 2007. The five years between 2004 and 2008, which started close to the market bottom, were notable, first for the strong market recovery, and then for a sharp downturn starting in November 2007. In these two periods, neither the lump sum nor the dollar averaging strategy showed distinct advantages.

Importantly, both approaches lost money in these markets. If the market goes straight down, dollar averaging produces smaller losses, because in such a market, the less one has in stocks, the better. However, if the market goes through cyclical ups and downs, like the 5- and 10-year periods in Table 6.1, it is unlikely that the dollar averaging strategy would provide much downside risk protection for investors. In a secular bull market, it would clearly be an inferior strategy.

The important conclusion to be underscored here is that both lump sum and dollar cost averaging strategies depend on the market going up. Indeed, if you assume that the market will keep going up, you should put the money to work right away and forget about dollar cost averaging. If the market goes down or through pronounced up and down cycles, such as during the 2000 and 2008 downturns, both strategies will generate only losses. An article in *Investor's Business Daily* summarized a study done by a major mutual fund company, which argued that dollar cost averaging is a superior strategy to what the author called "bad timing." The study was published in October 2008, and the article, "When Buy-and-Hold Beats Bad Timing," was run in February 2009, right in the middle of the worst bear market in a century. To make the case, the study used the long-term average return of 10.2 percent to project into a future of 30 years—starting in 2004.[3] Leaving out losses from the 2008 market disaster and assuming those returns, it is easy enough to make a case for buying stocks, dollar cost averaging or otherwise!

Return, Volatility, and Risk of Capital Losses

It is difficult to think of any human activity that is free of risks—from crossing the street, with the risk of being hit by a car; or boarding a plane, knowing it may crash; to the higher risk of injury or death in skydiving. In investments, even a safe instrument like a short-term Treasury bill has risks, even though it is guaranteed by the U.S. government. However, once an activity has acquired a certain degree of familiarity, the perception of its risk, as opposed to its actual risk of occurrence and loss, dims over time. Also, people perceive the same risk differently and have different levels of tolerance for it.

Given the myriad of ways to look at risks, more than half a century ago, Harry M. Markowitz, a finance professor at the University of California and Nobel laureate, posited an elegant theory, which evolves into what we know today as Modern Portfolio Theory (MPT).[4] The theory is simple and elegant, with a mathematically rigorous process that seeks to solve the thorny issue of how much assets are to be allocated among individual risky assets. However, to make the theory work, it assumes that investors are rational beings; there is no greed, no fear, and no otherwise irrational behavior. All investors look at the world of stocks through only two prisms: the expected return of the asset and its risk.

Expected Return

You may ask, expected return over what time period? MPT does not say, even though later modifications by others would show you how to solve the so-called multiperiod holding problem; that is, your investment horizon has multiple periods, and you have expectations of different returns for different periods. However, you need a lot of mathematical equations and a superfast computer to solve them. But the investment industry has a solution for it. Just assume that the annualized returns of stocks for the next 30 years would average 10.2 percent, as in the preceding *Investor's Business Daily* article, and hold on to your stock portfolio. That means you should not sell stocks in the interim; hold on to them!

Volatility

MPT has an ingenious way to define risk. It uses a mathematical construct, which supposedly measures the risk of an investment. It is called standard deviation of returns, or simply standard deviation; also known as volatility. (See the section titled "Standard Deviation.") But "risk" according to MPT is actually no more than a measurement of the variability of an investment's actual periodic returns from its simple average return over time. If a stock with higher volatility has a gain and another with lower volatility has a loss, you may not consider the former to be riskier. But, according to MPT, it would be; the mathematical reason for this outcome is that volatility on the upside is penalized as much as volatility on the downside, when in fact downside volatility is, well, more painful.

Thus, in the MPT world, a losing investment may not be any more risky than a winning investment, as long as both have the same volatility or variability of returns. Clearly, real people would think differently. They would be concerned about the risk of losses, and volatility is an incomplete and inadequate measure. But the risk of losses cannot be neatly factored into MPT mathematical equations.

Standard Deviation

Standard deviation is simple to calculate. It is the deviations of the actual returns of a stock or any investment from the average of its returns. To illustrate, suppose an investment X generates 20 percent, 25 percent, and 15 percent in years 1, 2, and 3. The average return of the three years is 20 percent. The deviations or differences between the individual years' returns and the average are 0 (20 minus 20), 5 (25 minus 20), and -5 (15 minus 20). These differences in percent are then squared (0, 25, 25), summed (50), divided by 3; and then take the square root. The standard deviation of this investment over this three-year period is 4.1 percent.

Now, let's consider investment Y that lost 20 percent, 25 percent, and 15 percent in years 1, 2, and 3: a totally opposite performance. The standard deviation of this investment is 4.1 percent, which is the same as investment X. Investment X gained 72.5 percent over three years while investment Y lost 49 percent, and yet X is said to be as risky as Y! Does it make any sense?

The DJIA generated annual returns of 22.6 percent, 16.1 percent, and 25.2 percent in 1997, 1998, and 1999. It then lost 6.2 percent, 7.1 percent, and 16.8 percent in the following three years. During 1997–99, the standard deviation of annual returns of the DJIA was 3.8 percent. (If calculated from monthly returns, the annualized standard deviation, which is the commonly used method, would be much higher, at 17.5 percent.) This was lower than the standard deviation of the ensuing three years of market declines, 4.8 percent, but not by much.

Nevertheless, this is *the* risk that underlies discussions about the risk of an investment, whether it is a mutual fund or a stock. How risky is a portfolio? Calculate its volatility! Mutual fund performance rankings are based on it. Returns are often adjusted for volatility and repackaged as risk-adjusted returns as if those returns were risk free.

To allocate investment funds across risky assets, MPT requires that all investors make decisions entirely based on the expected return and the standard deviation; then mathematics takes over. For any number of stocks, it constructs a continuum of portfolios with different weightings of those stocks; this continuum is known as the efficient frontier, and the portfolios on it are optimal.

Of course, professional portfolio managers do not construct portfolios this way. Their interest is to pick the best stocks—the most promising in terms of return. They are hardly conscious of the stocks' volatility, not in the way MPT intends for the construction of a portfolio. MPT is never meant to be, shall we say, a cookbook recipe. It is a brilliant conceptual framework to give insight into how rational people make decisions under uncertain conditions; namely, they evaluate the risk and the potential reward. But the investment industry uses the theory as a convenient tool in its business of selling stocks.

Volatility and Return

Furthermore, higher volatility does not necessarily produce higher return, even though that is a fundamental tenet of MPT, which says that higher risk, *aka* volatility, would lead to higher return over time. A number of academic studies pretty much confirm that volatility and return do *not* go hand in hand.[5]

We did a spot-check of the volatility of the S&P 500 index against three other stock indices that have higher volatilities, and the Barclays Aggregate Bond Index, which has substantially lower volatility. The three stock indices are Russell 3000, which represents the broad market; Russell 2000, which represents small cap stocks; and Russell 1000, for large cap stocks. We looked at the 15-year period from 1994–2009, with the market having up-down-up-down cycles; the 2000 to 2009 period; and the current bear market. This is shown in Table 6.2.

Comparing stocks and bonds, what is probably not expected is that bonds only slightly lagged stocks in the 15-year period between 1994 and June 2009, during which equities experienced two powerful multiyear rallies: from 1994–1999 and from 2004–2007. For bonds, the annualized return for this period was 6.07 percent compared to 6.45 by the S&P 500. (Without the equity rally in the second quarter of 2009, bonds would have outperformed stocks.) And the volatility of bonds was puny compared to the stock indices. Also, of course, during this bear market from November 2007 to March

2009, bonds outperformed stocks by wide margins. Interestingly, during the decade between 2000 and June 2009, bonds outperformed all the four stock indices, turning gains versus losses in stocks. Apparently, the 42 percent gain by the S&P 500 during the bull market between 2004 and 2007 along with the gain of 16 percent from the "market will come back" recovery in the second quarter of 2009 were not enough to outweigh the advantages of bonds.

	STOCKS				BONDS
	Russell 3000 Index	Russell 2000 Index	Russell 1000 Index	S&P 500	Barclays Aggregate Bond Index
1994-6/2009					
Volatility (Monthly Annualized)	15.66%	19.84%	15.71%	15.51%	3.88%
Return (Cumulative)	167.12%	142.21%	162.67%	163.35%	149.10%
2000-6/2009					
Volatility (Monthly Annualized)	16.29%	21.44%	16.42%	16.06%	3.83%
Return (Cumulative)	-22.67%	14.00%	-20.45%	-25.98%	76.83%
11/2007-3/2009					
Volatility (Monthly Annualized)	21.74%	29.34%	22.10%	21.24%	5.26%
Return (Cumulative)	-46.85%	-48.00%	-46.93%	-46.65%	7.56%

Source: Standard & Poor's

Table 6.2   Volatility and return of stocks and bonds

Thus, there was no meaningful connection between return and volatility, except that all the stock indices went down by roughly the same amount in the current bear market, regardless of market capitalization or volatility.

Volatility and Risk of Losses

As a measure of variability of returns, volatility does not measure the risk of losses or predict the potential return. To assess the risk that is most important to investors—the risk of loss, either substantial or total—there are statistical measures as well as commonsense ways to determine how much can be lost from an investment. One of these indicators is pretty simple and straightforward: the loss experience that an investment sustained in the past. What should an investor think about an investment that has a history of losing 30 percent or even more, with regularity? How meaningful is that data, as opposed to one that says it has volatility of 17 percent?

Unfortunately, the experience of losing stocks has scarcely entered discussions about stock investing or about the risks of stocks. If anything, periods of disastrous losses have been promoted by some as opportunities, as if the losses investors have suffered bore no consequences. Nevertheless, this is precisely the risky history of the stock market—extended periods of large losses that impact real lives and should not be ignored or downplayed as opportunities.

As we have seen in previous chapters, this is the kind of equity market that we have been through and possibly face going forward. The large losses also have critical implications on wealth building, as we will see in later chapters.

Risks of the Highly Improbables

To estimate the risk of losses, financial institutions use an indicator, called Value-at-Risk (VaR); it is also derived from the standard deviation. VaR has become a standard practice at large trading firms to estimate, presumably at a high level of confidence, the largest amounts they could tolerate to lose. To make these estimates, MPT assumptions are all important. The essential assumption is that the periodic returns of an investment (for example, monthly or daily) have the form of a symmetric bell-shaped curve, which is called normal distribution. Under this assumption, any investment has equal probabilities of a gain or a loss of a certain percent. This bell-shaped curve can be derived from the average return and the standard deviation; the VaR risk of losses can be estimated based on these two values.

Accordingly, at a confidence level of 95 percent, losses from an investment would not be larger than the difference between the average return of the investment and two times its standard deviation. Thus, there would be a 5 percent chance that, using the data for the 1997–1999 period, an investment in the DJIA could lose 8.3 percent in any month, or 65 percent annualized. Certainly, this magnitude of losses should catch the attention of any investor. However, that chance is estimated to be only 5 percent. This seemingly low probability calms a lot of minds and could easily lead to complacency. But perhaps the investment is not that risky—especially considering the gains that have been produced: 78.3 percent in three years!

This was the state of mind that undoubtedly occupied the thinking of managements at the financial institutions that invested in the sub-prime and other toxic mortgage-backed securities and their deriva-tives. Lulled by the seemingly low probability of the potential losses and the attraction of huge gains in recent pasts, what was possible was ignored. When the improbable happened, no one was prepared for it.

Then again, maybe such losses were not so improbable. How many times has the Dow recorded losses of 30 percent or more? Numerous times, if you look back far enough in history, but none in the three years preceding October 2007. It is the short-term memory built into the risk modeling that pushes the probabilities of losses into the long-distant past. An average person with common sense would think that after a winning streak in a game of chance, especially an unusually long one, the odds of unusual losses mount with each new bet. But in a world of assumed normal distributions of future events and short-term memories, a winning streak begets another. Every bet with the winning past as guide for the future is independent of one another, as if the opportunities are endless.

And that is how individual investors are advised about the risk of stocks. They are shown the historical returns of a past few years of large gains for enticement. Presented with the pseudo-scientific determination of such quantitative risk modeling as Monte Carlo simulation of recent histories, the probabilities of loss seemingly fade away. Investors are told how much they would miss staying out of the market and how only stocks can provide them with a secure future, because look at the gains that have been made! But the risks are real and present and mount with each month or year of addi-tional gains. And when the loss event materializes, the consequences can be devastating.

Diversification and Risk Reduction

Investors are often reminded of the need to diversify their invest-ments. Don't put all your eggs in one basket, as the saying goes. Presumably, diversification would help reduce the risk of the overall portfolio. If one investment lost value, the others would go up or would not go down as much. However, portfolio diversification by way of spreading a portfolio's holdings across a large number of stocks does not do much to reduce the risk of market losses; it preserves it. Also, often in the name of diversification, risk can actually be increased by including asset classes that have higher risks than what are already in the portfolio.

Security Diversification

Every stock has its own story, and any one stock can lose its entire value, like Enron or Lehman Brothers, or perform very well, like Google, while others are mere mediocrities. In MPT jargon, this is the security-specific risks or nonsystematic risks of a portfolio. If you hold only one or a few stocks in your portfolio, you run the risk of total losses—or substantial gains. However, if you hold a well-diversified portfolio of stocks, losses from some may be mitigated by gains from others. Accordingly, as posited by MPT and practiced in Wall Street, if a portfolio is diversified across a number of stocks representing the market, the nonsystematic risks of the individual stocks would cancel out one another over time, and what remains would be only the risk of the market.

This is how diversified stock mutual funds are set up. They buy such large number of stocks across the market that the portfolios are nothing more than the market itself. Though purported to be superior stock pickers, managers of actively managed mutual funds hold such diversified portfolios that any added value from good stock picking is washed away, reducing them to the averages of the market. After fees and expenses are subtracted from portfolio returns, diversified mutual funds lag behind market benchmarks, as time and again documented in academic studies and the press. At the same time, being fee-laden copies of the market, diversified mutual funds offer investors no protection from the market's risk of losses.

So, what is the point of investing in diversified mutual funds? If a portfolio manager is a great stock picker, why should he retain the risk of losses from the market and eliminate the added value of his talent, or alpha in MPT jargon, by diversifying away the potential of individual stocks?

Asset Class Diversification

As long as you own stocks, you are exposed to the risks of stocks-only risks. Therefore, it would make sense to diversify with other asset classes. In this respect, MPT offers a good insight and common-sensical guideline to reduce portfolio volatility. To achieve lower volatility, the portfolio should invest across assets that do not move in cohesion. If the assets move in tandem, the volatility of the portfolio is the average of the volatilities of the individual assets. In MPT speak, such pairs of assets have perfect correlation, and their correlation coefficient is equal to 1. If you can spread your portfolio among assets that do not behave in unison, the volatility of the portfolio would be lower than the assets' average. In the case of two assets, if they move in opposite direction—the case of perfect negative correlation or correlation coefficient being minus 1—combining them in certain ways could result in a portfolio that has no volatility.

Market experts also advise investors to diversify—but with other segments of the stock market. So, portfolios would include stocks of all varieties, from large- and mid-cap stocks to small cap, and value and growth styles. However, precisely because they are from different parts of the stock market, they bear the risks of stocks even if they are grouped in different categories.

In the real world, different segments of the stock market move together in almost perfect unison; sometimes it is less so, but when the stock market goes down, all segments of the market decline. As a check, we calculated the correlation coefficients of the S&P 500 index with the Russell indices representing the broad market, growth, value, mid-cap, and small stocks for the period between 1994 and June 2009; this period includes two distinct cycles of rising and declining stock prices. As shown in Figure 6.3, evidently these market segments are highly correlated to perfect unison. Diversification across these sectors would do nothing to reduce portfolio volatility or prevent losses in a market downturn. Indeed, during the crash between November 2007 and March 2009, the S&P 500 and all the Russell indices lost between 44 and 50 percent, whereas the Barclays Aggregate Bond index gained 7.6 percent. Over the 1994–2009 period, the S&P 500 actually outperformed all except Russell 3000 Value by a small margin. At the same time, the volatilities of the

Russell indices were about the same or higher than the S&P 500's volatility. Thus, diversification from the S&P 500 into the Russell indices added no value, except for lowering return and increasing volatility. For reference, during this period, the Barclays Aggregate Bond index returned 149 percent versus 163 percent by the S&P 500; its correlation with the S&P 500 was only 0.1.

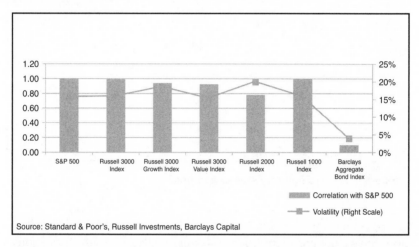

Figure 6.3   S&P 500: Correlations with different equity sectors (January 1994–June 2009)

To illustrate the possibilities of diversifying with noncorrelated assets, we examine a portfolio combining stocks (Dow Jones Industrial Average) and gold (exchange-traded fund GLD). Figure 6.4 plots the return streams of the two assets between January 2005 and May 2009. We also see the return stream of the Minimum Risk (volatility) Portfolio combining the two assets so that there could be no other portfolio of these two assets that has a lower volatility. In this portfolio, 62 percent was allocated to the Dow and 38 percent to gold.

The volatility of the Min Risk portfolio is 11.8 percent. It is lower than the volatility of both Dow and GLD, which are 15 percent and 19.2 percent, respectively. How is it possible that the portfolio volatility is lower than those of its underlying assets? The reason is that the correlation between Dow and GLD during 2005 and 2009 was almost 0—0.04, to be exact. Also, the cumulative return of the Min Risk

portfolio for the entire period is 12.5 percent, while the Dow lost
21.2 percent and gold gained 119.6 percent.

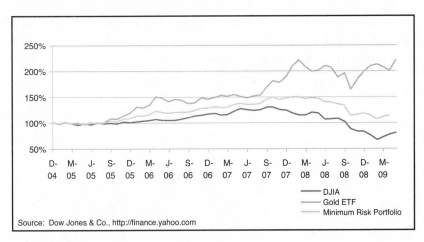

Figure 6.4   Diversification: stocks and gold

Although this illustration demonstrates the power of diversification across noncorrelated asset classes, it also begs the questions:
Why keep stocks in the preceding portfolio? Why have stocks when
their return streams are so uncertain and the prospect of losing is
likely? Why have stocks when the odds of poor returns have increased
substantially?

The Market Is Going Up!

Let's consider an alternative. By the end of 2004, the stock market had staged a strong recovery after the 2000 bear market. An
investor ("John") saw that his portfolio had recovered along with the
market. However, he was concerned that the rally was running out of
steam. The year was coming to an end. The Dow Jones was coming
back close to its historic highs in 1999. The Federal Reserve had been
raising interest rates every month since July. John talked with his
neighbor, who is an economist, about the economy, the rising federal
budget deficits, and everything else he could think of. He told his
neighbor that he did not want to go through the agony of the past few
years. "Joe, it's killing me! I don't want to see one-third of my savings

gone into thin air again!" As usual, his neighbor, the consummate economist, explained to him, "On the one hand, it is this; on the other hand, it is that." However, after much prodding from John, he said, "Why don't you think about keeping a small amount in stocks and putting the rest of your money in bonds?"

"Maybe you should put 80 percent of your portfolio in fixed income; there are reasonably good bond funds out there," the economist said. Then he mentioned the name of a famous bond fund and a couple of others. He also mentioned something about a fixed income portfolio with laddered maturities. "For the rest of it, keep 10 percent in stocks, and put some in emerging markets," the economist continued, mentioning that he thought the emerging markets would do very well. "If our stock market goes up, the emerging markets would do well. If things are bad, it doesn't matter if it is us or the emerging markets. They will all go down. With emerging markets, at least you can get more bang for your buck. And you can spice it up with gold; you can use the gold exchange-traded fund GLD," the economist said. "You know, the Fed has been raising interest rates; they are worrying about inflation," the economist added.

The next day, John, the investor, went to see his financial advisor and told him about the economist's suggestions. The advisor went berserk when he heard John putting so much in bonds. "John, you're my friend! I can't let you do this. The market is going up and up!" He calmed down a bit after John told him he would buy some emerging market fund that the advisor had recommended a few months ago. "John, the emerging markets are on a tear!" John asked his adviser, "What do you think about gold? I'm thinking about putting 5 percent in GLD in addition to 5 percent in emerging markets."

We don't know what John ended up doing. Rumors have it that the advisor has been leaving John messages at all hours, "John, the market was up another 200 points today!" But if John made the changes as suggested by the economist and very reluctantly agreed to by his advisor, by 2009 his portfolio would in all likelihood perform much better than had he made no changes and stayed in stocks.

The fact is that stocks are risky assets that have a substantial risk of losses, like gold, commodities, or emerging markets, which most investors are not likely to have in their portfolios. Nevertheless, they are opportunistic plays that can produce handsome returns, but also large losses.

So, why would you treat stocks as something you must always have in your portfolios?

The stock answer—no pun intended here—is that stocks always go up!

Will they? They haven't!

Long-Term Investing and Final Wealth

A paradox of long-term investing is that you may have a long-term investment horizon, but the market may cut it short against your wish.

You are told you can't expect to make money soon after purchasing a stock. And that, in the long run, stocks will produce better returns than bonds and protect you against inflation. So, you stay in the market for 10, 15, or 20 years, adding more money as time goes by and as the market goes up, hopefully. And soon, a good part of your life savings is now in the market. Then one day, out of nowhere— unexpected even by the experts and amid the cheers of even better times ahead—the market comes crashing down, and you've lost a good chunk of your savings.

So where does long term end and short term begin? Suppose an investor had planned to retire at age 65 and reached age 55 in the middle of the equity bear market in 2001. The usual advice to the investor would be for him to hold on to his investments, waiting for the market to recover. In 2008, this investor would be 62, three years shy of his retirement, when the market went into a tailspin. What actions should this investor take? Did his financial advisors tell him to sell his stocks in 2007? More likely than not, he was again advised to stay on and perhaps buy more.

"We can't imagine someone spending 40 or 50 years of their life saving up and then losing 40% to 50% of their money all in one year," said a portfolio manager who manages target-date funds for USAA mutual fund group. "Sometimes this industry gives this false hope of just sticking more in stocks and that will bail you out."[6] To this, another mutual manager countered, "That more aggressive stance is necessary to keep people from running out of money in the later years of retirement." Despite the market's recent battering, he continued, strong stock performance during bull markets will help compensate for losses in down years.[7] Fortunately, there are others in the investment industry who say those with more investment in equities underestimated the danger of a prolonged down market after several decades of strong return.[8]

In important ways, the distinction between long versus short term has meaning only in the context of trading versus investing. Even in this regard, portfolio turnover among mutual funds that are supposed to be "investors" and not "traders" is so high, the line hardly exists. Some funds turn over their portfolios several times a year. Even funds that have low turnover liquidate parts of their portfolios every few months or less.

Investors can only wait for the long term to arrive when they do not need to draw on their investments. To paraphrase John Maynard Keynes, the long term exists until you need the money to live on. From this perspective, the investment horizon varies with individual ages. Long term for a retiree is certainly not very long. For a 55-year-old, it may be only a few years if the individual plans to retire early. Shouldn't he cut back the bulk of his stock holdings now? At that age, how long can these investors wait for the market to come back?

The answer lies in whether the individual has to draw on the savings for income. If not, and the losses account for only a tolerable amount of assets, the person can wait. Otherwise, the long term is not long.

Another way to look at long versus short term is this: How much loss can you afford without affecting your income stream? If the affordable losses are only small amounts, as is the case for most in retirement or even long before then, the ability to wait for the market to come back is hardly meaningful. The long term for these savers simply does not exist.

The 2008 crisis led to untold numbers of people having to postpone their retirements because of stock market losses. Thousands of seniors had to resort to taking out the equity in their homes in the form of reverse mortgages to pay for living expenses after losses in the stock markets. Although these reverse mortgages carry high fees, federally insured reverse mortgages jumped 20 percent in March and April 2009, compared to the same period a year earlier.[9] The seniors clearly could not afford the risk of losses in stocks and had no ability for the many years of long-term horizon required in equity investing.

When Markets Are Upside Down

When the equity market is upside down, as we have seen in the past decade and in the 1970s, or as experienced with the Japanese Nikkei, risk is not about variability of returns. Losses can be substantial, and risk of losses is critical in making decisions. Throughout its history, the U.S. stock market has demonstrated its potential to generate handsome returns but also the risk of substantial losses. Equity returns can far exceed the inflation rate when inflation is moderate but can be big losers in a high inflation environment. The equity market does not go down forever or go up and up. Investment paradigms of beliefs that assume risks of stocks can be managed simply by holding on and waiting for the market to come back expose investors to substantial financial damages, as we have seen time and again. These risks need to be managed and factored into our investments and planning for our financial futures. We need to think about the risks added to our portfolios when venturing into other risky investments in the name of diversification. As long-term savers and investors, we need to think about events that happened in the long-ago past and the perspectives they provide about the risks in the future. Although we want to plan for the future in the long run—for we cannot get in and out of the market like hot-shot traders—we need to be cognizant of the dark clouds that appear on the horizon. We do not want to be hasty and rash, but our patience is not unlimited; neither is our financial ability.

Above all, we want to preserve our hard-earned savings and make sure we have enough income and cash flows to pay for expenses when we need them, not having to wait for the stock market to come back. We also want to build wealth by seizing attractive opportunities as long as their risks are within reason and do not potentially destroy our financial futures. We want our portfolios to withstand the vagaries of the equity market, as well as position us to save and build up our wealth for the future.

These are the issues we will discuss in the next chapter, where we will focus on investment approaches to deal with upside-down markets. We also will introduce absolute return as an investment philosophy and analytical framework, as well as an asset allocation strategy to help achieve these objectives.

7

Investing in Markets Upside Down

The roaring equity prices of the 1980s and 1990s have conditioned our expectations so much, it has been difficult to think of the stock market as anything but a perpetual bull run, with the good times always coming back after any declines.

For any of us who might have thought otherwise, our financial advisors would show us the double-digit returns of the preceding three and five years, and our doubts about the market would be shaken, at least a little bit. Neighbors (and, in my case, on a number of occasions, the airport limo drivers and the carpenters and the masons who did work on my house) would also be glad to help point us toward the wonderful ways of stocks. We would feel like maybe we were too conservative or didn't know what was going on, or worse, that we were missing out on a great party. Thus, any thought of an off-chance that we could lose big-time money with the stock market receded into the back of our consciousness.

It also helped to think that if returns on stocks kept going at those double-digit rates, we would have plenty of money for retirement—even be rich. We would say to ourselves, *Geez, this is how much I would have even if the return came "down" to 25 percent. Okay, I'd be happy at 20 percent. Well, I'll still be fine if I earn "only" 12 percent a year; I won't be as rich, but I'll be doing fine! I would still have plenty of money to pay for the kids' college tuition and many wonderful things I could do with the profits.* We would go through these ruminations with our calculators (sorry, spreadsheets!) on Sunday mornings and find new reasons to avoid saving more. If only we had known!

But as individual investors, we shouldn't blame ourselves too much in thinking these optimistic thoughts. The big boys at corporate pension plans and institutions like college endowments and foundations believed in the stock market, too. Even in the midst of the 2008 crash, the big financial advisory firms were projecting returns on stocks of 10 percent or more. How else could they attract clients if they do not continue to euphemistically promise high return?

Any suggestion that the long-term return on equities averaged about half that figure would likely have been greeted with silence, a rolling of the eyes, or worse. If we were to mention that between 1915 and 1999, the annualized return of the Dow Jones Industrial Average (DJIA) averaged only just a bit more, the conversation would probably have screeched to a halt, or we would have gotten a reaction from someone who was perhaps too polite to say we were mistaken or old-fashioned. We probably would not have a chance to point out that 1915 was the beginning of a decade and a half of market uptrend that rivaled the golden years between 1982 and 1999. And, of course, 1999 was when the market hit the highest mark on record before the tech bubble burst. Naturally, we still would want to keep a friend, so we would not want to add that if the calculations were extended to include the 2008 bear market, the annualized return would be cut down to much lower.

Then again, for anyone who is old enough to remember, much less to actually have experienced it, during the decade of stagflation in the 1970s, the return on stocks was less than two percent a year, which was far below the inflation rate of the time. Most investors would certainly have been far better off with short-term bank deposits. How about since the beginning of the new millennium? Well, maybe I should take a long walk in the woods!

A Walk in the Woods

The woods in the back of my house are really dense this year, because it rained all spring. It is summer time, but you wouldn't know it by looking out the window. The sky is overcast, the leaves are wet, and the air is damp and a bit chilly. The narrow trail that I use to cut through to my neighbor's house is hardly visible, with new growths and branches hanging over. There is hardly any sunlight shining through—not that there has been much sunshine at all for months.

But a long walk in the woods wouldn't change anything, leaving aside the bugs and the fallen trees that I might trip over. The mindset of a perpetual bull run is still ruling; it is just a matter of how long it will take for market pundits to get back to talking about when the market will come roaring back.

Nouriel Roubini reported that barely three months after the March 2009 lows, a number of analysts were contemplating how soon the Dow could get back to above the 11,000 level before Lehman went bust—even though, he noted, many analysts were suggesting that current earnings estimates and the stock rally seemed overoptimistic given the macro outlook.[1] But euphoria and panic have always been the emotions that drive stocks. "Stocks Recapture 9000 on Profit Surprise," screamed a newspaper headline,[2] as if surprises are not what stocks are made of. Estimates of higher price/earnings multiples followed upward earnings revisions and were projected to recover to precrash levels just in time for disappointments to set in and the market to come back down to earth.

Take, for example, the letdown in Microsoft's 2009 fourth quarter and Amazon's second-quarter earnings—their stocks crashed after their after-hours earnings announcements, but not before big run-ups in prices during the day. Unrealistic expectations aside, so far the major indices like the Dow by mid-2009 have been trading between the pre- and post-Lehman bankrupt levels now that the banks are not making new headlines. Yet, banks from Wells Fargo and JP Morgan to Bank of America and Bank of New York Mellon have been reporting new write-offs in their second-quarter 2009 earnings reports due to rising bad loans and other investments. Apparently, the market has found comfort in the belief that the government will step in if the banks get themselves into trouble again. Heads, they win; tails, taxpayers lose!

Financial advisors continue to be enamored with stocks, even though some claim they have turned a bit more conservative; they simply have no other advice to give their clients. "We are still very concerned about the status of the economic recovery and remain quite defensive as a result," said a financial planner who claimed he invested his clients' portfolios in "only" 40 percent stocks.[3] Another said he might put 40–50 percent of his clients' funds in stocks, with at least 30 percent of that in international equity funds; he added, "Cash is risky, stocks and bonds are risky, life is risky."[4]

Life may be risky, but investors do not want to gamble their life savings away. $100 in cash is $100 until you spend it. But $100 in stocks may turn into $50 before you know it. Many investors have already lost that much or more from stocks in this market downturn. Like Frank Baker, a 59-year-old who saw his portfolio cut from $1.2 million to $500,000. Is that an extreme case? How about Margaret Schaeffer, a 71-year-old retired teacher who recently took a part-time teaching job to avoid taking money out of her retirement account, which had lost one-third of its value?[5]

When the next downturn comes, those investors with too much in stocks in their portfolios will risk being wiped out. It is not that the next down leg is imminent, as some strategists have warned, or that it will come at a particular level. "The market [S&P 500] is up some 40 percent from the low it reached just last March. Rallies like this are wonderful, but this one, on consistently light volume, makes me nervous. Although the equity market has done well, commodities, especially oil, have risen, and bond yields have backed up."[6] The point is it will come at a time least expected, when investors are least pre-pared, causing the impact to be most devastating.

Nassim Nicholas Taleb, a mathematical trader, college professor and essayist, and best-selling author, wrote a wonderful and irrever-ent book about randomness. It's about how the highly improbable happens and how it explains almost everything. So far, I have only borrowed his book's title to use as part of the title of the first chapter of this book. I do further gross injustice to his work by quoting only one sentence out of over 300 pages of small print about life, philoso-phy, science, randomness, and charlatans in all walks of life, especially on Wall Street:

> ...I can make inferences about things that I do not see in my data, but these things should still belong to the realm of possibilities.[7]

The reason for that, in a nutshell, is that the human experience is so limited—according to the law of large numbers—that just because we think something has not happened, it does not mean it is not possible.

The stock market crashes, and surprises in the past 100 years were not possibilities—they were realities. They happened, and every time such events occurred, people were caught wholly unprepared. The 1929 crash, which led to suicides; Black Monday in 1987, which raised fears of a depression; the tech bubble burst of 2000; the sub-prime mortgage debacle; and the near-collapse of the world banking system in 2008—they were all preceded by warnings and warning signs, except that those who were supposed to know, and those who needed to know, paid no heed.

The point here is not that we should have or could have known the coming of these events. Maybe we should have or could have. At least some aspects about the bubble of house prices and the potential blowup of subprime mortgages were talked, written, and warned about in various circles, from the media, economists, blog writers, and so on. Ditto with the tech bubble burst in 2000, Black Monday in 1987, the tightening of the monetary screws under Paul Volcker's Federal Reserve, the hike of interest rates in 1994, and numerous other times and situations. Human nature as it is, all of these signs were ignored or treated as mere entertainment, or worse by most people. There was a great party going on, and all these warnings seemed like only spoilers. But when the crashes came, we were surprised.

We are bound to be surprised by events even if they stare us in the face, because they are so big, and we can see only a small part of their whole structure. Like staring at a section of the Great Wall of China, we can only see a few stones rather than the whole 4,000 miles of it. Even onboard a helicopter, we still can only see a few miles at a time. From an airplane at 30,000 feet high in the sky, at best we can see only an outline of the wall. Even after all that, we still do not know much about the colossal enterprise that it was, the human sufferings, the political and cosmic consequences of a tyrant's whims, and how all that changed the course of China's history. Yes, we can spend a few hours in the library, but who has time for that on a vacation trip, and where's the library anyway? We probably will only discover that perhaps we know even less than we had thought.

How is the Great Wall of China relevant to our discussion? Let me resort to a quote from a recent speech given by Janet L. Yellen, governor of the Federal Reserve Board and president of the Federal Reserve Bank of San Francisco on monetary policy and the housing bubble:

> First, some question whether bubbles even exist. They argue that asset prices reflect the collective wisdom of traders in organized markets who best understand the fundamental factors underlying asset prices. It seems to me that this argument is difficult to defend in light of the poor decisions and widespread dysfunction we have seen in many markets during the current turmoil.
>
> Second, it's an open question whether policymakers can identify bubbles in time to act effectively given that our models of underlying fundamentals are imprecise. For example, fundamental values of housing often are estimated by comparing the ratio of house prices to rents with a long-run average. This is a rather crude method, and some experts doubted that a bubble existed even when this ratio reached record highs in 2006. That said, by 2005 I think most people understood that—at a minimum—there was a substantial risk that houses were overvalued, although few anticipated that house prices would fall as sharply as they have.
>
> Third, even if we can identify bubbles as they happen, using monetary policy to address them will reduce our ability to attain other goals, so it makes sense for monetary policy to intervene only if the fallout is likely to be quite severe and difficult to deal with after the fact. For example, fluctuations in equity prices generally affect wealth and consumer demand quite gradually. A central bank may prefer to adjust short-term interest rates after the bubble bursts to counter the depressing effects on demand. The tech stock bubble seems to fit this mold. Still, some bursting bubbles are more virulent than others. It may be that credit booms, such as the one that spurred recent house price and bond price increases, hold more dangerous systemic risks than other asset bubbles. By

their nature, credit booms are especially prone to generating powerful adverse feedback loops between financial markets and real economic activity. If all asset bubbles are not created equal, policymakers could decide to intervene in those cases that seem especially dangerous.

Fourth, if a dangerous asset price bubble is detected and action to rein it in is warranted, is conventional monetary policy the best tool to use? Going forward, I am hopeful that capital standards and other tools of macroprudential [sic] supervision will be deployed to modulate destructive boom-bust cycles, thereby easing the burden on monetary policy. However, I now think that, in certain circumstances, the answer as to whether monetary policy should play a role may be a qualified yes. In the current episode, higher short-term interest rates probably would have restrained the demand for housing by raising mortgage interest rates, and this might have slowed the pace of house price increases. In addition, tighter monetary policy may be associated with reduced leverage and slower credit growth, especially in securitized markets. Thus, monetary policy that leans against bubble expansion may also enhance financial stability by slowing credit booms and lowering overall leverage.

Certainly there are pitfalls to trying to deflate bubbles. At the same time, policymakers often must act on the basis of incomplete knowledge, and it is now patently obvious that not dealing with some bubbles can have grave consequences. I would not advocate making it a regular practice to lean against asset price bubbles. But, in my view, recent painful experience strengthens the case for using such policies, especially when a credit boom is the driving factor."[8]

Yes, the evidence of the housing bubble was there; but maybe it wasn't. We should have done something about it. On second thought, perhaps we shouldn't. Or maybe just a little bit. It depends! All that wishy-washy from a Fed governor long after a historic event that wrecked the world banking system.

And this is how the economy and the financial markets are shaping up ahead of us. A lot of surprises, and untried solutions that may or may not work. Some may even have been shown to be misguided, but what else is there to do? Nevertheless, their consequences will be real and potentially have deep effects on our lives. We can discern the contours of the outline of what may lie ahead. But trying to pinpoint the peaks and valleys, how long it—whatever "it" is—is going to last is likely to be self-defeating and possibly harmful. We need to be prepared for surprises; most importantly, we need to protect ourselves.

How can we be prepared?

An Open Mind

Having an open mind is one way to be prepared—certainly not by following the formulaic 60 percent in stocks, 40 percent bonds, or the "if you are conservative, you invest 60 percent in bonds, 40 percent in stocks" garden variety of investing. The economy and stock market are at the crossroads of many forces at work not experienced by any of us alive, nor really understood even by those who have spent their lifetimes studying the past or were in positions supposedly to protect us from them. Otherwise, these events would not have happened, and we would not now be wrestling with their destructive impacts on our lives and futures.

We could choose not to invest in stocks at all for a while, at least not the usual way that leaves us exposed to devastating losses. Or we could avoid chasing after mutual fund managers who claim to be best-of-class only to see our investments managed by them lose more than the market. Or we could think twice, and again, about entrusting our money to such fancy funds as target date retirement funds, whose managers are more interested in outcompeting their peers with our money, leaving us with big unexpected losses, than in managing our retirement savings the ways they had promised.

Perhaps there are other investments or approaches of investing that meet our savings goals, although they may lag the stock market in euphoric years. But why should we try to compete with this amorphous entity called the stock market when its prospects can only be guessed at while our financial obligations are set in advance?

We certainly should not wholly depend on the so-called experts or take their words as gospel. They may provide certain services that may be valuable. But even the best of them mostly function on the premises of investment paradigms and assumptions, of which the values are, at best, subject to interpretation or outright questionable validity, as discussed in the previous chapter. They also usually are motivated by reasons that are not necessarily compatible with our needs and goals, from pushing products with high commissions to preaching the party line of their employers about certain investment strategies because they are told to do so. Their skills may not be at the level necessary to comprehend the consequences of the investments they recommend to us. Worse, their recommendations may come from canned solutions concocted from some vendors found on the Internet. (They used to come from the yellow pages.) They also cannot fully appreciate the particular complexities of our lives that may make us check the box that says "Aggressive" when in fact we are anything but.

We may simply mean that we want to have high return but are afraid of or cannot afford losses. The fact is we feel much greater pain having to endure a 10 percent loss than the pleasure of a 10 percent gain, especially when we are in danger of losing our jobs or are near retirement. A loss of 20 or 30 percent of our savings that has taken a lifetime of hard work and deprived cravings to accumulate is to us an unmitigated disaster.

But how else are we supposed to respond if the advisor tells us stocks will go up and stocks will outperform bonds, inflation, and everything else? We could not possibly choose the worse of two alternatives; bonds will be losers to inflation and the taxman, we are told repeatedly. Even if we check the "Conservative" box and say we want more bonds in the portfolios, the advisors will most likely try to talk us out of it as they are still doing now, even if we are of retirement age. And in making their argument, that everyone needs to have stocks in their portfolios, the advisors have the aid of influential firms providing them backup research with numbers, color charts, and statistics that we do not understand. How can we mortals not be impressed?

In a study dated April 2009, the large investment firm T. Rowe Price revisited its asset allocation strategies for investors across all ages.[9] First, it observed that "In 2005, a 65-year-old couple had more than a 50% chance of one of them living to age 90 and a 23% chance of one of them living to age 95, according to the Society of Actuaries." It went on, "The analysis reaffirms the glide path's equity allocations for a diverse set of retirees who do not intend to cash out their assets at retirement but instead seek a stream of retirement income over their life spans." And that asset allocation recommendation "starts with 90% of investors' assets in stocks for those more than 25 years from retirement, reduces that to 55% at age 65, 35% at age 80, and 20% at age 95 and thereafter."[10] And how did the analysis support this conclusion? By including the two periods that experienced the highest market returns, between 1955 and 1965 and 1982 to 1999. That was why there was also a caveat above one of the impressive graphs that might be missed by a few readers: "Based on historical returns, portfolios with the exposure to equities provided by the T. Rowe Price asset allocation glide path have tended to outperform similar portfolios with less equity exposure—while tending not to significantly underperform those more conservative portfolios over time in *poor markets* [italics added]."[11]

"Do not intend to cash out...at retirement"? So, when am I supposed to cash out? On my part, I have this indescribable feeling about having 20 percent in equities if I am alive at age 95! I still should worry about inflation and such things rather than the oxygen tank next to my bed or the nurse who wakes me up at ungodly hours to make me swallow those awful pills? Or perhaps the indescribable feeling comes from the heavenly perfumed nurse. Then maybe I still remember my 101 statistics course enough to recall that if at 65, a couple has a 50 percent chance of one of them living to age 90, then I or my wife *probabilistically* will die at 77.5 years old and the other will be deceased before then. So why should I worry about portfolio growth or outperformance at age 90?

But you have to admit the study's statistics are precise and impressive.

Above all, we want to be prepared for what the economic environment may bring, be it inflation or deflation. Deflation fears seem to have receded, and inflation talks have picked up. But it was not many months ago that the United States was gripped by fears of a deflation spiral like that of the 1929 depression, and headline Consumer Price Index (CPI) numbers still declined year-on-year in the latest releases by the Bureau of Labor Statistics. In either case, stocks could not do well amid surging prices, like in the 1970s, or when prices fall, as experienced in Japan.

Whatever surprises are to come, we want to preserve our capital, to survive, to retain the ability to wait out the storm, and to take advantage of opportunities that will surely emerge once those unprepared have given up in despair.

Capital Preservation Is Key

The movie *The Perfect Storm* was based on a true story of the journey of the swordfish boat, *Andrea Gail,* and its captain, Billy Tyne. Played by Oscar winner George Clooney, Captain Tyne and his crew, all desperate for money, decided to make a late-season expedition to bring back "more fish than you've ever seen," as he said to the nefarious boat owner. The weather was forecasted to be inclement, with a big storm brewing. They went anyway, totally confident in their seagoing ability. Unsuccessful initially, Captain Tyne exhorted his crew to go off to Flemish Cap, an area of the sea far "off the charts" because "that's where the fish are." Informed that the crew "started to get an ugly feeling out [t]here," the captain caustically remarked, "This is where it separates the men from the boys." The captain was right; the crew caught a boatload of fish. However, precipitated by a broken ice machine, they had to race back home to preserve the prized catch. The *Andrea Gail* braved its way through the mighty storm. The ship sailed into a confluence of two weather fronts and a hurricane, with 100-foot high waves. Captain Tyne and the crew knew they had one desperate act to save themselves, and they did it: They threw overboard the entire catch. "We'll come back the next time," the captain said.

In investing, survival has different shades of meaning.

To a retiree, survival may simply mean the difference between being able to pay the bills or a future with little assets to live on. A simple illustration should suffice.

Assume that a retiree had a portfolio with 55 percent in the S&P 500 and 45 percent in the Barclays Aggregate Bond index, as recommended in the T. Rowe Price analysis. If the retiree wants to withdraw 4 percent a year from his portfolio, which is a relatively low rate, the fixed income component would not generate enough income for his spending. Let's suppose that he got an interest rate of 5 percent on his bond holdings. This would work out to be only 2.25 percent. He would have to sell stocks to meet his requirements. He could not or should not sell any of the bonds because that would reduce his income.

What should this retiree do since the market decline? Hold on to his portfolio and wait for the market to come back? How? Cut back on his expenses or sell some of his stocks? The newspaper said that many of the retirees have had to return to work. In this economy, with millions of people having lost their jobs? Are retirees not supposed to work?

Ready Liquidity

Selling stocks in a portfolio to meet liquidity requirements is often recommended by investment advisors. To sweeten the prospect, the argument even cites tax advantages. "It's a mistake to think you should get the cash flow you need solely from portfolio income without ever touching principal [sic]. This is an emotional bias that for many can be difficult to overcome,"[12] so advised an investment firm in its recent mailings to prospective clients. "Instead, your focus should be on total *after-tax* return. For example, selling stock to meet cash flow needs can be a better alternative than taking income from your portfolio... because the transaction might be taxed at the capital gains rate rather than your marginal [ordinary income] tax rate."[13]

That's fine only if there are gains in the stocks! And there are gains to be taxed at capital gains rates. Selling stocks at a loss has disadvantageous tax consequences because of the deduction limit of only $3,000. Untimely selling of stocks to meet cash flow needs also can disrupt the overall asset allocation strategy of the portfolio. Furthermore, it reduces the portfolio's prospect of recovery.

The idea of selling stocks for liquidity is rooted in the notion that stocks always go up. And it encourages people to invest more in stocks, even if income generation is more important to the investors than capital gains. "You can get the income you need and grow wealth at the same time!" so goes the advice. "And pay less tax, too!" The swan songs are so appealing that even retirees who need a dependable stream of income are told to invest more in stocks—and, as a result, suffer financial destruction in their advanced ages, when they can least afford it.

That problem would not arise if the retiree built his portfolio around his income requirements. Suppose that the retiree in our illustration invests 80 percent of his portfolio in bonds and the rest in stocks. We need not perform any calculation to know that the retiree's bond portfolio would generate income for him to withdraw 4 percent a year.

The retiree would not have to touch his stocks. He would be able to hang on to his stock holdings if he believed the stock market would come back and he would realize handsome profits. If worse comes to worst, he could leave the stocks to his heirs to deal with—even though he might wish from time to time that all of his portfolio were in bonds so that he could draw more interest income to take a vacation now and then.

In the meantime, he would not have to throw his fine swordfish catch into the swirling ocean to survive.

How Much Can I Afford to Lose?

Younger people may not need to draw on their savings for living expenses, although they should pay off their credit card debts and student loans before putting money in stocks; or for that matter, they should have a cash cushion in case of unemployment. But youth has the advantage of having a sense of indestructibility. That does not mean that they or their spouses don't feel the pain from the losses. Spouses have wonderful ways of reminding each other of the mistakes the other has made.

Smart risk takers know what risks to take. From downhill racers to skydivers, extreme athletes take measures to protect themselves from harm by wearing appropriate gear and undergoing arduous training, even though they have trainers and coaches; their lives are at stake! They don't go into risks unprotected; their coaches don't allow them. Do your financial advisors look after you the same way? Professional gamblers know what odds to bet. Casino goers limit their bets to the amounts they can afford to lose; otherwise, they become gambling addicts, with severe consequences on their lives and families. In lotteries, people spend small amounts in the dim hope of winning big. They realize that the chance of winning is small and behave accordingly. Some do buy more tickets than they should, but they don't spend their life savings.

When the odds for losses increase, and when the ability to withstand or the amounts of affordable losses decline, the bets on risky plays should become proportionally smaller.

Everyone has limits of how much loss they can afford and how much pain they can bear. These are not measured by standard deviation or volatility. I don't care much about standard deviation, as long as I win! And when I am losing, I only care about how much I lose, not the standard deviation of my losses.

So, how much can you afford to lose?

I do not have a neat and precise way to calculate the maximum loss affordable for everyone in every circumstance. But I have a rule of thumb that starts out pretty simple. Whatever I think I can afford to lose in percentage terms, I double it, and that is what I put into risky stuff like stocks, international securities, commodities, and whatnot. I call it the 2-to-1 rule. The rest of it goes into safe investments. Readers may note that it is risky assets I am referring to, not just stocks.

John C. Bogle, founder of the Vanguard Group, was reported to have his own rule of thumb. Just subtract your age from 100, and the difference would be the percentage amount of stocks you should have.[14] Mr. Bogle is 80 years old. I think 20 percent is a bit much for his age. Then again, he is rich, so he probably can afford it; he might not need that money to live on. Fidelity Investments manages more than 17,500 employer retirement plans with 11.3 million investors. In the first quarter of 2009, Fidelity found that of the new money coming into these plans, the allocation to equities declined to 70 percent, from 75 percent.[15] Also, it reported the allocations to equities in its portfolios according to the age brackets of participants in the first quarter 2009 as follows: 77 percent in equities for those between 25–29 years old; 76 percent for ages 35–39; 70 percent for ages between 45–49; 59 percent for ages 55–59; and 53 percent for ages 60–64.[16] These allocations explain how the values of equity holdings by households lost 29.5 percent or over $5 trillion between 1999 and 2008, according to the Flow of Funds Accounts published by the Federal Reserve. Readers may note that these figures include the gains from the market recovery between 2003 and 2007.

As to my own rule of thumb, I must confess my threshold of pain declines rapidly with age. Although my allocations to risky assets used to be a 2-to-1 ratio, they have decreased fairly rapidly with every passing year.

Also, my threshold of pain from losses drops precipitously if the future seems bleak and the prospects of gains look grim. Modern Portfolio Theory (MPT) actually tells me that I should consider these variables when constructing a portfolio for the next holding period; I need to factor in the expected return and the risk, or volatility in MPT speak, for the next holding period, leaving aside the risk of losses. So, if my investment horizon is 15 years, I should break it down into shorter intervals, say, three-year periods, for each of which I should have different expectations about volatility and return. My financial advisor has been telling me that I can't do that. Although he is a devoted believer in MPT and often cites beta and alpha and such Greek alphabet letters to impress and convince me of the potential returns of his recommendations, he said no one could tell what the stock market would do the next few years, Yet, he expected the market to go up and equity returns over the next 15–25 years to be about 10 percent a year or more. I don't know how he knew that, and I don't remember him warning me about the market drops in 2000 and 2008.

Dependable Income Stream

After I have more or less defined the percentage of losses I can bear, or hopefully would not lose sleep over, using a rule of thumb like the 2-to-1 ratio, I want to make sure I will have enough income to live on. Suppose I can build a bond portfolio that gives me an income stream of 5 percent a year and I need 4 percent for liquidity. As such, I would need to put 80 percent of my savings into bonds and the remaining 20 percent in risky assets. If the fixed income portfolio generates only 4.5 percent a year, I would need to invest about 90 percent of my assets in bonds to get a 4 percent annual income stream from my portfolio. I can go through a number of bond variations to get a higher yield, including accepting some lower-rated bonds.

But the point is that if I want to have a dependable stream of income, I need to allocate the bulk of my savings to a source of income generation that is more predictable than stocks.

However, I do not need to stop there. With this strategy as the baseline, I can develop an absolute return strategy portfolio whereby I can explore other opportunities (which will be discussed in later chapters) that will possibly improve my investment returns while I can retain the confidence that I have enough income to draw on for my spending and liquidity needs and the ability, if not the pleasure, to withstand market setbacks. That's what managing risk is all about: the ability to survive it and do better with it.

Importantly, I always try to remember that the past is not the future, no matter how great it had been.

The Past Is Not the Future

"Past performance is not indicative of future returns." This is a standard disclosure by investment advisors to make sure they are not accused of making promises or guaranteeing future results. That they cite historical returns of better times to support their recommendations does not seem inconsistent to them. But this is one warning that I take very seriously.

Alas, the future is impossible to predict, while the past is so comforting. The road we know is always more reassuring than the unknown. But the less we know, the more cautious we should be. We don't drive at full speed when the fog obscures our view or the road is slippery wet with heavy rain. We may not want to rely on the economists, the practitioners of that dismal science, who are better known for recording recessions and stock market gains than predicting them. But they give us information and voice their concerns. Sometimes we can tell if they always talk up or talk down the market, regardless of conditions; those are the economists we want to avoid. Most of all, we want to be wary of pat answers or presumed certainties like, "The market always comes back."

But we must deal with the future, in all its uncertainty and incomplete information. This is where questions can be asked and assumptions challenged. Hopefully, in the process, we will gain better insight and perhaps come to the conclusion that the risk is not worth taking or the potential return in the future might not be worth the effort.

As MPT dictates in its deterministic formulation, if an asset has lower expected (future) return, allocations to it should be reduced, other things being equal. Although MPT has its flaws, its logic of lower return means lower allocation makes imminent sense. So the next time your advisors cite elegant and seemingly infallible mathematical equations and statistics to back up their recommendations of equity allocations that are higher than you feel comfortable with, you might ask them about the return and volatility (they'll say "risk") assumed in those equations. You should not be surprised if those numbers are pretty close to historical data of past equity bull markets of rising stock prices.

Know Your Objectives

Remember the fable about the hare and the tortoise? You don't need to run as fast as the hare to get to your destination, or waste your energy like him. The familiar Figure 7.1 recasts the fable in a different context: the race between stocks and bonds over the past 20 years. Figure 7.2 shows the annualized returns of stocks and bonds in the past 10-, 15-, and 20-year periods, ending June 2009. Although the race appears to be close, bond investors actually have consistently gained while equity investors have lost money, most dramatically since 1999—$5 trillion at the national level.

Figure 7.1   Stocks and bonds: a 20-year journey

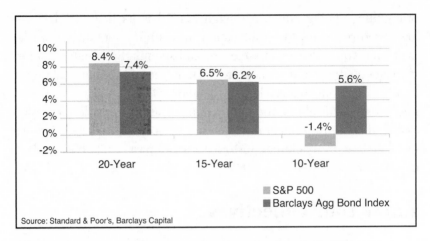

Figure 7.2   Stocks and bonds: annualized returns 1989–2009

However, even if you want to run as fast as the hare, you probably will not be able to.

The U.S. economy is burdened with unprecedented and unsustainable debts and lower growth prospects. We discussed these issues in the first four chapters. At some point in time, the stock market has to come to terms with this reality. Over the next 2–3 years or less, the stock market may get relief rallies from the booster shots provided by the government's massive stimulus programs, deficit spending, zero-percent interest rates, and the Federal Reserve money-printing machine. Although not without heightened volatility, the rallies might have the semblance of a sustainable market recovery. But the flash point may coincide with the baby boomers reaching retirement age in the next few years when they will qualify for full social security benefits. Those who own stocks are holding back if they can, but many will start liquidating their equity investments to fund their retirements as their hopes for a strong market recovery wane. Concurrently, the economy may simply show a slower rate of growth, as the International Monetary Fund (IMF) and other economists are projecting, partly because the effects of the stimulus programs will begin to wear off.

Meanwhile, the economy will be drawn in two opposite directions. One is the imperative to pay down debts. The other is the imperative to acquire more debts, to finance the increasing deficits of the federal and state budgets and the government-sponsored Fannie Mae and Freddie Mac and entitlement programs, to sustain the economic recovery, and to refinance household balance sheets, which were devastated by the 2008 market meltdown as well as high unemployment. A slip into imbalances of these finely tuned demands will have repercussions on the currency and interest rate markets, and the resulting impacts will be magnified in stock prices driven as usual at such times by fear and panic. With zero interest rates, the Federal Reserve will only have at its disposal the tools of jawboning and printing money, while the executive branch may be in the grip of paralysis and impotence for lack of funds after so many stimulus and deficit spending programs. If brought in to bear on a crisis, these measures will be like adding fuel to a smoldering fire; the strength of the Federal Reserve has been spent with its overstressed balance sheet, and the market will severely question its credibility. No more booster shots for the patient!

Investment and Saving Objectives

I don't know if you want to risk more heart-stopping crashes from these black clouds that are hanging over our heads just because some experts say it isn't so bad and you should believe in America. We all do believe in America, but we want to make sure our capital assets are preserved to protect our futures and families. Opportunities will come, and those that are genuine will be sustainable. We will be able to take advantage of them if our capital is now protected and will then be available to exploit them. There is no point of putting up our capital to the shredder of short-term moves or being the guinea pig of someone's idea about cheap valuation. Equity valuation is by no means cheap given the risks of the macro-economic conditions going forward. The conventional measures of equity valuation have come down somewhat from the highs in previous years, thanks to the low levels of interest rates. The rally in the stock mark since the March 2009 lows has also benefited from the relief that the worst may be over. However, a continuation of further strength in prices needs a pick-up in sales revenues from economic growth and consumer spending.

According to John Dear, appointed in March 2009 to be the chief investment officer of the gargantuan institutional investor, $174 billion California Public Employees' Retirement System (CalPERS), "CalPERS is not a market-timing organization...the outlook for earnings has got to get more realistic because of the amount of de-leveraging that has to occur in households and financial institutions. And there's no way that can be worked off without affecting consumption. With consumption being 70 percent of the economy in the U.S., it's hard to see that we're going to get great earnings growth. We're not going to see a powerful rebound in equities prices. They should go up if confidence continues to improve—and cash on the sidelines is going to get pulled in, because no one's going to want to miss the rally. But are there conditions to sustain it? I'm doubtful of that."[17]

Under these circumstances, you may want to review your investment and saving plans and the investment returns you think are achievable. The returns of stocks during the past decade were negative, while historical long-term equity return averaged about 6 percent annually. Going back 20 years, including the roaring stock market of the 1990s and the Internet hype, stocks and bonds produced similar rates of return. Are your savings accumulating enough to meet your goals? Are you relying on high-investment returns to make up for the shortfall in your savings? Perhaps you shouldn't.

If you target a high rate of return, you may end up with disappointments—the returns dismal and the losses detrimental to your retirement plans. To preserve capital, you may want to think about accepting a lower rate of return for a while—but hopefully not forever. Also, having in mind a more realistic rate of return might help you avoid getting caught up in euphoria or despair. Additionally, it could open a host of ideas, strategies, and opportunities besides chasing after the stock market. We will return to this subject in Chapter 9, "Absolute Return: Manage Risks and Build Wealth."

Risks and Volatility

Over time, it makes sense that now and then you look at your portfolio to see if you still like what you have in it. Things may have changed in the investment marketplace and in your life, so your goals and needs may change accordingly.

There are no hard and fast rules you can find in books or on the Internet about how often you need to do portfolio reviews. However, most of us look at the balances of our portfolios at least quarterly, if not more often. We might even look at them daily to enjoy the feeling of getting richer every day without having to do any work.

But really looking at your portfolios means you might need to make some important changes. During the good times of rising stock prices, we find the allocations to stocks rising above what we initially intended to have. So, we let the stock allocations ride higher, only to see the market go down. We then say to ourselves, *I should've rebalanced my portfolio, cutting back the stock allocations!* Conversely, the stock market keeps going up, and we lament, *I wish I hadn't cut back.*

It is a no-one-wins situation, and it is a much-talked-about-but-little-is-done kind of issue that financial advisors have trouble dealing with. They cannot conclude whether to rebalance—that is, change the allocations in their portfolios quarterly or annually—or whether rebalancing itself is a better strategy than leaving things well enough alone. The reason they have trouble in making up their minds on this issue is because they look at the return aspect. For example, you have a 50/50 portfolio with 50 percent in stocks and 50 percent in bonds. Because of the rising stock market, a year later, the portfolio has 60 percent in stocks and 40 percent in bonds. So you rebalance the portfolio back to 50/50. The next year, the market goes up again, and you find that the portfolio would have been better off with the 60/40 split. *What have I done?*

Rebalancing is not about market timing, chasing after the market to maximize return!

Rebalancing is about managing your portfolio's risk, the risk of losses. Your portfolio risk has gone up to 60/40. It is now above what you had intended, and you want to cut it back. If the market keeps going up, you still participate in the run-up as you had intended at the 50/50 allocations. If the market goes down, you are only exposed to the risk that you *had* felt comfortable with. It is a win-win strategy.

Rebalance Your Risks

When you focus on your risk objective, or the amount of risk you feel comfortable with, you will develop a good sense of when to rebalance. Again, there are no hard and fast rules, just like there are no rules about when to enter and exit the market. Once a year is usually a good time to make a thorough review of your portfolio allocations, even if there are no changes whatsoever, which is unlikely. Certainly when the market is going through major changes, more frequent reviews might be needed.

You might not want to let the allocations deviate too far from the intended targets. My rule of thumb is 10 to 15 percent deviation. The higher the allocations to stocks and other risky assets, the lower the deviations are allowed. And because you cannot anticipate how fast the deviations occur (they depend on the market), you might want to return to the targeted allocations in increments like 2 or 5 percent at a time, although this is not carved in stone either.

In addition to a review of the allocations to risky assets, you might want to think about whether stocks are necessarily the be-all investment for you. What about stock substitutes that generally move with stocks, although not in tandem, have fewer risks (both in terms of risk of losses as well as volatility) and smaller returns than stocks, but are higher in risk and return than U.S. Treasury securities or investment grade bonds? Above all, they might meet your return and risk objectives. This exercise might open up alternatives that were not readily apparent before. One such stock substitute is junk bonds; just recognize that they are not bonds like corporate triple-A rated securities but hybrid instruments—part bond, part stock. The same principle applies to other equity investments, such as international stocks. We will return to this subject in Chapters 9, 10, and 11.

Portfolio review and rebalancing become more important as you advance in age. People of the same age still have widely different lives, careers, and health circumstances, and their risk objectives can vary accordingly. Your tolerance for losses and the degree of comfort you feel about volatility have a bearing on how much in risky assets you want to hold in your portfolios, as compared to your contemporaries. And, for any individual, those circumstances change over time, sometimes drastically. These life events appropriately need to be considered in the reviewing and revising of individuals' margins of risk tolerance.

Ultimately, risks should be the focus of your periodic portfolio review, from what kinds of risks are in your portfolios to how much in risky assets you want to have.

Absolute Return Investing

It is risks that we need to focus on and manage when the market is upside down. Come to think of it, risks always need to be managed. It's akin to a skier on a vertical course downhill who needs training and all kinds of paraphernalia to protect himself or a car that needs good brakes whether it is in normal city traffic or on the highway.

Let's think about an investment approach that emphasizes management of risks and does not set us in a race against some stock market index. We want the risks of our portfolios to be managed, not left to the vagaries of the market or to chances. We want to make sure serious efforts are made to minimize the risks of losses that can be so detrimental to our futures, not left unattended or to presumed certainties about the equity market's prospects. And we prefer that the variations of the periodic rates of return are minimized. That is, the money we count on next year will be greater or at least not much different from what it is now.

Under any market conditions, that strategy should allow us to take care of our liquidity needs and generate income when we need it without having to sell risky assets when they are down in values. Because our requirements are fairly predictable, we want to make sure the sources of funds to meet those requirements follow some sort of predictable patterns. Just like in business, we would prefer that the revenues and expenses temporally match so that we don't face liquidity shortfalls. This is no different from making sure that your paychecks are deposited in time at the bank to meet the mortgage payments and such expenses.

Above all, we want to have in place a strategy that can allow us to withstand divergent market conditions while we retain an ability to have our lifestyles unaffected even in market crashes.

This is absolute return investing.

In Chapter 9, we will focus on absolute return investing and how to develop the strategy and put together such a portfolio. But first we need to discuss investment risks, which we do in Chapter 8, "Beware of the Risks."

8

Beware of the Risks

Bank certificates of deposits have been considered safe investments—or so it seemed until the collapse of Washington Mutual, Wachovia, and other banks in the banking crisis. The fact that consumer deposits in banks (and savings associations) were guaranteed up to $100,000—this limit was temporarily raised to $250,000 until 2013—by the Federal Deposit Insurance Corporation (FDIC) did not seem good enough to many depositors. They feared that their money would nevertheless be lost or tied up too long in a busted bank, at least until the mess was worked out. And when a money market fund like the Reserve Primary Fund "broke the buck"—that is, its Net Asset Value dipped below the $1 threshold expected of money market funds—it seemed no investment was safe anymore. Also, supposedly conservative mutual funds like target date funds suffered losses much more than expected as if they were just the same as other equity mutual funds. Suddenly, risk took on new meanings. Where can investors find safe and conservative investments?

Facing huge losses from the stock market decline and seeing a good part of their savings disappear, investors are not only fearful for their futures without the money they need, but they also become concerned about other risks of their portfolios, which until this point seemed nonexistent, or at least not enough to worry about.

What are the other risks that are lurking behind investors' portfolios? What can investors do about them?

Systemic Risks

As the banking crisis in 2008 hit the stock market, investors were caught by surprise with other asset classes that in previous market downturns had held up well, but this time they were also broadly affected and declined. For one, fixed income securities recorded unusual losses. During the crisis months of September and October, the major bond indices of blended-quality corporate bonds and government securities recorded losses, including those of intermediate maturities. High-yield bonds declined almost as much as the S&P 500 (see Figure 8.1). Even U.S. Treasury notes and bonds saw their yields higher and prices down.

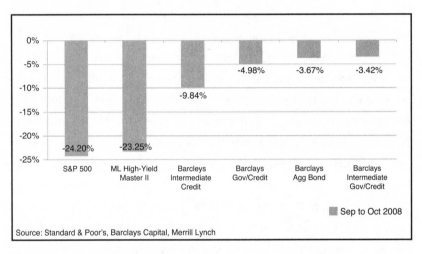

Figure 8.1   The ires of October

The only securities that improved in value, of sorts, were short-term Treasury bills. As fears drove investors to safe havens to park their cash, three-month Treasury bills rates dropped to near zero. However, the lower short-term rates were surely not an improvement to those who rely on bank CDs for their income. The upside was that short-term investments offer the liquidity of cash. And in the case of reasonably good-quality bond portfolios, fixed income investors have the income streams from the bonds' interest payments, notwithstanding the unrealized depreciation of the principal.

Hedge funds, which were supposed to weather such a stock market downturn better than mutual funds, also suffered significant losses. In the 2000 bear market, hedge funds held up and produced positive returns, versus losses by the S&P. It was not so this time. In fact, as a result, many hedge funds had to close up their operations because of severe losses and investor withdrawals. Even gold faltered badly as the crisis became full blown. In the past, gold has been a favorite safe harbor in times of turmoil. Yet during the several months that were the worst of the crisis, gold prices dropped precipitously, from over $1,000 to just over $700.

In 2008, the subprime debacle infected the banking system, which is the heart of the entire U.S. economy and the world. In this instance, if the U.S. government had not intervened to shore up the system and had the doomsday scenario materialized, the system would have unraveled; every productive activity in the economy would have come to a screeching halt. To continue daily living activities, people needed cash. Liquidity was at premium and people would have run on their banks, causing banks to collapse. Investors would have also needed to sell their noncash holdings, whether they were stocks, jewelry, or whatnot, to raise funds. U.S. Treasury securities became investments of choice, not much for their investment values, but for their perceived status as a safe haven. As a result, in international markets, the dollar appreciated in value as foreigners flocked to the currency of the largest economy in the world.

In times of systemic risks, dislocations grip the economy and the investment marketplace. Pricings of assets of any quality become distorted because buyers and sellers are not motivated by value, but by fear and panic. Better-quality securities decline as much as, or seemingly more than, lower-quality assets, simply because they are easier to sell; and cash-rich buyers' offers at unreasonable discounts may still be accepted by buyers in dire straits. In the meantime, low-quality assets have no bids, although prices might still be marked at long-obsolete levels, only to be swept up later by dire market conditions and sold at huge discounts.

It was different this time; for the first time since the 1929 Depression, the entire system was looking into the precipice of total collapse. It was certainly different from the 2000 bear market that resulted from the burst of the tech stock bubble. Although a recession followed the crash in the stock market, the recession itself was relatively short, and there was no crisis in the financial system. The crash in 1987 of Black Monday fame, although severe, was short lived and did not spread into Main Street, as it was often (dismissively) said at the time. Even the long period of market losses in the 1970s were not the results of systemic risks of a system collapse. Followed by a decade of economic expansion from the economy's trough in the first quarter of 1961 to the peak in the fourth quarter of 1969, the economy went into an equally long period of slow growth and inflation. Productivity growth slowed to 1.8 percent a year while inflation went into the high double digits. Stock market losses ensued that were substantial and lasted longer than a decade.

The 2008 market crash was precipitated by the collapse of inflated house prices and an economy rooted in excess leveraging in every sector, public and private. After the banking system was infected with unbearable debt and losses, the upside-down pyramid teetered on the brink of bankruptcy, bringing the entire economy to the proverbial cliffs. By 2009, the outlook of economic growth was uncertain. Although slow growth was widely expected, it was hampered by fears of inflation and rising interest rates alternated by bouts of Japanese-style deflationary concern.

But the next bubble of debt is already brewing. The economy's debt burden is rising, not declining, while pressures are mounting from foreign creditors, especially China, for the U.S. to reduce its fiscal deficits and public debt. Thus, the need for reigning in debt is well recognized. However, debt reduction or deleveraging—even just a deceleration in the rate of debt growth—could have severely adverse effects on economic growth. It is a vicious circle that might break and drive the system out of its existing indelicate balance.

What can you as an investor do in times of systemic upheavals? First, recognize that systemic risks do exist. The best way to prepare for such times is not to take on more risks than you can afford. Like the proverbial perfect storm discussed in Chapter 7, "Investing in Markets Upside Down," once in it, only those who are prepared are most likely to survive. Access to liquidity is paramount. That means your bank accounts should be in strong and sound financial institutions. You want to have a dependable source of income if you are in retirement. For those in the workplace, you need a cash reserve to fall back on if your job prospects look uncertain. Stocks will be neither a reliable source of liquidity or income nor an investment offering quick payback experienced in years past.

Market and Manager Risks

Just as important, keep in mind that your equity mutual funds will not be any help toward containing your losses in times of market declines and systemic turmoil. As a rule, fund managers are more worried about the individual stocks in the portfolios they manage than the risk of losses from market declines and a host of other risks that cause losses to a portfolio, such as the risk of currency losses in international funds. As discussed in the previous chapter, this is because managers hold a large number of stocks such that their portfolios behave like the market. In Modern Portfolio Theory (MPT) speak, there is a term to describe how much a mutual fund resembles the stock market. It is called beta, the second Greek alphabet; the market has beta of 1.

Essentially, MPT postulates that the return of a stock is driven by beta plus a risk-free rate like one-month Treasury bills. If a stock is less (or more) impacted by the market, its beta would be lower (or higher) than 1. However, in the short term, the beta-adjusted return of a stock is not necessarily the same as the market; there is a residual, a random number. Over time, these short-term residuals cancel one another out so that in the end, the beta-adjusted returns of the stock and the market converge. Applying this to mutual funds, a fund's portfolio is also said to be driven by the market; but the residual random number is repackaged into the Greek alphabet letter alpha. When a mutual fund's return exceeds that of the market, the fund is said to have alpha or excess return, even if the outperformance is all due to the fund's greater risk exposure to the market—and it is attributed to the fund manager's stock-picking prowess, not its higher risk. Conversely, if the fund's beta is 1 or higher and it still lags the market, it qualifies as a case of double indemnity; you pay higher fees, take more risk, and get less return than an index fund.

Performances in Bear Markets

In reality, few mutual funds have betas of much less than 1, and few have excess returns. Even funds with different betas, which cause divergent performances in rising markets, tend to fall with the market in downturns.[1] As a result, in severe market declines, losses of mutual funds tend to track the market; the riskier or higher the betas of the funds, the larger the losses.

One strategy to reduce beta is simply to reduce exposure to the market by raising cash. However, mutual fund managers are generally reluctant to raise cash and reduce the amounts of their funds' exposure to the market. They fear that they will miss getting back into the market when it recovers and rallies, a situation that occurred often during periods of rising stock prices in the 1980s and 1990s when stocks recovered quickly after relatively short periods of decline. Lest this happen and undermine the performances of funds managed by managers who seek to aggressively manage the market risk, mutual fund companies require their portfolio managers to file some form of notice with management before they can raise the cash holdings in their funds above 10 percent. Filing this preaction notice and facing possible embarrassment if they turn out to be wrong, managers are content to leave things well enough alone, watching their funds go down with the market in periods of lower prices. Their hopes are that their funds will lose less than the market; in that case, it will be an occasion for celebration and advertising for their prowess of beating the market.

As a result, in bear markets, investors can do little but watch helplessly as their investments lose value. Invariably, the only advice, more like a consolation that they get from their advisors, is to hold on; the market will come back. Right, but only if you have the time to wait!

In this connection, it is noteworthy to cite a study by Standard & Poor's, which only confirms the results of numerous studies by academia and practitioners about mutual fund performances.[2] The Standard & Poor's study observes, "...One of the most enduring investment myths is the belief that active management has a distinct advantage in bear markets due to the ability to shift rapidly into cash or defensive securities. We dispelled this myth in 2003 using the case study of the 2000 to 2002 bear market. The downturn of 2008 provided another case study."[3] If anything, the 2008 experience was a bit worse, because the number of underperforming funds that lost more than the market climbed to 70.9 percent compared to 67.5 percent in 2000–2002 (see Figure 8.2).

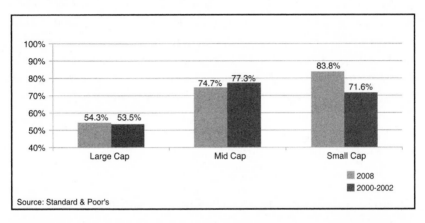

Source: Standard & Poor's

Figure 8.2   Bear markets: percent of equity funds underperforming their benchmarks

Performances of Top-Rated Managers

Even the presumed stock-picking prowess of professional managers has not shown itself to be of much help. In the bear market of 2008, even mutual funds highly rated by firms like Morningstar lost as much money as the market.

Morningstar evaluates funds according to risk-adjusted returns over different periods and rates them on a scale of one star being the worst to five stars being the best. You might assume that investing in the best-rated funds should provide your portfolio at least some protection in a severe market downturn. What if you go through the trouble of rebalancing your portfolio at the beginning of each month so that it contains only no-load domestic equity mutual funds with five-star Morningstar ratings? As reported by Mark Hulbert for *The New York Times*, in the fourth quarter 2008, such a portfolio of best-rated funds would lose 22.3 percent, compared to a loss of 21.94 percent by the S&P 500.[4]

Similarly constructed portfolios using other well-known ranking systems gave by and large the same results. The Value Line fund rating system produced a portfolio that lost 22.2 percent. Another approach, based on momentum, picks the best funds according to their performances over the previous 6–12 months; presumably the momentum will tend to keep the funds outperforming for up to an additional year. The model portfolio of a newsletter that picks funds according to this momentum methodology lost 22.3 percent. Other systems that have received academic endorsements for their ranking methodologies fared no better. One such approach is a mathematical technique called the Kalman Filter. The funds that were ranked best by this approach registered a loss of 22.2 percent in the quarter. Another one that has shown promising results in academic research is the Return Gap approach. The funds constructed from this model lost 20.6 percent in the fourth quarter.[5]

Performances over Different Market Cycles

A great many studies have shown that actively managed mutual funds have not outperformed the market averages, except perhaps a few. Recent data analyzed by Standard & Poor's gave updated results.[6] As shown in Figure 8.3, over the two 5-year market cycles of 1999–2003 and 2004–2008, two-thirds of all domestic equity funds underperformed their benchmarks. In some subcategories, like small cap funds, the underperformance was much worse in the 2004–2008 market cycle.

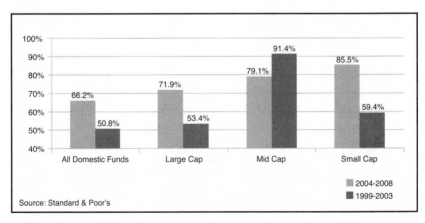

Figure 8.3   Market cycles: percent of equity funds underperforming their benchmarks

As individual investors, if you have persisted in searching for those rare gems of out-performing managers among the thousands, you might share the frustration expressed by the market expert who said, "My problem is that I don't know which ones are going to do well next year."[7]

In fact, chances to discover such managers for your portfolios are virtually nonexistent. To have a high degree of confidence that a manager indeed has the skills to beat the market, you would need to see a track record beating the market by an average of 4 percent a year for 15 years.[8] However, of the 452 domestic equity mutual funds in Morningstar data that have 20-year-long track records (as of January 2009), only 13 of them exceeded the return of the S&P 500 at least 4 percentage points on average a year.[9] That makes for odds of 3 in 100. As unlikely as the chances are to discover these rare managers, how do we find them before the fact? By the time their exceptional skills are in evidence, most likely they're ready to move on to other endeavors.

The weight of these data and academic studies have long suggested that investors would be better off investing in index funds. At least investors can get the market returns, losses as well as gains, for a relatively small fee.

With active managers, not only is there a greater than 50/50 chance that the funds you choose lag the market, but they may be among the worst. In 2002, the 100 worst-performing domestic equity funds lost 53.3 percent, more than twice the loss of 22.1 percent by the S&P 500.[10]

Nevertheless, the myth lives on. According to data from Morningstar, there are 7,495 actively managed funds managing $4.5 trillion but only 304 traditional index funds holding about $508 billion in assets.[11]

Performances Across Strategies

Thus, mutual funds not only underperformed their market benchmarks over market up-and-down cycles, they also stacked up greater losses than benchmark indices during market declines. These unwelcome results make it difficult for investors to manage risks of market losses by selecting managers who can weather stormy market conditions.

Additionally in severe market downturns, all major market segments decline. Figure 8.4 shows the cumulative losses of major U.S. and world market indices in periods from 2000–2002 and from November 2007–March 2009. The losses by the S&P 500 are shown, along with the Russell indices that represent the broad market (Russell 3000), growth and value styles, and mid cap and small cap stocks (Russell 2000). The MSCI World index is also included (excluding the United States), as is the MSCI Europe Asia Far East index (EAFE) and the emerging markets index.

As evident in Figure 8.4, in the 2008 period, all market segments declined by large amounts. The S&P 500 lost 46.6 percent; its loss was exceeded by all the other indices, except Russell 3000 Growth, but by only a small amount. The international indices fared much worse. The EAFE index declined by 55.8 percent; the emerging market index lost 57.4 percent. In the 2000 bear market, the international indices also lost heavily, exceeding the decline of the S&P 500. Among the Russell indices, the value, mid cap, and small cap indices fared better because they were not dominated by growth stocks of Internet companies like the Russell growth index.

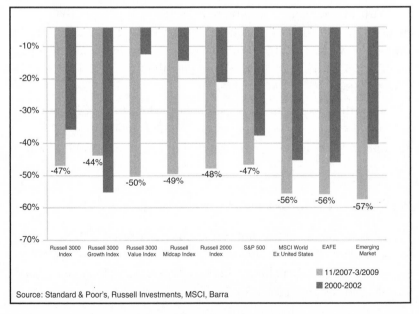

Figure 8.4   Returns: major equity indices in bear markets

"Fake" Diversification

If investors cannot depend on their managers to manage the market risk of losses in their equity portfolios, what can investors do to protect themselves? Intuitively, reducing the allocations to stocks and such risky assets would lower the risk of portfolio losses. Shifting more assets to safe investments like money market funds, banks' CDs, and cash, as well as to less-risky fixed income securities, would certainly provide greater protection and reduce loss potential. For sure, if markets for risky assets rally, this more defensive strategy would miss out on opportunities for profits.

These portfolio moves are part of a strategy known as asset allocation. It has become an article of faith that asset allocation is the most important contributor to a portfolio's performance. In a study that has become the source of authority for financial planners and others, it was concluded that on average 93.6 percent of a portfolio's return over time is due to the allocations of assets among stocks, bonds, and cash in the portfolio, not stock picking, rotation among different market sectors, market timing, or any other strategy.[12]

As critical as asset allocation is to portfolio returns, it also is crucial in managing the risks of a portfolio. If asset allocation is performed correctly, it can tailor the risk of a portfolio to the investor's individual risk appetite. Incorrectly done, it increases the portfolio risk to an extent unknown to the investor.

In its original conception, asset allocation divides assets among three principal asset classes, namely stocks, bonds, and cash. Most traditional portfolios are allocated between cash and short-term money market instruments; stocks of various types; and fixed income securities that include U.S. treasuries and corporate bonds of different ratings (see Figure 8.5).

Although the lower risks of fixed income decrease the overall portfolio risks, low correlation of fixed income to stocks is also critical to portfolio risk reduction.

Conversely, diversification among correlated asset classes increases the risks of the overall portfolio if the added investments have higher risks, even if the overall allocations to risky assets remain unchanged. This is an important point because asset allocations of many portfolios have been extended to include asset classes that are highly correlated and have higher risks. A recent study examined five asset classes—namely, large cap U.S. stocks, small-cap U.S. stocks, non-U.S. stocks (EAFE), U.S. bonds (Lehman Brothers Aggregate Bond Index), and cash. The study concluded that 90 percent of the volatility of a portfolio can be explained by its asset allocation policy—a result that is intuitively expected and consistent with the preceding discussion.[13]

Asset Classes

Cash and short-term investments

Treasury securities

Top-rated corporate bonds

Other investment-grade bonds

High-yield bonds

Large-cap stocks

Mid-cap stocks

Small-cap stocks

International stocks

Investment Styles

Core

Value stocks

Growth stocks

Figure 8.5   Diversification by asset classes

Suppose a portfolio starts out with holdings in cash equivalents, treasury securities, high-quality corporate bonds, and large cap stocks. The risk of this portfolio depends on how much is in stocks. However, if the portfolio adds holdings in high-yield bonds, which have a higher risk than Treasury securities and have a higher correlation with stocks, the risk of the portfolio increases even if the overall allocations to fixed income and stocks remain unchanged. Similarly, if the portfolio is diversified out of large cap stocks to include small cap and international stocks, its risk accordingly increases, because these asset classes are both more risky and have a high correlation to large cap stocks.

Thus, when the stock market is in a long-term secular rising trend, increasing risks by adding these asset classes increases the return potential of a portfolio. However, the key point is that there is an increase in the risk of losses, and it needs to be recognized as such. In an uncertain market environment, investors should be well aware of the increased risk, and they may opt to be more cautious in adding risky investments to their portfolios.

For years, the endowments of Harvard, Yale, Princeton, and Stanford[14] have practiced the art of asset allocation and diversification with great success, to the envy of their peers and serving as portfolio models for investment advisors. For the fiscal year that ended in June 2008, the Harvard endowment had a 10-year track record of generating 13.8 percent a year on average. The annual returns of the Princeton and Yale endowments were even greater, at 14.9 percent and 16.3 percent, respectively. By comparison, the S&P 500 turned a meager 2.9 percent a year in the same time span. The consistent and outsize returns of these endowments were the more impressive given the large size of their assets. At the end of 2008, Harvard had $36.9 billion in its endowment, whereas Yale had $22.9 billion and Princeton $16.3 billion. Their portfolios included not only traditional stocks and bonds but also hedge funds, private equity and real estate, and other real assets. At the Yale and Princeton endowments, 75 percent of their assets were invested in hedge funds, private equity, real estate funds, and commodity-related investments. Importantly, in terms of exposure to equities with equity-like investments, these two endowments were over 95 percent exposed to the stock market; Yale had virtually no bond exposure because of the leverage on its portfolio. The Harvard endowment had 55 percent in the alternative assets. For reference, at nonprofit endowments, allocations to alternative assets accounted for an average of 35 percent of their assets. Importantly, the Ivies and the other endowments allocated similar amounts to hedge funds. The difference in alternative assets rests solely with the much greater allocations by the Ivies to private equity and real assets—all illiquid investments with long-term commitments. Also, the Ivies had little cash on hand, and they used borrowing for cash needs.

In the 2008 crisis, the successful strategies at these endowments hit a deep air pocket. For the fiscal year that ended in June 2009, Yale's endowment reported an investment loss of 24.6 percent. The endowment blamed the poor return on losses from investments in real assets such as real estate and timber, which fell 33.9 percent. Its energy investments alone dropped 47.4 percent, while private equity holdings dropped 24.3 percent.[15] Harvard reported a loss of 27.3 percent for fiscal year 2009. Its private equity investments lost 31.6 percent, whereas its real assets dropped 37.7 percent.[16]

"History is less useful now," commented Byron Wien, former strategist at Morgan Stanley, on the three Ivy League endowments' asset allocation strategies and investment performances (see Figure 8.6).[17] A similar crisis of confidence has played out at the $6.6 billion endowment of the University of Chicago that led to significant realignment of the endowment's assets and resignation of some investment committee members.[18] "We had underestimated the value of liquidity and overestimated our degree of diversification," lamented Andrew Alper, chairman of Chicago's board of trustees and member of its endowment committee.[19]

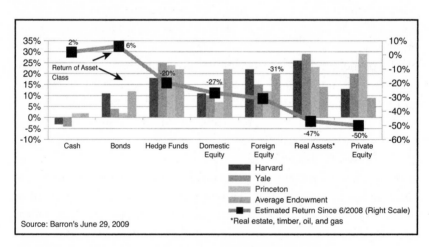

Figure 8.6   Ivy League endowments: asset allocations

This historical record thus refutes the value of diversification across sectors of the stock market to achieve reduction of the risks of losses of equity portfolios. The reason: They all move together, even if sometimes not in perfect unison. In market downturns, investors get no protection from such diversification.

Illusory Profits

A rising stock market is really fun. On quiet Sunday mornings, while the kids are still asleep, we tally the investment gains of the past weeks—again and again. On Monday mornings, the first thing we do is call the advisors only to hear the market is up again. So, we buy some more stocks. We keep buying as the market keeps going up, and we pay higher and higher prices. And along the way, we add riskier stuff like small cap and international stocks.

When the bear market of 2000 and 2008 came, we found out that we have lost more than a popular market index like the S&P 500, as if that magnitude of losses was not enough.

Figure 8.7 shows some sobering statistics on a national level of illusory profits in rising markets and losses in market declines. As published by the Federal Reserve Board in its quarterly Flow of Funds accounts, equity holdings by households include equities directly held in brokerage accounts and those held indirectly in mutual funds, life insurance annuities, bank personal trusts, and pension and 401(k) plans. At the end of 2002, total equities had declined to $10.6 trillion, a loss of 38.3 percent from 1999. For comparison, the S&P 500 lost 31.2 percent. And these numbers excluded the fresh capital added each year, so the losses of household equities were under-reported. Directly held equities fared even worse, losing 41 percent. It was the same story in 2008. Household equities lost 41.2 percent in 2008, compared to 37.7 percent by the S&P 500. During this same time, indirect equities in funds and corporate retirement programs, which are managed by professional managers, had larger losses at 42.2 percent. All told, in the 10 years since 1998, the increases in the values of household equity holdings were wiped out by the end of 2008.

So, all the profits we thought we had on those quiet Sunday mornings and additional capital we put in along the way evaporated with the declines in the stock market.

In a roller coaster market, the illusions of profits are even more ephemeral, and the risk of losses can be disproportionately larger. In a market trending down, at least we might be scared enough to stay away. When equity prices keep rising, maybe we are alert or cautious enough to take some profits off the table, so to speak; or at least we don't have to deal with losses. However, when the market is upside down, like Japan's stocks in the past 20 years or the U.S.'s from 1965–1982, as well as in the past decade, the risk of buy-high-sell-low disproportionately increases. The fear of missing out, the desire to recoup the losses, and the urgings of market pundits who predict further gains ahead—all are strong emotions and motives that distract calm minds and disciplined planning.

In the end, like the hare in the classic fable, all that jumping around is for naught.

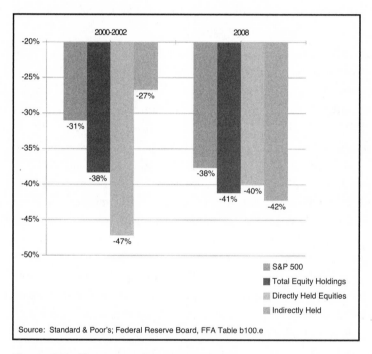

Figure 8.7   Illusory profits, greater losses

Liquidity and Safety

A standard but flawed aspect of investment advice during the bull market—and still common nowadays—is that little attention is paid to the liquidity needs for living expenses and other commitments. Thus, if you need money for spending, all you need to do is sell the stocks that have risen in prices. The gains would be taxed at the capital gain tax rate, which is lower than the ordinary income rate applicable to interest income. Additionally, return on fixed income is projected to be lower than stocks', as has historically been the case during times of rising stock prices. To support a spending rate often recommended at 4 or 5 percent, this line of reasoning has led to stock allocations larger than they would be otherwise, with smaller allocations to fixed income. Invariably, the stream of income generated from the bond portfolio is not sufficient to support the income needs of the investors. So, the shortfall of income would have to be made up from stock selling.

Access to Liquidity

That this strategy is flawed because of its dependence on ever-rising stock prices has escaped much scrutiny. Even if it is not in a bear market, the stock market does not go up in a straight line, and any stock can go up or down by 5 or 10 percent or more in a day. How often should an investor sell individual stocks or mutual funds to fund his monthly expenses? And which stocks or funds should he sell? Should only the losing stocks be sold even if they might have been purchased just a short while earlier? What if such stocks might be better retained because they may be poised for a run-up? How about those that have had great gains for years, since the resulting gains would be subject to even lower long-term capital gain taxes? What if they should be retained because of their long-term potential? The exercise becomes so complicated and so fraught with risks that the argument makes sense only because it appeals to the interests of the stock brokers.

In a highly uncertain market environment, when stocks go up and down like roller coasters, or in a prolonged sideways or bear market, the strategy is outright imprudent.

A great many businesses have been known to go bankrupt because they overinvest to achieve growth and expansion, and as a result they lack short-term liquidity to meet the needs of their ongoing operations. However, businesses usually have established reasonably priced credit facilities, including commercial papers or credit lines with banks. Individuals have only their credit cards and home equity to access credit. The former charge notoriously high interest rates, and the latter expose the borrower to the higher risks of losing their homes if the stock market declines and their financial situations further deteriorate.

As the 2008 crisis depressed stock prices, many investors became aware of the lack of liquidity in their portfolios, as well as to the inadequacy of the income generated from their investments. Unwilling to sell stocks and lock in the losses, they also were reluctant to sell the fixed income securities in their portfolios. For some, caught in this liquidity trap, many have had to delay their retirement or come back to work, often at jobs they don't want, to make ends meet.

Illiquid Securities

For investors who invest in less-liquid securities and with funds that have liquidity restrictions, the lack of liquidity access can be even more troublesome. Less-liquid securities, such as junk bonds, can often be sold only at discount to value. Even municipal securities issued by states in difficult budget conditions, like the state of California, may be sold only at deep discounts. Hedge funds invariably have liquidity restrictions, sometimes quite onerous ones. Commonly, hedge funds require notice periods, as short as a month, or a year, before investors' requests for withdrawals are honored. Even then, investors may have to wait for a month or a quarter before payments are made. Redemption requests may be suspended altogether. Investments in private equity, real estate, and other real assets face even more restricted liquidity.

These are the circumstances faced by the endowments at Harvard and other universities. Lack of liquidity at these endowments will pose great challenges to them for years to come. Their portfolios are low on cash, and they are loaded with illiquid securities that are difficult to price and even more difficult to sell at fair market values. Yet they face commitments to contribute to as much as half of their universities' operating budgets, compared to 5 to 10 percent at smaller colleges.[20] This is a reason why they aimed for a high return, to cover annual withdrawals averaging 5 percent a year to meet these budget obligations, plus the desire to achieve a return above the infla-tion rate. Princeton, for example, has a targeted annual return of 10 percent.

Onerously, these endowments also had to wrestle with commit-ments to continue to contribute to their private equity and real estate investments. These are the so-called capital calls that investors in private equity funds pledged to honor, upon demand by the fund managers. At Harvard, the commitments totaled $11 billion at the end of June 2008; at Yale, $8.7 billion, and $6.1 billion at Princeton. These are huge sums, amounting to between 44 to 55 percent of these endowments' shrunken assets, projected to be around $25 bil-lion at Harvard, $17 billion at Yale, and $11 billion at Princeton.[21]

The illiquidity of these assets will continue to affect the flexibility of these endowments for years to come. Unable or unwilling to sell illiquid securities at discounts, these endowments are burdened with borrowings to meet current needs, with underperforming assets, and with a limited ability to take advantage of new investment opportuni-ties. Such prospects have far-reaching effects on these universities and on those investors in similar situations. The universities have had to resort to budget cuts, freezing salaries, and laying off employees (as at Wellesley), reducing financial aid (as at Middlebury College), and such things as eliminating hot breakfasts at Harvard dining halls. Out-siders may not make it easier for them. Moody's Investors Services recently downgraded the rating of Dartmouth University's bonds from triple-A to double-A1. It said, "The organizations have fared pretty well, but they need to assess the relative benefit of certain investment strategies."[22]

Safety of Cash Balances

Most individual investors do not have illiquid investments, such as private equity or hedge funds like big institutional investors. How-ever, many keep their cash balances, money market investments, and even stock and bond accounts at troubled financial institutions. The banking crisis and the resulting forced closures of a number of banks, including the giant Washington Mutual, highlight the risk exposure of these assets. So far, the number of bank closures numbered less than

100 from 2007 to July 2009; there were none in 2006. This figure is still much lower than the 534 banks closed by the FDIC in 1989 and, of course, negligible compared to the thousands of banks closed in the 1929 Depression. This comparison, however, is not meaningful because of a variety of reasons, including the bigger size of the banks nowadays.

Nevertheless, the bank closures have spread out across the country, from West Virginia to Washington, from New Jersey to California, Idaho, Minnesota, and other states. The spate of continuing bank failures has also depleted the FDIC's reserves. According to the FDIC, from almost $60 billion in the fall of 2008, the FDIC's reserves were just over $10.8 billion in the second quarter of 2009, just enough to cover about two-tenths of one percent of bank deposits. Also, the number on the FDIC's list of troubled banks had swelled by one-third to 416 from 305 in the first quarter of 2009.

Because the FDIC insures accounts of up to $250,000 deposited in a single bank (see Table 8.1), larger balances are subject to risks of losses due to bank failures. Depositors need to observe these limits to ensure their bank balances are protected. A supplement and alternative to bank accounts are money market funds, many of which offer check writing facility, although they are not insured by FDIC. However, the funds' assets are supposed to be separated from the other accounts of the sponsoring investment firm or brokerage house. Also, some of the money funds managed by large firms have been reported to hold significant amounts of their assets in repurchase agreements collateralized by potentially troubled mortgage-backed securities. Thus, to avoid the possibility of irregularities in the handling of clients' assets, as well as bad investments that may force a fund's Net Asset Value (NAV) to dip below the $1 threshold, it would make sense for investors to keep money market funds at multiple large institutions. The size of these institutions gives them the ability to step up and provide funds to their money market funds if the latter "break the buck" as the Reserve Primary Fund had. Another possibility is to invest in government money market funds, which only buy U.S. Treasury securities.

Single Accounts (Owned by one person)	$250,000 per owner
Joint Accounts (Two or more persons)	$250,000 per co-owner
Certain Retirement Accounts (Includes IRAs)	$250,000 per owner
Revocable Trust Accounts	$250,000 per owner per beneficiary up to five beneficiaries (More coverage is available with six or more beneficiaries subject to specific limitations and requirements.)
Corporation, Partnership, and Unincorporated Association Accounts	$250,000 per corporation, partnership, or unincorporated association
Irrevocable Trust Accounts	$250,000 for the noncontingent, ascertainable interest of each beneficiary
Employee Benefit Plan Accounts	$250,000 for the noncontingent, ascertainable interest of each plan participant
Government Accounts	$250,000 per official custodian

Source: Federal Deposit Insurance Corporation

Table 8.1   FDIC deposit insurance coverage limits (through December 31, 2013)

Manage Risks to Preserve Capital and Build Wealth

Risks are paramount and ever present in investing. In good times, risks recede into the background and into the subconscious; they draw little attention and seem nonexistent. However, it is the persistent management of risks that aids in preserving the capital that is invested in risky assets, and this helps avoid panic in times of crisis.

We have reviewed the many facets of risks, from systemic risks and market and manager risks, to the risks of "fake" diversification and the illusions of profits, as well as the liquidity and safety of your capital. In the next chapter, we will focus on "absolute return" as a framework and asset allocation strategy to manage risks and build wealth.

9

Absolute Return: Manage Risks and Build Wealth

Magellan Fund of Fidelity Investments was made a darling of mutual fund investors by its manager, Peter Lynch. The legendary stock picker achieved a feat that none of his peers could match: beating the S&P index every year, partly by doing deep-dive research in small cap stocks and by taking big positions in them. During the bull market of the 1980s and 1990s, the strategy paid off handsomely for its manager and investors. Thus, it became a consternation to Magellan's 4.3 million investors and the media when the fund built up a large cash and bond position in 1995 to nearly one-third of its total assets of $56 billion. This change in strategy was taken by the new manager, Jeffrey N. Vinik, who took over after Mr. Lynch retired from active portfolio management, because he worried about "considerable speculation in the stock market overall."[1] He explained his decision by citing "'unprecedented amounts' (of money flowing into funds like Magellan), which has led to high expectations and low levels of fear among investors—the opposite environment from late 1994, when the fund was aggressively positioned in the market."[2] He also wrote of "euphoria surrounding the stock market in general and certain sectors in particular."[3] Criticism of Vinik mounted as the market kept climbing and Magellan's returns lagged the roaring S&P 500, despite the fact during the nearly four years of Vinik's tenure, Magellan's value increased by 84 percent and outperformed most of its competitors. In 1995 alone, Magellan returned 36.8 percent, slightly behind the 37.6 percent gain by the S&P 500, but ahead of 80 percent of the funds in the growth-stock category.[4] Apparently that was not good enough for the relative-to-the-benchmark critics. Vinik quit and immediately launched a hedge fund, which turned out to be hugely successful. His successor quickly sold off the fixed income positions and returned the fund to its former style, which was credited for Mr. Lynch's incredible winning streak.[5] Fast forward to May 2009, Magellan had lost more money than the S&P 500 for the 1-, 3-, 5-, and 10-year periods, according to Fidelity.[6] For the previous 12 months, Magellan lost 38.18 percent versus a loss of 32.57 percent by the S&P 500, and that included the rally since market lows in March. It now earned a one-star rating from Morningstar for its 3-year performance.

Had Mr. Vinik's critics foreseen the coming of a decade of bear market and how wealth accumulated over many long years can be quickly devastated, they might have applauded his actions. Unfortunately, they were more concerned about Mr. Vinik lagging a benchmark index, producing less than 5 percent in 1996 before he resigned in May, as compared to 12 percent by the S&P 500.

Following the convention of the bull market, and according to its believers, lagging the market benchmark was not indicative of a good manager. It didn't matter how ephemeral the gains were; they were, in fact, only paper gains because investors did not get a chance to spend them on groceries and such necessities of life. The game is to chase after the benchmark year after year and exceed it, no matter how much risk a manager might take. Beating the index is the hallmark of a good manager, and that is how managers can claim big bonuses. If the market tumbles, it's the investors who lose money, and the managers can always blame it on the market conditions. As it happened, in such instances, investors would always be urged to hang on, for "the market always came back."

Absolute Return

The bear markets of 2000 brought into sharp focus a different perspective about performance relative to a benchmark and the risks of capital losses. Wealthy investors became attracted to strategies and managers who at least attempted to manage the downside risk of the market. Put bluntly, they were simply tired of riding the market up and down to see large chunks of their wealth evaporate while their mutual fund managers did nothing before and after. Managers even bragged about beating the market by a few percentage points after losing 30 percent or more. That attitude runs counter to the way most wealthy investors make their money; many are business owners and executives of industrial enterprises. The money they make is real money from hard work, not paper gains, and they are pretty unhappy when they lose such large amounts. Less-wealthy investors think the same way about their money!

For over half a century, wealthy investors, starting with industry luminaries like Lawrence Tisch of Lowe's Corporation and movie stars like Deborah Kerr and Lana Turner, have invested in a different style of investing.[7] The managers practicing this style of investing seek to avoid losing money if the stock market declines by selling short certain stocks while holding onto the usual long (buy) positions; some even have managed to produce handsome positive results. Although practiced for half a century with demonstrable success, short selling was a complete anomaly to the mutual fund world. Mutual fund managers buy stocks and hope for the market to go up. If the market goes down and their holdings lose value, so be it! They are happy when the market goes up. But equity investing has aspects of a game of chance. As long as you stay in the game, the winnings accumulated after so many hands are subject to losses. Until you cash in the chips, the money is not real.

Investors think of investment gains as real money. Gosh, they count on it for their retirement and other purposes, like sending their kids to college. That's why they don't want losses.

And they care little about relative performance. This attitude is most pronounced among investors who have accumulated a significant net worth, including retirees. Their focus is to achieve reasonable returns for their investments to retire, to maintain their lifestyles and such financial commitments as charitable causes, with minimal risk to their capital. They do not focus on market benchmarks to compare with the returns on their investments. They could not care less about the relative performances of such indices as the S&P 500 or the NASDAQ. The most important yardstick for their investment returns is what they need for their lifestyles and perhaps some growth for their capital. To get richer, they work harder on their jobs and expand their businesses instead of taking undue risks with what they already have.

This sensible and pragmatic objective is paramount among individual investors. That is why most individual investors are happy with their mutual fund managers as long as these managers produce positive returns even when these returns lag the market indices. They don't fire their managers when they make money. They become concerned only if their investments start to have losses. Thus, while the S&P 500 is a household name, most individual investors do not know the difference between this index and the Russell 1000 or the Russell 3000, which are commonly used by institutional investors to evaluate their managers.

As a matter of fact, the obsession with benchmark returns has its genesis from the sell side of the market. That is, as funds vie for attention from investors, they compare their returns with the S&P 500 index or against their peers. They advertise heavily and proclaim superior talent if their results exceed the market benchmarks. Little, if any, is mentioned about the risks they take to produce these results, such as how a stock like AOL was suitable for a value portfolio during the Internet bubble. As a result, every money manager chases after market indices. While the market keeps going up, prudence is no more a virtue, and falling behind some index is not a mark of wisdom or foresight.

Large and presumably sophisticated institutional investors also are enamored with performances relative to market indices. On the advice of consultants armed with statistics on the historical returns of different strategies, from small to large cap stocks, to value versus growth investing, institutional investors compare their managers against market indices and among the managers' peer groups. Indeed, managers who rank below the average of their peer groups, even if they take lesser risks, usually end up being shunned from consideration for additional investments from their existing clients, or worse, being fired. And risk in this context is not the risk of losses, but the volatility or variability of returns from month to month or quarter to quarter.

A better manager is viewed as the one who outperforms the indices and the peer group. If the market goes down, losing money is not bad performance, as long as the loss is less than that of the market.

However, individual investors, wealthy or otherwise, are less sanguine about losses. One cannot buy anything with losses, and one certainly cannot become richer. This is where hedge funds come in. The single most distinguishing characteristic of hedge funds from traditional long-only stock and bond investing is that their investors expect positive returns regardless of market conditions, up or down.

Because of this emphasis on absolute returns regardless of market conditions, hedge funds are also called absolute return strategies, although they do not always deliver them. In 2008, hedge funds, on average, lost 20 percent. But as a group, they have been successful enough. For example, during the 2000 bear market, the Hedge Fund Research Inc. (HFRI) Equity Hedge Index, which tracks long/short equity funds, reported positive returns of 9.09 percent in 2000 and 0.4 percent in 2001 and a loss of 4.71 percent in 2002. The comparable figures for the S&P 500 in those years were losses in all years of, respectively, 9.09 percent, 11.88 percent, and 22.1 percent. By the way, this HFRI index gained 44.22 percent in 1999 versus 28.69 percent by the S&P 500, but that was an unusual year.

The central thesis of absolute return is to avoid losses. Hedge fund managers try to achieve this loss avoidance objective while seeking high return by short selling and other techniques of risk management. Again, they may not be always successful in achieving these objectives; some have even failed so miserably that they have closed down. But this is the key difference that sets them apart from traditional long-only mutual funds: the aim of avoiding losses while seeking high return. A consequence of loss avoidance is the significant reduction of variability of returns from month to month and from year to year; it has much less of the volatility of long-only mutual funds.

These aspects of absolute return—loss avoidance and lower volatility—have important consequences on wealth building and maintenance of steady income streams, as you will see.

Wealth, Volatility, and Market Declines

At its best, an absolute return approach aims to produce positive return regardless of market conditions, even though in a market uptrend the return could lag behind a stock market benchmark like the S&P 500. Conversely, in a market decline, it would still have a gain. Any losses are supposed to be limited. The concept of limiting losses in a market downturn is particularly crucial to retirees or institutions that need to take out certain amounts of money periodically to meet spending expenses or other commitments. We can think of this concept in a practical way: If we want to take out some of our money next month or next year—we do need time to plan, to put in the necessary trade or withdrawal orders—we sure would prefer that the money is there and the amount is not lower than what it is now. High-volatility investments like stocks somehow have a way of going down in values when we need the money most!

Adverse Impact of Volatility and Losses on Wealth

Suppose an investor had his savings of $100 invested in the S&P 500 starting on January 1, 2000; call this Scenario 1. Although the timing was most inopportune, he nevertheless would recover his capital some six years later and go on to see his initial investment grow to $119.90 at the market peak in October 2007. Overall, it was not a great investment, for the annualized return was only 2.34 percent a year, worse than three-month Treasury bills rates. But he made money!

Now compare this outcome with the alternative, whereby the investor had to withdraw from his savings monthly at the annualized rate of 5 percent from the beginning—the exact rate of withdrawal does not change the conclusions, only the numerical values—by selling stocks, stock by stock or proportionately across his equity holdings. Let's call this Scenario 2. By October 2007, at the new historic highs of the Dow and the S&P 500, his savings would have dwindled to only $64.58. After almost five years of rising stock prices!

Let's now suppose in Scenario three that by the beginning of 2004, the investor realized that he could not continue on this path and stopped making withdrawals. This would turn out to be fortunate timing because the market recovered and began a climb for the next four years. By October 2007, the investor's savings was recouped to $88.96, still below the initial $100 amount, but certainly far higher than the $64.58 sum had he continued to make withdrawals.

Figure 9.1 recaps the three scenarios and shows the patterns of volatility on wealth over time. These case scenarios illustrate the different impacts experienced by investors during the distribution or spending phase of the life cycle. When you start making withdrawals, the higher the volatility and the more damaging it is to your wealth, as well as your ability to access liquidity and income.

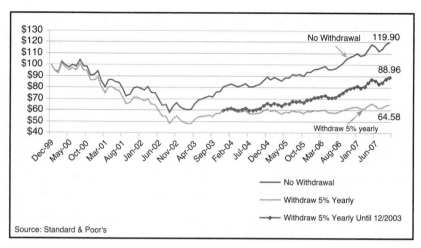

Figure 9.1   Wealth effects of periodic withdrawals

While wealth is being accumulated, investors have the ability to wait for the market to recover; whether they should, or even believe in a market recovery, is a different question. However, during the spending years when periodic withdrawals are made to pay for expenses, a bear market—or a market that goes sideways, up, and down, but is little changed at the end—would have detrimental impacts on savings, even if the market subsequently recovers. In a bear market, the investor would need to find an alternative source of income or eventually face financial ruin. As it turned out, by March 2009, in the "no withdrawal" Scenario 1, the investor would again see his investment taking a big hit from the high of $119.90 in October 2007 and tumble to $63.97. Yet this amount was not lower than the worst he experienced in September 2002, which was $57.55. He had recovered from that disaster; he would again recover! He can wait for the market to come back! Hasn't it always?

However, if the investor had continued to make withdrawals, his savings would have dropped to only $29.28 by March 2009. This is the kind of wealth destruction that would be extremely difficult to accept.

Wealth Benefits of Stable Return

What if the investor had gotten out of stocks at the end of 1999 and invested in fixed income securities? With short- and long-term interest rates exceeding 5 percent at the time, the investor would have been able to make his monthly withdrawals at the 5 percent annualized rate and see his savings exceeding $100 in October 2007 instead of $64.58 and still above $100 in March 2009, in lieu of $29.28.

However, financial advisors and market pundits would discourage retirees from getting out of stocks entirely (ask Jeff Vinik!), even at the edge of a market catastrophe, arguing that retirees need the higher long-term return of stocks to protect their savings. The problem with this argument is that retirees don't have long term. A cursory glance at a life expectancy table should surely serve as a reminder of this fact. Retirees can ill afford to wait for the market to recover!

The market returned a total of 19.90 percent between January 2000 and October 2007. This works out to be an annualized compound return of 2.34 percent or 0.2 percent monthly. Suppose that in January 2000, the investor locked his savings in an investment, say, a bond that produced 2.34 percent of interest a year (which would be way below the then-prevailing market rate), and took out the equivalent of 5 percent annually as before. We call this Scenario 4 shown as the straight line in Figure 9.2. (He would have to sell part of his principal to make up for the difference between 5 percent and 2.34 percent.) By October 2007, his savings would be valued at $77.00, which would still be a loss from the initial amount of $100, but it would be 19 percent better than the $64.58 that resulted from investing in the stock market.

Let's stay with this Scenario 4, whereby the investor remains invested in an absolutely mediocre investment producing only 2.34 percent a year. Between January 2004 and October 2007, the stock market gained 32.82 percent, or 7.68 percent annually—three times the bond's return. This would be a reason for financial advisors to emphasize the poor choice of getting out of stocks completely. Be that as it may, the lack of volatility in investment returns—although at a mediocre 2.34 percent annually—has earned the investor an additional 19 percent for his wealth, despite a strong market rally that took the major indices to new historic highs.

Thus, variability of periodic return would have great impact on investor wealth during the distribution phase. For any given expected rate of return, higher variability can lead to wealth destruction. Conversely, the more stable the return, the higher the odds of preserving wealth.

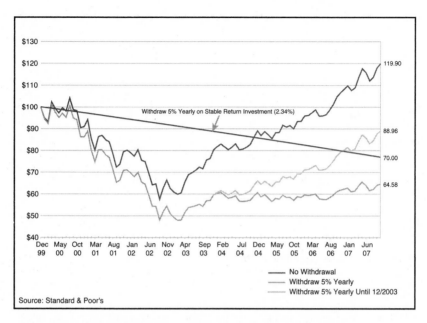

Figure 9.2   Wealth benefits of stable return versus stocks

Paths to Final Wealth and Short-Term Illusions

During the wealth accumulation phase, when there is no periodic withdrawal, variability has no impact on final wealth—that is, wealth value at the end of the planning horizon or at retirement. This is simple mathematics. In the last 20 years, between 1990 and June 2009, the S&P 500 produced returns of 7.29 percent annually.

If the investment was at a constant annual rate of 7.29 percent, the final outcome would still be the same. Likewise, if the sequence of the return stream were reversed—that is, starting with the return in June 2009, going through the 2008 and 2000-2002 bear markets, and ending with the return in January 1990—the final wealth would still be the same amount.

But of course, wealth levels in the interim periods would be vastly different. This is illustrated abundantly clear in Figure 9.3. It shows the three paths to final wealth: The first is calculated using the historical monthly returns of the S&P 500; the second uses the reserve of the historical returns; and the third uses monthly constant returns equivalent to 7.29 percent annually.

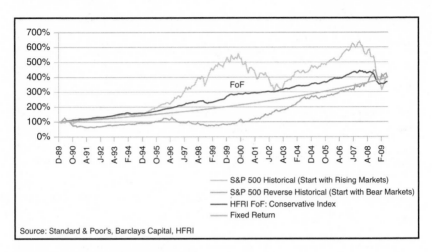

Figure 9.3   Paths to final wealth

The gaps in accumulated wealth between the two paths of historical and reverse historical returns over time are huge, depending on
whether the accumulation started at the beginning of a bull or bear
market. If the first 5 or 10 years of the accumulation phase is an up
and down market, like between 2000 and 2009—or worse, a steadily
declining market—the hoped-for prospect of eventual recovery in
some future year is not very comforting. What if, as the famed
Nouriel Roubini, professor of economics at New York University,
liked to say, when asked if he saw the light at the end of the tunnel for
the U.S. economy, "it's from an incoming freight train...?" Even
patient investors may not have the wherewithal to wait out such market doldrums.

Contrast these two scenarios with the fixed return alternative
whereby the investor started his wealth accumulation plan with, say,
an investment that produced 7.29 percent annually. The investor's
final wealth in June 2009 would be exactly the same as if he had been
in stocks, except that he would not have experienced the glee of
seeing his investment skyrocket during the 1980s and 1990s or
felt the agony of the 2000 and 2008 bear markets As it happened,
the Barclays Aggregate Bond Index—shown as the Fixed Return line
in Figure 9.3—generated annualized return of 6.96 percent during
this 20-year period.

Another alternative shown in Figure 9.3 is for the investor to invest in conservative funds of hedge funds represented by the HFRI FoF: Conservative Index. As implied in the name, this type of funds invests in specialist hedge funds that seek low volatility of returns. In this 20-year period, the HFRI FoF index produced annualized returns of 6.91 percent. Its volatility was 4.1 percent compared to 15 percent by the S&P 500 and 3.9 percent by Barclays Aggregate Bond.

Thus, with low-volatility investments, the investor would be more confident that going forward, his net worth would remain and his income would be available. With stocks, both the investment and the income would have been open to questions and doubts.

Build Final Wealth with Absolute Return

This analysis points to the critical role of stable returns in wealth accumulation, as well as in investment and retirement planning. It is not so much the unusual return gained in short-term intervals—unless they can be repeated over time—that determine the final wealth. It is the compounding effects of returns that determine the amount of final wealth. Thus, it is important for investors to think about the final wealth target they desire and the lowest risk strategy available to achieve it. Setting such a target explicitly may possibly unearth and highlight opportunities that would satisfy an investor's investment objective without the unnecessary risk. For many investors, fixed income securities may perfectly fulfill this role, regardless of whether they are aggressive or conservative, as long as their goal is to achieve and preserve a target of final wealth. In some market environments, fixed income might be the best investment in terms of potential return. With the benefit of hindsight, such an opportunity was readily available at the beginning of this decade, even when yields on quality corporate bonds were relatively modest at around 7 percent. But returns on fixed income clearly turned out to be far superior to stocks. A retiree could withdraw 5 percent a year and still see capital grow; for savers, their savings accumulate. But who would want to invest in bonds when the stock market's bull run seemed never-ending?

The answer: Investors who give careful thought to retirement planning and wealth accumulation and the true nature of high volatility and high risks of losses of stocks. Such investors would probably defy conventional financial advice and seriously consider putting the bulk of their assets in investments that produce an equivalent rate of return, yet more dependable.

Consider the case of the endowment of the college Cooper Union for the Advancement of Science and Art in Manhattan, New York, and how it shunned the model of investing of the Ivy League college endowments so much admired by the world. As reported in *The Wall Street Journal*,[8] after the tech stock collapse and the World Trade Center terrorist attack in 2001, the college's endowment dropped by more than one-third and officials consulted bankruptcy lawyers. It took this disaster to heart. In 2006, at the high of the stock market's climb toward new historic highs, the endowment began to take a series of actions to raise cash and move about one-quarter of its portfolio into hedge funds with focus on generating absolute return. "We knew that if we took a big risk and lost, we couldn't recover," said Cooper Union's president. For the nine months ending in March 2009, these hedge funds had a loss of 18 percent compared to a loss of 36.34 percent by the S&P 500 and a loss of 27 percent by the median endowment. Cooper Union's experience stood in stark contrast to the big losses suffered by the large endowments like Harvard and Yale, with their investments in private equity and real assets as previously recounted. The endowment's investment committee chairman criticized the investment model followed by the Ivies as "deeply flawed" because of its inadequate emphasis on a college's cash needs, like a retiree who relies on rising stock prices to pay for his expenses.

For those who missed the opportunity at the turn of the century and 2007, now is another opportunity to avoid the possibility of financial agonies.

Thus, for investors who seek to build final wealth, the choice is quite clear: either enjoying relatively worry-free years of accumulating wealth or retirement with a relatively dependable rate of return or alternatively suffering through uncertain periods of wild market gyrations.

Thus comes the idea of absolute return investing. Instead of chasing after some market benchmark, absolute return investing seeks to achieve final wealth with minimal risk of losses and lower volatility of returns.

Paths to Absolute Return

All roads may lead to Rome, to paraphrase the old saying. But the roads taken depend on individual circumstances and, let's face it, the greed for gains and the fear of losses.

Plain Vanilla

For many retirees, a perfectly appropriate investment strategy may be 30-year U.S. Treasury securities; in this low-yield environment, they generate 4.5 percent of interest income. It looks like a terribly mediocre rate of return. But it is not a lot different from the return of stocks in the past 15 years; in the foreseeable future, stocks may not generate anywhere near that level. The retirees can also add some TIPS (Treasury Inflation Protected Securities). Spice it up with a few quality corporate bonds, and the yield can get to 5 percent.

But the point is not comparing it with stocks or any market benchmark index. If an investor seeks an absolute return in the single digit rate, most likely it can be achieved with high-quality fixed income securities. This is, in fact, what many investors do, often using municipal bonds to avoid taxes, and nothing else. Although this may sound extreme, it is a favored investment strategy of many celebrity investors in the art and entertainment world.

What about inflation and growth of capital? Should retirees worry about such issues and take so much risk with stocks in the face of heightened uncertainty ahead? Can they just clip the coupons and let their heirs collect the face values of the bonds upon maturity? The face values of the bonds will be there, but the stocks might not. Hopefully by that time, the younger generations will have paid off some of the debt that their parents' and grandparents' generations have accumulated to unprecedented levels, surpassing even those generations in the Depression era. Come to think of it, our offspring should be glad if they don't have to take care of us in our old age, for by that time, Social Security benefits may have been depleted. Celebrities in

the entertainment world protect themselves from inflation by working. Perhaps people of a working age should think about the same
strategy instead of relying on outsized investment gains for their
future retirement. Those gains may be illusory, and in their place
might only be agony in the future. Many people in high-risk profes-
sions like sports, entertainment, and other high-profile endeavors
have already taken risks with their careers and the sources of their
income and lifestyles; should they also take risks with their safety
nets? That is why many have opted to invest in municipal bonds.

By the way, if we worry so much about the depreciative impact of
inflation on bonds, should we also not be concerned about its effects
on stocks, like the inflationary times of the 1970s? In those times,
stocks only gave us anxiety and frustration without the coupon payments for the bills. At any rate, to achieve growth of capital in changing market conditions, there are other alternatives, as discussed later
and in the next chapters. Reliance on stocks for inflation protection is
not the only investment option or always the best.

As it happens, for active investors, the availability of Exchange
Traded Funds (ETFs) that short sell bonds can be used to hedge
against the interest rate risks. Presently several ETFs allow shorting of
Treasury securities, both on a leveraged and nonleveraged basis. For
two-time leverage, there are ProShares UltraShort 7-10 Treasury
(ticker: PST) and UltraShort 20+ Treasury (TBT). ProShares Short 20+
Treasury (TBF) is a nonleveraged short. For three-time leverage, there
are Direxion Daily 10-Year Treasury 3X Bear Shares (TYO) and the
Direxion Daily 30-Year 3X Bear Shares (TMV). Effective use of such
ETFs could provide investors with protection against changing interest
rates on laddered maturity bonds as well as on professionally managed
bond portfolios.

Diversified Bond Portfolios

On a larger perspective, we thus should not forget an absolute
return strategy that precedes stock investing but has been much
despised during all the years of runaway rallies in stocks. Bonds!

It has been said *ad nauseam* that stocks are for the long term.
Let's give bonds the same benefit of the doubt and examine the track
records of bond returns over full market cycles. Figure 9.4 shows the

cumulative returns of the Barclays Aggregate Bond Index and several world stock indices—namely, the S&P 500, MSCI EAFE, MSCI World Index ex. U.S., and MSCI Emerging Markets. We look at the following five periods: two periods of rising stock prices (1995–1999 and 2003–2007); two periods of declining stocks (the 2000–2002 bear market and the 2008 crisis between November 2007 to March 2009); and additionally the full 15-year cycle from 1995–June 2009.

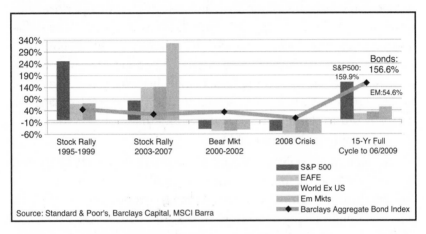

Figure 9.4   Stock versus bond returns: market cycles

A few findings from the chart are not at all surprising. One is that bonds underperformed stocks substantially in periods of rising stock prices, but they produced positive returns in times of declining stock markets. A key objective of absolute return is to produce positive return regardless of the conditions in the stock market. Historically, neither hedge funds as a group nor the new breed of absolute return mutual funds have been able to accomplish this feat—albeit the track record of the latter is short. Bonds could not do that either, as in 1994 when the Barclays Index lost 2.9 percent. But bonds did not experience losses in any of the five periods being examined.

One finding may be surprising to stock enthusiasts: Returns on bonds were about the same as the return on the S&P 500 in the full 15-year cycle: 156.6 percent cumulatively versus 159.9 percent by the S&P. Bonds also beat out the international indices handsomely and by wide margins. Adjusted for volatility, or risk-adjusted return in MPT speak, the Barclays Index outperformed the stock indices by substantial margins.

As if it needs to be pointed out, this is a historical record, fairly selected as it may be (because it includes times of rising as well as declining equity prices), but the future may well be different. In an inflationary environment, prices of long-term bonds fare poorly in the interim, but stocks should not do well either. At the same time, quality bonds of varying maturities should generate steady streams of income at little risk of principal losses if held to maturity—whereas inflation-sensitive stocks may or may not turn in strong performance while the rest of the equity market may languish. Conversely, in deflationary times, few stocks would do well, whereas quality bonds could turn in strong performance as well as reaping the benefits of increased purchasing power. In a market like the past 15 years, if there is any margin in favor of stocks, it might very well be marginal, so steady return should be the clear choice—that is, unless you bet on the return of the 1980s and 1990s.

As such, an absolute return portfolio may very well be a fixed income portfolio. It might consist of a number of short-term notes and bonds of maturities laddered to mature over a number of years, plus some high-quality bond funds managed by respected firms, several of which are well known to the public. The laddered maturity component would provide ready liquidity and income whereas the bond funds would provide income access and a way to diversify to enhance yields. A bond fund that mimics the Barclays Aggregate Bond Index may fit the requirement. Such an index bond fund may be supplemented by bond funds that are actively managed in response to changing interest rate environments.

A word of caution is in order: Not all bond funds are managed the same way. Actively traded bond funds may turn out to be speculative. Because some bond funds excessively speculate on the direction of interest rates, trading losses may result, possibly large enough to wipe out the income stream as well as some of the principal. Furthermore, high fees are never welcome, but in bond funds, they are often the only factor that differentiates bad funds from better ones. Junk bonds are only part bond; they bear interest coupon payments but can be as volatile as stocks and are subject to high risks of default. International bond funds have a high risk of losses because of the currency risk that a traditional bond manager may or may not have the skills to manage; they may not even manage it. Yet currency values can fluctuate as much as stocks, and the currency risk is often the most important component of the returns of international bond funds. These funds are similar to domestic bond funds only because of the word "bond" in their names.

Hedge Funds

The success of hedge funds in avoiding the crushing losses of the 2000 equity bear market prompted accelerated interest in their absolute return orientation, although not always successfully. In general, hedge funds seek to achieve equity-like returns with significantly lower volatility and risk of losses. We will return to a more detailed discussion of hedge funds in the next chapter. For now, it is worthwhile to introduce the concept of investing with hedge funds by taking a look at the so-called conservative funds of hedge funds (FoFs).

As the name implies, these fund of funds (FoFs) invest their capital with single-strategy specialist hedge funds with a more conservative orientation. These specialist hedge funds tend to favor the so-called relative value trades such as fixed income arbitrage and long/short strategies with low exposure to the stock market as in equity market neutral. These FoFs are relatively easier than single strategy hedge funds for individual investors to gain access; the major investment banks offer them with relatively low minimum investments of a few hundred thousand dollars. They are also expensive. Investors pay management fees and possibly incentive fees to the FoFs in addition to the fees to the specialist hedge funds. Although conservative in philosophy and orientation, the conservative FoFs are not always successful in avoiding losses. In 2008, as measured by the HFRI FoF Conservative Index, these funds lost 19.86 percent—not as much as the stock market, but shockingly high nevertheless to their investors.

Figure 9.5 recasts the returns of the conservative FoFs against the Barclays Aggregate Bond Index and the S&P 500 from 1995–June 2009. For each index, it is assumed that withdrawals of 5 percent are taken out each year. The returns of the FoFs are net of fees, whereas fees are excluded from the other two indices' returns. This 15-year period is noteworthy in that it includes two distinct cycles in the stock market, thereby casting a long-term perspective of the returns of distinct asset classes of highly different levels of volatility over time.

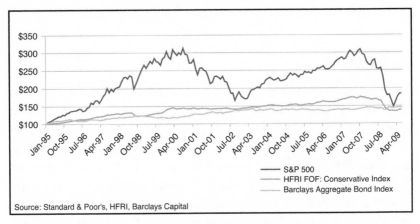

Source: Standard & Poor's, HFRI, Barclays Capital

Figure 9.5   Returns: stocks, bonds, hedge funds

In the end, the final wealth generated by each of the three strategies was not substantially different. The bond index ended in June 2009 at $145.30, whereas the FoFs came in somewhat behind at $138.32. The S&P 500 was valued higher, at $183.40, but its volatility and gyrations were simply awful compared to the other two. If the return calculations had March 2009 as the terminal date, the S&P 500 would barely edge ahead of the Aggregate Bond and FoF indices. It doesn't seem worth the trouble!

Generally, FoFs tend be most vulnerable in times of systemic risks when most asset classes decline in value; effectively, risk assets have no place to hide. Hedging becomes less effective, except that those funds that do not hedge fare worse than those that do. This was the case with hedge funds in the 2008 crisis. When only pockets of the global markets were hit with lower prices, like the 2000 bear market, FoFs tended to perform better, by virtue of their diversification across different asset classes and strategies, as well as the risk management at the specialist hedge funds. Between 2000 and 2002, the HFRI FoF Conservative Index had gains each year, with 18.9 percent in 2000.

Keeping in mind the systemic risks, the HFRI FoF Conservative Index represents hedge funds that can be used as near-substitutes for fixed income, for reasons of low volatility and risk of losses. Figure 9.6 recaps the history of the FoF Index since its beginning in January 1990, against the Barclays Aggregate Bond Index and Merrill High Yield Master II, an index of high-yield bonds. In terms of returns, the FoF index and the high-yield index produced similar returns until the second quarter of 2009 when the high-yield index recaptured some gains. The FoF index pretty much outperformed the Barclays Bond index for the entire period, until the 2008 crisis. Importantly, in terms of volatility during this period, the FoF index and the Barclays Bond index have similar annualized volatility: 4.07 percent versus 3.87 percent. The volatility of the high-yield index was more than twice as much, at 8.99 percent. Incidents of losses experienced by the Merrill index were more often and larger than those seen in the FoF index. For instance, the high-yield index lost –6.9 percent in September 2001, compared to –0.5 percent by the FoF index and –2.6 percent in June 2001 versus –0.1 percent. From June and July 2002, the high-yield index went down by –11.2 percent as compared to a loss of –1.1 percent by the FoF index. In the second half of 2008, the Merrill index declined by –27.4 percent compared to a loss of –19 percent by the FoF index.

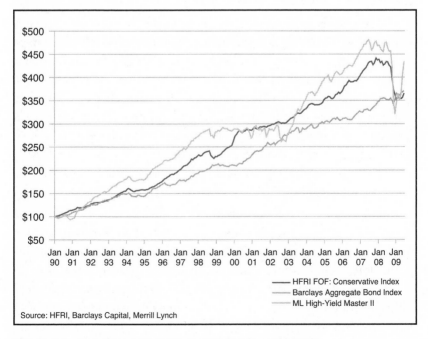

Figure 9.6   **Volatility and risks: hedge funds and bonds**

Thus, for the absolute return portfolio, we may add to the bond component a diversified group of hedge funds with different tilts in their return orientation; among them are conservative FoFs. We nevertheless must be wary of their vulnerability to systemic risks, although they are vulnerable to a lesser extent than stocks. For some investors, this potential risk may not be acceptable, leaving them with the fixed income portfolio as the only viable absolute return strategy. However, in most market conditions, hedge funds can be an attractive part of an absolute return portfolio. They produce equity-like returns over time while managing the downside risks, as we have seen in the 2000 bear market and 2008, although less successfully.

"Absolute Return" Mutual Funds

The success of the hedge fund industry and investors' growing interest in alternatives to traditional long-only stocks have spawned a new breed of mutual funds that mimic hedge fund strategies to generate some targeted rate of return. These mutual funds call themselves absolute return, as opposed to return relative to a market benchmark, even though there is nothing absolute about their return. In 2008, these funds lost an average of 11.7 percent.[9]

Hedge funds in general don't claim to be absolute return. They seek positive returns in diverse market conditions and take advantage of market opportunities favorable to their strategies to profit outsize gains, sometimes in high double-digit percentages. To achieve these returns, hedge funds use two principal strategies that are absent in traditional mutual funds: short selling and leverage. Their investment styles are also more flexible. They trade frequently and have high portfolio turnover across different market segments and asset classes, from stocks to bonds of wide-ranging quality and ratings, or international securities and derivatives.

Short selling involves selling short those securities that are expected to decline (rise) in values more (less) than those on the long side of the portfolio. In this case, the favorable relative performance of the long versus short side would add to returns regardless of whether the stock market went up or down. The portfolio could benefit even more if the short sells decline in value while the long positions rise. But the opposite could happen: The long positions could decline while the short side goes up. In this case, the portfolio would have a loss even if the stock market overall rose.

In hedge funds, the leverage can be high, especially those specializing in fixed income securities. Leverage can work both ways. It can increase return in multiple times proportionately with the amounts of leverage. Conversely, it can cause losses correspondingly.

Leverage can take a variety of forms. It can be simply that a fund uses margin borrowing to add to its trading capital. The borrowings might be bank loans many times the value of the investment capital, with each newly purchased security serving as collateral for additional loans. Derivatives like futures and options are also common tools of leveraging, which permit high levels of leverage without tying down much capital for collaterals. Leverage can also be achieved with structured securities whose returns are derived from the price movements of different securities across the global stock, bond, and currency markets. Embedded in these structures are often varying amounts of leverages and derivatives intended to enhance return.

Absolute return mutual funds ("mutuals") claim to also use "progressive risk management with modern investment tools, including derivatives."[10] However, it is hard to tell exactly what they do and how they use these techniques. The reason is their prospectuses are hardly informative about their strategies. As an analyst at Morningstar said, "Lack of transparency is a concern."[11]

One thing that seems apparent is that absolute return mutuals are structured as funds of funds, whereby they allocate their capital to different mutual funds presumably within the same fund family. As such, they can move across different asset classes, from stocks, bonds, and international investments. This is how they can claim that they access the talent of the experts in different areas of the global markets. However, the underlying in-house mutual funds may or may not be very good. As mutual funds, they may not be able to hedge effectively, thereby missing out on the very strategy that makes hedge funds work: short selling across different securities. They may not use leverage as much or as well as hedge funds.

In this regard, absolute return mutuals are different from funds of hedge funds in several aspects. The FoFs only invest with third-party specialist single-strategy hedge funds, presumably the best that the FoF managers can find. These specialist hedge funds are "hedge" funds—that is, they undertake risk management to protect the downside risks of the underlying assets. To the extent that the mutual funds underlying the absolute return mutuals do not or cannot manage their risks positions properly, the mutuals are exposed to the risks of other asset classes—perhaps unknown to them.

Absolute return mutuals seek to avoid the risk of losses in case of a stock market decline by taking on different kinds of risks from a variety of asset classes, not by hedging these risks. Thus, although they hope to reduce risks of losses with these strategies, the opposite could happen, through bad luck, poor skills, or excessive risk taking. For one, by migrating to other asset classes, such as commodities or real estate, they are exposed to the market risks of these markets, just as stocks are exposed to the risk of losses of the stock market. The skill sets that are required to invest in these different markets are very much distinct from equity investing.

Using these strategies, the stock market's risks are not necessarily neutralized in absolute return mutuals. Rather, these risks are simply replaced by the risks of other markets and the trading strategies that the managers employ. How these risks are balanced out to reduce the volatility of the overall portfolio is to a great extent a matter depending on the skill sets and experience of the managers of absolute return mutuals.

Hedge fund managers usually have different backgrounds than traditional long-only equity portfolio managers. Although the latter are usually well trained in the analysis of companies and their stocks, hedge fund managers are experienced in short-term trading, risk management, and the use of leverages. Importantly, they are experienced in short selling as opposed to managers of traditional mutual funds, who are conditioned to picking stocks that are more apt to go up with the market.

Importantly, the FoF managers are themselves skilled professionals in doing due diligence and evaluation on the managers they hire for their FoFs. It is not apparent that the managers of the absolute return mutuals are as proficient in this art. Furthermore, as discussed in Chapter 8, "Beware of the Risks," it is difficult to pick out top-performing mutual fund managers. It is thus an open question whether the absolute return mutuals can add much value from aggregating a group of mutual funds.

Traditional long-only stock mutual funds expose investors to the equity market's volatility and its risk of losses. With absolute return mutuals, investors are exposed to different kinds of risks: the risks of losses caused by actions of the managers, the so-called manager risks, in addition to the risks from the markets of the different asset classes. The return of absolute return mutuals, therefore, depends predominantly on the skills of the managers—the skills in short selling and such strategies, and the skills to navigate among different market segments. For example, a manager of a fund investing in stocks and bonds needs to be knowledgeable in both stocks and bonds, but more importantly, he should be sufficiently sophisticated to know when to get in and out of stocks and accordingly decrease or increase the allocations to bonds. Such market timing skills are traditionally absent in the mutual fund world.

The 2008 market crash and the success of hedge fund have stimulated the growth of absolute return mutuals, amid concern about their performances, their complexities, and whether they can deliver on these promises. However, it is difficult to analyze their records as a group because, unlike hedge funds, they are not classified under one category. For example, Lipper Inc. of New York, the mutual fund ranking firm, lumps the 30 funds it counted as absolute return with other categories like market neutral, global income, and other funds.[12] Morningstar also does not have a separate category for absolute return mutuals, although 15 funds have the word "absolute" in their names.[13]

Absolute return mutuals also have a short history; they have no five-year track record. According to Morningstar, their three-year average annualized return was 4.14 percent.[14] Hedge funds have been in business for half a century, populated with names like George Soros and many other celebrity managers. They also have benefited from organized data collection about them and their performances for some 20 years, with the HFRI reported on their indices of hedge funds since 1990. There are also other index publishers with more or less similar index construction methodologies.

A recent study by Standard & Poor's of absolute return funds in Europe did not note any outstanding feature about them. Of the 21 funds tracked by S&P, in the 12 months ending in February 2009, none met the return benchmark set by the managers, which was one or two percentage points above the London interbank offered rate.[15] Three-fourths of them invest in bonds![16] Also, according to Strategic Insight Mutual Fund Research and Consulting Group LLC in New York, misleading promises, poor expectation management, and disappointing performance resulted in nearly $100 billion in net redemptions and several liquidations in 2007 and 2008.[17]

Don Phillips, managing director of Morningstar Inc. in Chicago, summed it up well when he said, "There is an element of absolute-return strategies that looks like some of the gimmicks the fund industry has seen before." And, "Right now, there are a lot of red flags to consider, but if they can be overcome, absolute-return strategies could redefine the fund industry."[18]

Absolute Return with Opportunistic Profits

Absolute return is not a strategy like growth versus value stocks. It is an investment philosophy, an objective; but it also serves as a foundation to develop an asset allocation strategy and build a portfolio to achieve the specific objectives discussed earlier. It says that we want to avoid market losses or minimize the risk of losses from the market; we want this risk of losses to be managed, not to be left to chances. And we want to mitigate the volatility of the periodic rates of return. Because our liquidity needs, and the resulting withdrawals, follow predictable patterns, we would rather that the sources of funds that we depend on also follow similar predictable patterns. And we don't compare what we get from our portfolios against the returns of some indices, although we look at them for information about the different markets. In some ways, these indices are not even real. They don't include the fees we have to pay to mutual funds, and they may be constructed in ways unlike the way we invest, like the S&P 500 assigning weightings according to market capitalization values. We may prefer reducing the amounts allocated to stocks with rising market cap because we want to take profits off stocks that have risen in value. So, why do we want to compare our investments with these indices?

As in business, we strive for the revenues and expenses to be temporarily matched. At the same time, we look for opportunities to make prudent investments to grow the business to take advantage of opportunities that come our way. When the economic conditions turn hostile, we hold back our expansion plans and become more cautious in decisions concerning expenses, liquidity, and anything to do with the future. Thus, absolute return investing can be positioned to take opportunistic risks, to make prudent investments in risky assets to the extent that we can absorb unexpectedly large losses without affecting our lifestyles. Absolute return investing is not about not taking risks. It's about taking risks we can afford to lose and when the potential return is commensurate with the risk. Importantly, we don't want our financial futures to be undermined by taking such risks.

Our goal is not a hare's, catching every piece of scenery along the way. Our goal is "getting there," with as little pain as possible.

So, our absolute return portfolio primarily includes a fixed income component for liquidity and income, as well as capital preservation. For quality bonds, we should be able to count on getting our money back at predetermined times. As bond traders like to say: Bonds mature, stocks do not.

Our individual circumstances may give us the financial resources to invest in hedge funds as a vehicle to enhance return without bearing the volatility of stocks. At the same time, we need to be wary of their vulnerability to systemic risks. Chapter 10, "Absolute Return and Alpha," will discuss in more detail different strategies available in hedge funds, offering different possibilities for return enhancement.

If our financial situations allow us to have left-aside capital that we can afford to "forget" or to lose a substantial portion thereof, stocks and other high-risk investments may be excellent candidates in an opportunistic way. That is, we take profits on them when we become uncomfortable, regardless of how promising their markets' prospects may be. And we avoid them when the outlook for their future is grim and the return prospects are mediocre. Above all, we don't have to invest in them and run the risk of substantial losses. Chapter 11, "Beyond the Traditional," is devoted to these investments.

Figure 9.7 depicts the possible boundaries of the absolute return portfolio framework assuming the needed financial flexibility. There are three buckets, each with a different return and risk profile. The fixed income allocation is shown to be 40 percent. However, it can increase as much as required, possibly to 100 percent to assure liquidity and income. The allocation to hedge funds should be bounded at 40 percent. Beyond this boundary, perhaps up to 50 percent, hedge funds may actually dampen the upside potential of the absolute return portfolio and increase its risks. For a detailed discussion of this issue, please refer to my hedge fund book, *Evaluating Hedge Fund Performance*. The allocation to opportunistic risks should be bounded at 20 percent, although it can be tailored to an investor's ability to afford losses. To opportunistically enhance returns, rather than increasing the allocation to the opportunistic risks bucket, there is a more viable option: Where feasible, change the composition of the hedge fund allocation to include more hedge funds that seek to maximize return while emphasizing the downside risks with active hedging. Opportunistic risks may include traditional stocks, emerging markets securities, and nontraditional investments. Their payoffs can be large, but their risks are commensurately substantial or difficult to manage.

Chapter 10 provides a detailed look at the potential return and risk profile of the absolute return portfolio with these boundaries.

Within these boundaries, the absolute return portfolio is poised to take advantage of opportunities in the fixed income component, in hedge funds, as well as in the allocations to opportunistic risks. What it does not do is leave risks of losses to the vagaries of the markets and be married to traditional long-only stocks without their risks being managed. For hedge funds, the differences in returns between best, worst, and average managers (dispersion of returns) are so great (see the next chapter) that there is always the danger of selecting the wrong manager; Madoff is just one of many such scam artists. However, appropriate due diligence and evaluation of fund strategies present opportunities to select good managers who could add not only strong returns but also possess the capability to manage risks. Both are critical to meet the absolute return objective and represent opportunities to achieve return over and above peer groups' performances embedded in the HFRI indices.

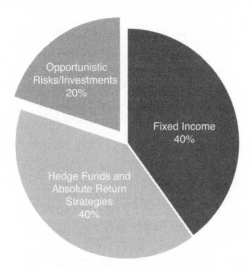

Figure 9.7   Boundaries of the absolute return portfolio

We have discussed the detrimental effects of risks on the final wealth that we rely on for retirement and to maintain our lifestyles and the beneficial impacts on wealth of absolute return. We also discussed the strategy of absolute return as well as laid out the composition of the absolute return portfolio and its boundaries. We now turn in the next chapter to a key component of absolute return investing, generating alpha with hedge funds.

10

Absolute Return and Alpha

In 1966, a journalist at *Fortune* wrote an article about "the best professional manager of investors' money these days," a "quiet-spoken seldom-photographed man named Alfred Winslow Jones," and called his investment partnership a hedge fund.[1] Carol Junge Loomis, an editor and writer at *Fortune* for over 50 years, whom the *New York Post* touted as a "legend in financial journalism," went on to cite Jones' investment track record and gave an explanation of his strategy as to why short selling and leverage can be used "for conservative ends."

In 1949, Jones formed a general partnership starting with $100,000 of capital. His portfolio was both "hedged" with short selling of stocks to reduce the risk of losses from market declines and "leveraged" with borrowed money to enhance return.

According to Loomis, in the first year, Jones' partnership earned 17.3 percent, "but this was only a suggestion of things to come." Jones' hedge fund turned out to be a huge success. For the five years ending in May 1965, Jones made 325 percent, besting the 225 percent return of Fidelity Trend Fund, managed by Gerald Tsai, which had the best record of any mutual fund during those years. This was thanks to the market pulling back in 1962, causing Gerald Tsai to have a big loss and yield the lead to Alfred Jones. Jones also had a loss that year because he misjudged the direction of the market, and the short positions were not large enough to turn a profit for him. Nevertheless, the hedges worked out well enough that the loss was small. Jones' 10-year record as of May 1965 was 670 percent, almost twice the 358 percent return of Dreyfus Fund, which was the mutual fund leader at the time.

Alpha Investing

How did Alfred W. Jones do it? By combining short selling and leveraging to reduce his exposure to the market risk. This sounds *nonsequitur*, perhaps because many hedge funds these days get into trouble by doing the same thing—although not exactly the same thing, upon further scrutiny. As explained by Loomis, suppose you have $100,000 in capital and are able to borrow another $50,000. Jones' strategy was to put $110,000 into stocks he liked and sell short $40,000 of stocks he thought were overvalued. As a result of these trades, Jones was able to cut down his market risk exposure from $100,000 to $70,000.

In the jargon of today's investing, the beta or market risk exposure in this illustration was only 0.7, yet Jones was able to generate substantial alpha—that is, the excess return over and above the market (adjusted for beta). In Jones' case, alpha was generated from the use of short selling and leverages, which he had been able to apply skillfully. That's why alpha is also referred to as manager "talent" in today's jargon.

After Loomis' article was published, hedge funds popped up everywhere, "almost overnight a raft of would-be hedge fund managers, most of whom [sic] were convinced that Jones had discovered the millennium. Some who then went on to start funds now acknowledge that they paved their way into business by using the article about Jones as a sort of prospectus, relying on it for help in explaining and selling the hedge fund concept to investors."[2] Within four years, *Fortune* estimated 150 partnerships were launched trying to mimic Jones' success, including George Soros' Quantum Fund.[3]

"Swimming Naked"

Then trouble hit the new industry in 1969. Starting in December 1968, the Dow plunged for 1½ years. By the time the bottom was reached in May 1970, the Dow had lost 36 percent. That got a lot of hedge funds into trouble. The new hedge funds began their lives at the beginning of a new upward leg in the general market "when the craze for performance swept the investment world...," and managers "...got overconfident about their ability to make money."[4] Many found

Jones' model of leveraging conducive to elevating return in a bull market but found short selling not so attractive, as well as difficult to execute. So, they were leveraged, but "swimming naked," with little or no short positions to protect themselves. Even Jones wondered if his shorting was misguided and if it would have been smarter to bear the full risk of the market.[5] Jones' second thoughts about hedging cost him dearly in 1969, along with most of the hedge funds; the oldest public hedge fund lost –47 percent, supposedly the very worst. Some managers even began to question the very idea of hedging. "Hedging is vastly overrated as a concept.... I stopped believing it after we got bloody and beaten from short selling,"[6] said a manager of two hedge funds and a large investment counseling firm.

But the industry survived, although their ranks thinned out. According to one estimate by the end of 1970, the 28 largest hedge funds saw their assets under management drop by 70 percent.[7] During the next decade, the industry operated in relative obscurity. Growth, however, resumed in the early 1980s and accelerated with the equity bull market and global financial liberalization. Many of the new funds engaged in trading across asset classes and national borders to take advantage of global shifts in stocks, bonds, and currencies, not just confining their activities in stocks like Jones did. They also employed financial derivatives, over-the counter markets, futures, and options as hedging tools, not just the short selling of stocks. Most notable of the hedge funds were Quantum Fund run by George Soros and Julian Robertson's Tiger Fund and its offshore sister Jaguar Fund. In later years, global macro funds, as they came to be known, evolved to be a major player in the hedge fund industry. In 1990, Hedge Fund Research, Inc. reported assets under management by hedge funds had grown to almost $39 billion and an estimated 610 funds.[8] From then on, the notorious failure of Long Term Capital Management in 1998 could not stun the growth of the industry, nor could the bad press about the alleged role of George Soros and other hedge funds in the Asian crisis and the currency bets against the Thai baht. Prime Minister Mahathir Mohamad of Malaysia got to call Soros a "rogue speculator." He lamented, "We have worked 30 to 40 years to develop [our] economy, and here comes someone with a few billion dollars and, in just two weeks, he has undone most of our work."[9] A decade later, hedge fund assets had grown to almost a half-trillion dollars with an estimate of about 3,900 funds.[10]

Tests of a Bear Market

The industry's growth got another boost from the 2000 bear market. As the market drop asserted itself month after month, savvy investors did not fail to notice that many hedge funds produced positive returns—sometimes exceeding 20–30 percent, or more—found only during the tech stock bubble. More broadly, as a group, hedge funds went through the market downturn generating mostly positive returns on average. The HFRI Fund Weighted Composite Index (HFRI Composite) reported a gain of 4.98 percent in 2000 and 4.62 percent in 2001. In 2002, it showed a loss of –1.45 percent against a loss of –22.1 percent by the S&P 500. The HFRI Equity Hedge index, which includes long/short equity funds, also managed to have gains in 2000 and 2001 and a relatively small loss of –4.71 percent in 2002. Other indices that included funds that were market-neutral or diversified across market segments (HFRI Equity Market Neutral, Relative Value and Multi-strategy) actually showed gains in all of the three years. A recap of the returns of the HFRI Composite index, S&P 500, and Barclays Aggregate Bond Index during the 1990s and the 2000 market decline will readily explain the impetus for the explosive growth of hedge funds (see Figure 10.1).

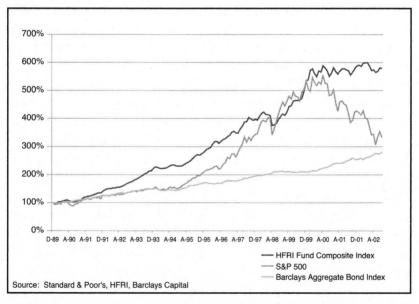

Source: Standard & Poor's, HFRI, Barclays Capital

Figure 10.1   Hedge funds versus stocks and bonds: 1990–2002

A Full Market Cycle

Having weathered the 2000 bear market, hedge funds entered into another period of even faster growth, with assets under management growing by leaps and bounds. By the second quarter of 2008, hedge funds had amassed a record $1.9 trillion of assets, according to Hedge Fund Research, Inc. It had taken the industry half a century to grow its assets to about a half-trillion dollars but less than eight years to multiply by four times. Their investment returns also matched the expectations of investors: producing positive returns when the stock market declined and pretty much kept pace with equity returns when the market climbed. For the five years between 2003 and 2007, the HFRI Composite index gained a total of 75.7 percent, while the S&P 500 generated 87.7 percent. But viewed from a full market cycle beginning in 2000, the performances of hedge funds were even more persuasive (see Figure 10.2).

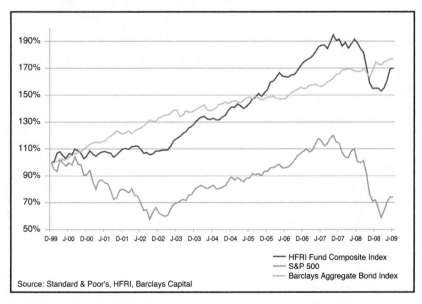

Source: Standard & Poor's, HFRI, Barclays Capital

Figure 10.2   Hedge funds versus stocks and bonds: 2000–2009

The 2000 and 2008 market crashes were so devastating to equities that the equity market's recovery between 2003 and 2007 hardly made a difference. The patience of the investors who had been staying with the stock market for the long term had been in vain. In the meantime, investors who had ventured into investing in hedge funds enjoyed a decade of steady gains. (And so did bond investors by clipping coupons while staying out of the fun and games.)

Challenges of a Global Market Crash

When the global markets hit a wall in 2008, asset prices across the risk spectrum tumbled. Although originated in the housing market in the United States, assets prices across the globe from stocks to bonds, commodities, and energy sharply declined. The only exceptions were assets considered safe havens, such as the U.S. dollar, cash, and government bonds of the developed countries. Even Treasury Inflation Protection bonds could not resist the decline as deflation fears gripped the global markets. This is shown in Figure 10.3. Worst hit were emerging market stocks (represented by the MSCI Emerging Markets index) losing –54.5 percent for the year; following right behind with a –45.1 percent loss were developed market equities (the MSCI EAFE index).

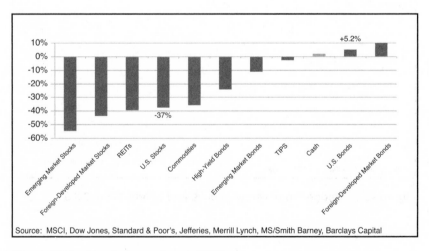

Source: MSCI, Dow Jones, Standard & Poor's, Jefferies, Merrill Lynch, MS/Smith Barney, Barclays Capital

Figure 10.3   Asset class returns: 2008

REITs (Dow Jones REIT index), U.S. stocks (S&P 500), and commodities (Reuter/Jeffries CRB index) clocked in similar losses, at –38.1 percent, –37 percent, and –36.1 percent, respectively. High-yield bonds (Merrill Lynch High Yield Master II) also tumbled, losing –26.4 percent. However, with the flight to quality and aggressive cuts in interest rates by world central banks, both U.S. and developed foreign markets' bonds held up well.

Amid this turbulence, hedge funds could not escape the whirlwind and registered unexectedly large losses. In 2008, the HFRI Composite index lost –19.03 percent, with a six-month losing streak between June and November, which was unprecedented in its history. Most strategies had losses, including market-neutral equity funds, which dropped –5.92 percent for the year. As expected, the short sellers gained 28.41 percent. The global macro funds as a group also acquitted themselves well with a gain of 4.83 percent.

Notably, dispersion of returns among hedge funds was extremely high. Although the bottom 10 percent of funds lost an average of –62 percent, the average gain of the top 10 percent gained 40 percent. Figure 10.4 paints a wide array of return differentials among hedge funds, even those in the middle of the pack. (Note: The funds in Figure 10.4 are only about one-quarter of the number of funds reporting for the HFRI Composite index.) Whereas many hedge funds had a dismal year, some of the best-known funds put in stellar numbers (see Figure 10.5).

The crisis in 2008 and hedge fund losses highlighted big changes in the hedge fund industry from their days just a couple of decades earlier. Many funds had ventured beyond stocks and bonds to trade energy and commodities and derivatives without owning underlying assets. They still retained the technique of short selling to protect their portfolios as well as profit from market reversals, and leverages to enhance returns. But these strategies have been taken far beyond the objective of lowering the market exposure. Leverages may simply be used to enhance returns—even with little or no short positions—as often as not many times the value of the capital. Short selling also evolved to include shorting certain asset classes against long positions in other instruments, such as shorting stocks against bonds as in capital structure arbitrage, or shorting U.S. Treasury securities against other bonds to take advantage of yield differentials. The shorts can

also be executed through derivatives, whose performances can reinforce losses on the long positions rather than mitigating them, as in
credit default swaps. Or the transactions can be negotiated between
two private parties, one of which may fail to live up to its obligations,
like Lehman Brothers.

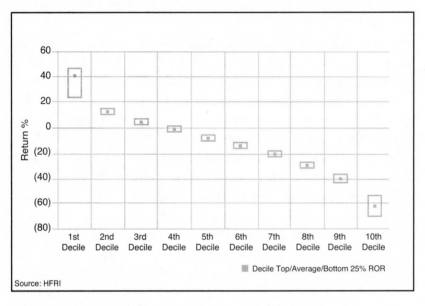

Figure 10.4   Dispersion of hedge funds' returns in 2008

In times of crisis, the relationships among these securities that
had prevailed in more normal times were dislocated, not to mention
the fact that prices of many assets had been marked up to inflated levels after several years of rising prices and then came crashing down.
Hedges, thus, became ineffective, leaving leverages to do their usual
work, multiplying the losses. On top of that, hedge fund managers
had become aggressive to generate returns to beat out the competition as well as to make more money for their managers and to attract
new investors. "We grew into this culture of gunslingers.... All anyone
really wanted was performance, and managing risk was a drag on performance," said the founder and president of a large hedge fund.[11] It
was not unlike 1969 of A.W. Jones' days.

Fund Name	2008 Return	Strategy	($ Millions) Fund Assets*
Horseman Global	31.3%	Equity Long/Short	$3,863
Paulson Enhanced	12.5%	Merger Arbitrage	$2,535
Paulson Advantage Plus	37.8%	Event Driven	$2,171
GMO Tactical Opportunities	36.5%	Equity Long/Short	$2,161
Altis Global Futures Portfolio–Composite	51.9%	Managed Futures	$1,340
Balestra Capital Partners	45.8%	Global Macro	$ 800
Pivot Global Value	51.9%	Global Macro	$ 754
Quality Capital Mgmt– Global Diversified	59.5%	Global Diversified	$ 747
Element Capital Master	34.9%	Global Fixed Income	$ 694
Odey European	58.9%	Equity Long/Short	$ 580

Source: Barron's Hedge Fund Rankings 2009   *As of February 2009

Figure 10.5   Top-performing hedge funds in 2008

The ranks of hedge funds also had swelled, to over 10,200 funds with single-strategy managers numbered over 7,600 strong, as estimated by Hedge Fund Research, Inc.; the rest are funds of funds investing with the specialist funds. Many of these funds were caught in the crisis unprepared, lost money, and ended up closing their operations. An analysis by Morningstar is illustrative.[12]

On the heels of the explosion of assets under management by hedge funds, Morningstar launched its rating service in January 2008. All in all, it assigned a rating from 1 to 5 stars to 1,732 funds. A whopping 615 funds disappeared in the ensuing 12 months! Morningstar noted that by and large, hedge funds closed up shops because of any of these reasons or a combination thereof: "a) Their performance is so poor that they cannot keep current shareholders and are unlikely to attract new investors in the foreseeable future; b) their performance is so poor that even though the funds have retained most of their investors, the managers have little realistic hope of surpassing the fund's high-water mark over the next few years and thus will not earn their performance fees; or c) management is embarrassed by the performance results and does not wish for outside parties to see its funds."[13] The analyst also observed that the lower the rating a fund received from Morningstar, the likelier it would be closed. Additionally, the larger the losses occurred in a strategy, the greater the incidents of dropouts. As intuitively sensible as these observations are, the numbers did not always support them. For example, short sellers had a stellar year, yet Morningstar reported an 83 percent dropout rate. HFRI Distressed Securities had 25.2 percent loss, which is not great but not the worst; yet Morningstar data base had a 62 percent dropout rate. On the other hand, HFRI Emerging Market index produced a loss of 37.26 percent, but Morningstar found a dropout rate of only 27 percent.[14]

Some of the fund closures are big operations by prominent names in the business (see Figure 10.6). The Madoff Ponzi scandal also claimed some prominent victims from the hedge fund ranks. The biggest loser was Fairfield Greenwich's $6.9 billion Sentry Fund. Tremont Group's of more than 10 hedge fund vehicles may have lost more than $3.1 billion. Kingate Global Fund also joined the list with a loss of $2.7 billion.[15] Overall, figures compiled from Hedge Fund Research, Inc. database recorded fund closures of 1,847 between the beginning of 2008 and the first quarter of 2009, bringing the number of funds in operation down to just over 9,050 funds.[16] Furthermore, funds of hedge funds closed in record numbers, with an attrition rate of 8 percent in 2009 first quarter. Assets under management also declined. From $1.93 trillion at the peak in the second quarter of 2008, hedge fund assets dropped to $1.43 trillion at the end of 2009 second quarter.[17]

Recovery?

The second quarter of 2009 marked the first increase of assets flowing into hedge funds, to the tune of $100 billion. The number of fund closings also slowed down to half of the pace in the last quarter of 2008.

Investment returns began to turn around in the first quarter of 2009 amid continuing losses in the stock market. In the first quarter, stocks continued to decline until the middle of March before making a sharp turnaround. Still, the S&P 500 recorded a loss of 11 percent for the quarter, versus a gain of 0.7 percent by the HFRI Composite index. Not every one of the HFRI indices recorded a gain for the quarter, but any of the losses were pretty small compared to those of the S&P 500. The HFRI Relative Value index, which includes market neutral strategies, turned in positive returns every month of the quarter.

Firm Name	Fund Name	Strategy	Peak
Fairfield Greenwich Group	Fairfield Sentry	Madoff Feeder Fund	$6.90
Drake Management	Global Opportunity, Low Volatility, Absolute Return	Macro/Multi	$4.70
Citigroup	Old Lane Partners	Multistrategy	$4.40
D.B. Zwirn	Zwirm Special Opportunities Fund	Multistrategy	$4.00
Tontine Capital Management	Tontine Capital, Tontine Partners	Equity Long/Short	$4.00
Ospraie Management	Ospraie Fund	Commodities	$3.80
Highland Capital Management	Crusader, Highland Credit	Credit	$3.50
Peloton Partners	Peloton ABS, Peloton Multistrategy	ABS, Multistrategy	$3.50
Tremont Group Holdings	Rye Investment Management	Madoff Feeder Fund	$3.10
Kingate Management	Kingate Global Fund	Madoff Feeder Fund	$2.00

Source: Deal Book

Figure 10.6   Large hedge fund closures

This return to stabilization turned out to be sooner than some observers had feared. Some had feared that the liquidation of hedge funds could reach 70 to 80 percent.[18] Citadel Investment Group, which managed $18 billion in 2008 and had seen its assets under management drop to $12 billion, recorded strong performance, gaining 44 percent in the first 7 months in 2009.[19] As a result, it agreed to release parts of clients' funds that had been locked in 2008 due to losses of over 50 percent by its flagship funds. For funds investing in distressed securities, conditions had much improved and liquidity was more available. Investor redemptions slowed down, and there were actually net inflows in the second quarter.

Absolute Return with Alpha

With the ability to produce returns competitive with traditional long-only stocks at lower volatility over time—in other words, generating alpha—hedge funds can add value to traditional stock and bond portfolios. For absolute return investing, hedge funds can play an active role.

Technically, volatility of returns refers to the fluctuations of the rates of return from period to period. It also means that your investment may be higher or lower the next time you look at it. To investors who need to withdraw from their savings for spending to maintain lifestyles, low volatility is important. This is because if you count on taking the money out the next month or the next year, you definitely want your money to be there and its value to be greater, or if not, about the same as it is now. With high-volatility investments like stocks, the future values of your individual investments as well as your portfolios are much less predictable.

Lower Volatility

Figures 10.1 and 10.2 demonstrated that stocks, as represented by the S&P 500, are far more volatile than bonds and hedge funds. In Figure 10.7, volatility is calculated by using standard deviation for the S&P 500, Barclays Aggregate Bond index, and the major representative HFRI hedge fund indices. The calculations are for three periods: two periods of rising stock price (2003–2007 and 1990–1999), and the entire history of the HFRI indices from 1990–2009. We already know that the hedge fund indices had gains during 2000–2002 and outperformed in 2008 when stocks declined, and thus would show lower volatility in these periods. The volatilities of the S&P 500 in the three periods are shown on a solid line; this line is above the bars representing the volatilities of the hedge fund indices. Only the Emerging Markets index experienced higher volatility from 1990–1999. The two bars at the end of each section represent the HFRI FoF Conservative and Relative Value indices; the dashed line represents the volatility of the Barclays Aggregate Bond index. These three indices recorded quite low volatility; all are under 4 percent in the three periods.

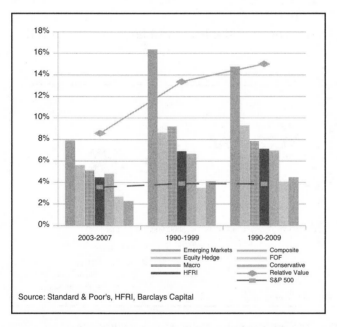

Figure 10.7   Volatility: stocks, bonds, and hedge funds

Low Correlation and Portfolio Benefits

When a traditional portfolio of stocks and bonds is supplemented with an asset class that has lower volatility and lower correlation to stocks, the change will lead to reduced volatility. If the added asset class has returns similar to stocks, the return of the resulting portfolio can also be enhanced. In addition to lower volatility, most hedge fund strategies (indices) have significantly low correlation with stocks. We will pick two hedge fund indices to illustrate the potential benefits of adding hedge funds to a traditional stock/bond portfolio. They are the Equity Hedge index and the FoF Conservative index.

Suppose we start with a portfolio with 60 percent in stocks (S&P 500) and 40 percent in bonds (Barclays Aggregate Bond Index). We modify the stock allocation by keeping 20 percent in stocks, adding 40 percent in hedge funds. Thus, we have a portfolio with 20 percent in stocks, 40 percent in bonds, and 40 percent in hedge funds. These allocations represent the boundaries of the absolute return portfolio discussed in the previous chapter. The 40 percent allocation to hedge funds is split equally 20 percent to each of the Equity Hedge and the FoF Conservative indices.

The key characteristics of the two portfolios are summarized in Figure 10.8.

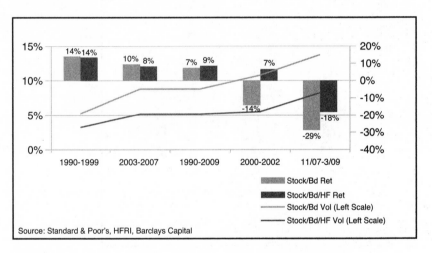

Figure 10.8   Absolute return versus traditional stocks/bonds

We examine five periods: the equity bull market from 1990–1999; rising stock prices from 2003–2007; the 20-year period from 1990–2009; the 2000–2002 bear market; and the crash of 2008 from November 2007–March 2009. Most apparent from Figure 10.8 is that in all five periods, the volatility of the stock/bond portfolio (shown on a line) is significantly higher than the volatility of the stock/bond/hedge fund portfolio.

In terms of returns (shown in bars), the stock/bond/hedge fund portfolio kept pace with the traditional portfolio in both of the two periods of rising stock prices; but it outperformed for the 20-year period. The returns of the two portfolios, respectively, are 400 percent versus 305 percent cumulatively, or 8.61 percent annually versus 7.45 percent. During the two bear markets, the stock/bond/ hedge fund portfolio outdistanced the traditional portfolio, especially between 2000 and 2002.

Diversified Hedge Funds

For investors who want to diversify into hedge funds, a good starting point is a fund of hedge funds. As such, you would acquire instant diversification across a number of hedge funds with different strategies and asset classes. The HFRI FoF Conservative index can be thought of as a diversified portfolio of the major hedge fund strategies, although not all the subcategories. The funds in FoF Conservative tend to be conservative in their objectives and investments. As such, they mostly engage in such strategies as equity market neutral, fixed income arbitrage, convertible arbitrage, or other market-neutral strategies. In 2008, the FoFs as a group had significant losses regardless of their risk objectives, conservative or aggressive. In more normal times, the FoF Conservative index tends to have lower volatility and lower return expectations than the more aggressive FoF categories. The lower-volatility feature can help investors ease the entry into the unfamiliar ground of hedge funds.

To give the hedge fund component (as in the stock/bond/hedge fund portfolio) an equity-like aspect, you can add the Equity Hedge index, which is the hedge fund strategy that has a semblance to an all-stock portfolio with the "hedged" and leveraged" components. However, the amounts of hedging and leveraging can vary substantially from fund to fund. They also differ in terms of geographical regions and investment approaches; they may include equity derivative instruments, equity substitutes, as well as hybrid securities. Commonly known as long/short equity, any two such hedge funds are likely to have differences in material respects. Thus, it is critical to perform due diligence and close examination of any hedge fund to uncover its risk orientation, how it generates return, and whether it is an equity fund or otherwise—in short, you want to make sure it is suitable for purchase.

As discussed, of the 40 percent allocated to hedge funds, half of this allocation went to the HFRI Equity Hedge index. Figure 10.9 shows the volatilities of Equity Hedge and the S&P 500 in the same five periods as earlier. In all these periods, the volatility of Equity Hedge was lower. In years of stock market rallies, as well as in bear markets, Equity Hedge kept pace or outperformed the S&P 500. Although not measured up to A.W. Jones' performances in his best days, this Equity Hedge index demonstrated the potential of investing in long/short equity hedge funds to protect the downside risk, as well as to enhance return over time.

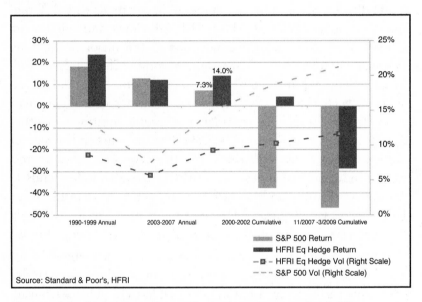

Figure 10.9   S&P 500 versus equity hedge: return and volatility

Beyond Equities

Starting with a fund of hedge funds with a conservative leaning and a long/short equity allocation as a foundation, investors can use other hedge fund strategies to enhance return. Hedge Fund Research, Inc. classifies hedge funds into four main categories: Equity Hedge, Event Driven, Macro, and Relative Value. Although together they account for 30 substrategies, the list may not even be inclusive enough. Also, many hedge funds actually provide "hedges," whereas others lean toward directional bets on the markets with potential for large losses, and yet others are better considered as "alternative investments." Funds using "hedges" are typically less volatile (lower standard deviation) than directional funds. As standalone investments, they do not add incremental risks to existing portfolios of similar securities. For example, as a "hedge," long/short equity should not be incrementally riskier than the S&P 500. Directional funds, on the other hand, do add value if they generate alpha and have low correlation with the investors' existing investments. However, "alternative" hedge funds often depend on illiquidity to generate returns or involve specialized market niches.

Also, although long/short equity funds tend to focus on the global equity markets, there are funds that trade across asset classes. For our present purpose, we will discuss three distinct groups of funds:

- **Convertible arbitrage**—Convertible arbitrage funds navigate in both stocks and bonds. Convertible bonds are interest-paying fixed-income securities with an equity component; they are convertible into common stock at a predetermined price. If the stock does well, the convertible bond behaves like a stock; if the stock does poorly, the convertible bond behaves like distressed debt. The arbitrageurs buy the bonds when they are traded below the implied value of the associated equities and simultaneously short the stocks of the same companies. Both sides of the trades are liquidated when the stock/bond relationship returns to normal. These funds historically have lower volatility than long/short equity because their strategy is by and large neutral to the stock market. In 2008, that relationship broke down in the midst of the credit markets' meltdown and the government's ban on short selling of stocks. The basis of the strategy, as a result, unraveled while funding costs increased, margin requirements rose, and redemptions from clients forced the selling of the bond securities. The return of the HFRI Convertible Arbitrage index for 2008 ended up showing one of the worst drops, losing –33.7 percent, only a bit less than the Emerging Markets index. However, conditions improved markedly in the first half of 2009 as credit markets thawed; equity volatility picked up, which is favorable to convertible arbitrage, and there were fewer players in the sector. The

HFRI Convertible Arbitrage index turned out to be the highest return strategy in the first half of 2009.

- **Event driven**—The so-called "event-driven" strategies also navigate in both the stock and bond markets. As the name implies, an event-driven strategy seeks to capture profits generated from price movements of securities of companies experiencing significant corporate events. Common events are mergers, combinations, or acquisitions. Other transactional events include bankruptcies, corporate restructurings, share buybacks, and spinoffs. The securities in these event-driven transactions include common and preferred stocks, as well as debt securities and warrants. Leverage may be used by some funds. Managers may hedge against market risk by using derivatives like options and their variations.

Funds that specialize in merger and acquisition arbitrage simultaneously go long and short in the companies involved in a merger or acquisition. Their trades are long in the stock of the company being acquired and short in the stock of the acquirer. The objective is to capture the price spread between the current market price of the targeted company and the price offered by the acquiring firm. By shorting the stock of the acquirer, the market risk is hedged out, and the trade's exposure is limited to the outcome of the announced deal. The principal risk is deal risk. Should the deal fail to close, the trade would lose. Merger arbitrage funds also invest in equity restructurings, such as spinoffs, leveraged buyouts, and hostile takeovers.

Another event-driven strategy involves distressed debt. These hedge funds invest in securities of companies experiencing some form of financial distress, such as reorganizations, bankruptcies, distressed sales, and other corporate restructurings. They may go long or short on these securities, which range from publicly traded corporate bonds, bank debts, common stock, preferred stock, and warrants. The strategy may be subcategorized as "high-yield" or "orphan equities." Leverage may be used, and some funds use market hedges like options and financial futures.

Companies in financial distress typically need some legal action or restructuring to restore their financial viability. Their securities trade at substantial discounts from par value because of difficulties in calculating their fair values, lack of street analysts' coverage, or an inability by traditional investors to manage their legal interests during restructuring proceedings. As a result, these distressed securities present opportunities for substantial profits if hedge fund managers with specialized skills in laws, corporate finance, and investment banking can discover the underlying values and steer the turnarounds in their favor. A typical strategy consists of buying the distressed securities, holding them through the whole restructuring process, and selling them after they have recovered closer to fair values. Managers may also take arbitrage positions within a company's capital structure, typically by purchasing a senior debt tier and short selling common stock, in the hopes of realizing returns from shifts in the spread between the two tiers.

• **Global macro**—The world is indeed the oyster of global macro funds. Global macro hedge funds face no limits on their strategies as they go long and short in stocks, bonds, currencies, and derivatives. They traverse across national boundaries, among developed countries as well as emerging markets. They use leverages as the opportunities arise to increase returns. Unlike some other hedge funds, global macro managers rely on the "top-down" global approach to a world view. They make forecasts on such developments as the world's economies, currency devaluations, government changes, political fortunes, or global imbalances in the supply and demand for key commodities. We will return to global macro funds in the next chapter.

Figure 10.10 recaps the histories since 2000 of these three strategies along with long/short equity funds, using the applicable HFRI indices. As evident in the chart, each of these strategies performed differently in different market environments. For instance, convertible arbitrage performed well in the 2000 equity bear market but tumbled in 2008. Event-driven funds advanced strongly in a generally rising equity environment but succumbed along with long/short equity in the current crisis. Global macro funds held up amid pressures on stock and bond prices in 2008, but otherwise they were hardly distinguishable from the others. Their differentiated performances reflect their differences in strategies and thus present opportunities to adjust the return and risk prospects of the absolute return portfolio, if so desired.

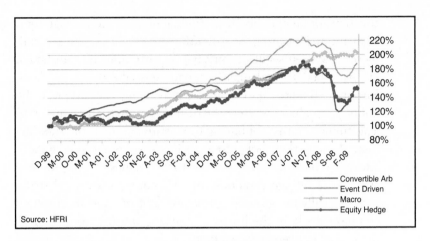

Figure 10.10   Returns of four hedge fund strategies

Having viewed a positive profile of hedge funds, we need to recognize certain complexities and risks of hedge funds that are not encountered in the mutual fund world.

Caveat Emptor

To say that hedge funds are different from mutual funds is an understatement; hedge funds have evolved much since the days of Alfred W. Jones. As alluded to before, the hedge funds of today are vastly different in terms of the amounts of hedging and leverages, the types of securities, the geographical regions, the types of risks, the investment strategies, as well as the terms and conditions they demand from their investors. It would take a book to go into these issues with some detail. See my book *Evaluating Hedge Fund Performance*, which discusses these topics in depth. However, there are immediate concerns that investors more familiar with mutual funds should be aware of.

Liquidity

Investors who are used to redeeming their investments from mutual funds at the end of a trading day and have access to the sale proceeds the next will be surprised to find out that hedge funds can hold back your money until they decide to release it. In the 2008 crisis, many hedge funds, large like Citadel or smaller ones, which faced mounting losses and the inability to liquidate their holdings suspended investor redemptions. These liquidity suspensions clearly are unwelcome. Even in normal times, investors face other restrictions. The most severe are from funds specializing in less liquid securities, like distressed debt; long/short equity funds are usually less restrictive. One such restriction is the lock-up period during which investors cannot withdraw their investments. The lock-up period can be as short as a couple of quarters or as long as five years; most are about one year. Before hedge funds make the disbursements, investors must give them redemption notices, usually about a quarter in advance. Some notice periods can be as long as a year, although smaller funds or funds dealing in liquid securities may ask for a much shorter notice time. Even funds of funds require redemption notices, due to the requirements from their underlying hedge funds. There is also the liquidity gate, to prevent all or a majority of a fund's investors from withdrawing at the same time. A liquidity gate of 25 percent means that only up to 25 percent of the fund's capital can be redeemed and any excess amount will be suspended.

The lock-up and redemption notice requirements can be managed by long-term investors, in the regular financial planning process. Indeed, to meet spending needs, investors can easily redeem once a year from their hedge fund investments, albeit with advance notices. In this regard, the history of hedge funds' lower volatility and lower risk of losses works to an investor's advantage. Nevertheless, hedge funds should not be considered a source of liquidity of first resort. Liquidation of hedge fund investments should be considered only in major asset allocation decisions, or in case of portfolio liquidation for estate planning reasons. Market timing, in general, has not demonstrated much success; with hedge funds, success is scarcer even among professional managers of hedge funds.

Transparency

Hedge funds are opaque, even to their sophisticated investors, such as foundations and endowments. Not only do single-strategy funds not disclose the securities they hold to their investors, many also do not disclose the data on a confidential basis to third-party risk monitors (hired by institutional investors to assess the risks of their hedge fund investments). Many hedge funds' strategies are difficult to understand and to decipher even by trained professionals. Long/short equity and equity market neutral sound more familiar but can be obscure. Many call themselves long/short equity but, in fact, are leveraged-long-oriented, such as a strategy with 200 percent in long positions and 100 percent in shorts. Market neutral may sound low risk but can be risk prone—a disaster waiting to happen if the strategy is concentrated, for instance, in option writing. Quantitative funds are dark incomprehensible black boxes, even though they can be very successful, with steady and strong returns. In this case, most investors have little to rely on, other than the managers' reputations and track records.

Because of the lack of transparency, due diligence and evaluation of hedge funds are critical. In a nutshell, due diligence has to do with making sure the hedge fund being considered for an investment is what it is supposed to be—that is, what is claimed in its marketing material. Important issues include the legitimacy of the hedge fund's strategies; its back office operations, especially fund accounting and security pricing or marking-to-market; as well as the viability and sustainability of its business organizations, operations, and practices. A fund should also be subject to close scrutiny about the soundness and viability of its strategies, as well as the risk management and controls in place so that investors can develop a good idea about the sustainability of its future return prospects. Concerns about potential fraudulent practices also underlie the need for due diligence.

Fees

Hedge funds charge high fees. In addition to a management fee from 1 to 2 percent, or sometimes higher, there are incentive fees of about 20 percent, or higher, of the profits. Fund of funds generally charge lower management fees; if any incentives fees are levied, they are usually lower or subject to a hurdle rate. For example, if a fund returns 11 percent with a hurdle rate of 3 percent, the incentive fee is assessed on the 8 percent above the hurdle rate. However, fees of funds of funds are in addition to the fees charged by the underlying hedge funds.

For investors used to low-cost index mutual funds, high fees by hedge funds may be difficult to deal with. However, it is useful to remember that the returns of the hedge fund indices are "net of fees," and all investments should be judged after the fees are factored in. Also, mutual funds can levy other fees in addition to investment management fees, such as expenses, load charges, and 12b1 fees for early redemptions. Yet, the stock indices are reported before any fees are factored in.

Access and Follow-Up Evaluation

Hedge funds are not as easily accessible as mutual funds. It does not help that they are prohibited from advertising. In fact, only accredited investors are allowed to invest in hedge funds. The principal conditions to qualify as an accredited investor are assets of at least $1 million and annual income of at least $200,000. Additionally, minimum investment requirements are extremely high compared to mutual funds. Many hedge funds require a minimum of $1 million to start. Bank-sponsored funds of funds or single-strategy hedge funds may require less but still be in the hundreds of thousands of dollars. They also levy additional fees; but this arrangement also applies to third-party mutual funds distributed by banks and brokers.

Once these issues are overcome, the individual hedge funds still need to be sought out. It used to be that the population of hedge funds was smaller, and investors relied on their personal contacts and word of mouth to locate hedge funds. Those practices still prevail today, to good effect, but sometimes they help conceal sinister schemes. In fact, investors with the convicted Ponzi scam artist Bernie Madoff were "by invitation only" or through introduction by "friends of friends of friends." Yet it takes 162 pages to list the names of Madoff's victims. Nevertheless, there are commercial services listing hedge funds and select data about them, obtainable on their Web sites. Even with this information, investors still need to perform due diligence and evaluation on any potential hedge funds.

Once a hedge fund is selected, it is useful to keep in mind that hedge fund managers operate within the constraints of the capital markets. Although they have specialized skills to discover and profit from anomalies in certain segments of the broad stock and bond markets, such opportunities must exist for them to exploit. When the conditions in these market niches are favorable, these hedge fund managers are well positioned to earn excess returns. If they take additional risks by leveraging in multiples of the capital base, the excess return could be extraordinary. In times of sudden shifts in the direction of the broad markets, such as during the 2008 crisis, it is likely that these market niches experienced dislocations. Only the most talented managers were positioned to cope with these inflection points in the markets. The average manager, however, would likely record excess negative returns, as the 2008 returns of hedge fund indices have shown. Aggressive managers—those who put on additional leverages to maintain returns when the opportunities in their market niches dwindle, such as when credit spreads have narrowed to historical lows—would likely endure unmitigated losses. These were conditions that contributed to the HFRI- Distressed index tumbling to a loss of 25.2 percent in 2008.

In mutual funds, market benchmarks like the S&P 500 are useful to assess managers' performances. In hedge funds, reference to a benchmark of their peers, such as those published by Hedge Fund Research, Inc., no matter how well constructed, is only a point of departure and is unlikely to capture the reasons or drivers accountable for a fund's performance. Returns of hedge funds are attributable to a variety of factors, from the conditions of their market niches and the broad global markets to the amounts of leverage, trading styles, and proclivity to take risks. Such individual variations cannot be captured just by looking at a market or peer index alone. Furthermore, hedge fund investing is about capturing an absolute positive rate of return even when the market goes down. As the market experiences periods of unusual volatility, different management styles will produce different results. Understanding these styles would greatly enhance the ability to judge how well certain hedge funds perform in times of market dislocations.

It is this need to understand what is behind the returns reported by hedge funds that makes it challenging for individual investors. Compared to just looking at market benchmarks for mutual funds, the time and resources required to decipher hedge funds can indeed seem overwhelming. To fill this gap, banks and brokers have stepped in to provide advice and recommendations for specific hedge funds. However, no matter what these sellers promise, a good watch word is "caution."

Risks of Hedge Funds

Hedge funds do have risks, in spite of the return histories of the indices as presented earlier. The media also often portray hedge funds as risky. Here are a few of the risks:

- **Poorly performing funds**—Although many hedge funds have performed well, many others have performed poorly. The unexpected losses, fund closures, and suspension of investors' requests for redemptions during the 2008 crisis only give further credence to this warning. As demonstrated in Figure 10.4, the differentials between the top and the bottom funds were so large in 2008 that it is not entirely unfair to say that hedge funds are risky. Closures of large hedge funds run by people with impeccable credentials or sponsored by investment banks like Bear Stearns only underline the absolute need for avoiding bad funds.

- **Frauds**—Newspaper accounts abound with stories about frauds in the hedge fund industry. The misdeeds usually included misrepresentation of managers' backgrounds, investment track records, assets under management, and circumstances that were designed to inflate the attractiveness of the investments. The end game was always to misappropriate investors' funds for personal use and other unintended purposes. Such was the case in a complaint filed by the SEC against Ashbury Capital Partners and its 23-year-old president and portfolio manager Mark Yagalla, whereby Yagalla was charged with misappropriating a substantial portion of the millions he had raised from 20 investors for personal use.[20]

Sometimes the frauds arise from attempts to conceal losses and to attract new investors. That was the case against Michael T. Higgins of San Francisco, California, whereby he was charged by the SEC in civil and criminal actions that he claimed to have produced returns of 54 percent in 1998 when in fact he had losses.[21] Sometimes the misdeed would be comic were it not for the losses that investors suffered as a result. Ryan J. Fontaine, who was charged with fraud by the SEC, was a 22-year-old college student living with his parents who claimed to have $250 million under management and had produced an annualized return of 39.5 percent for 13 years, including an average of over 21 percent for two years during the 2000 bear market.[22]

But frauds can be committed by hedge fund managers whose backgrounds are beyond reproach, at least on the surface, and whose investment strategies are sound. That was the case of Beacon Hill Asset Management, whereby the Securities and Exchange Commission charged it with deliberate falsification of its investment results to conceal losses in its reports to investors.[23] In the aftermath of the collapse of Bear Stearns, the managers of its two largest hedge funds that invested heavily in subprime mortgage-related securities were charged by the SEC with several counts of wire and securities fraud.[24] The two funds were Bear Stearns High-Grade Structured Credit Strategies Fund and Bear Stearns High-Grade Structured Credit Strategies Enhanced Leverage Fund. According to the SEC, their bankruptcies "caused investor losses of approximately $1.8 billion." Among the complaints, the SEC alleged that the two managers "...misrepresented the funds' deteriorating condition and the level of investor redemption requests in order to bring in new money and keep existing investors and institutional counterparties from withdrawing money. For example, Cioffi [the senior portfolio manager] misrepresented the funds' April 2007 monthly performance by releasing insufficiently qualified estimates—based only on a subset of the funds' portfolios—that projected essentially flat returns. Final returns released several weeks later revealed actual April losses of 5.09 percent for the High-Grade Structured Credit Strategies Fund and 18.97 percent for the High-Grade Structured Credit Strategies Enhanced Leverage Fund." In the same complaint, the SEC alleged that the two managers "...misrepresented their funds' investment in subprime mortgage-backed securities. Monthly written performance summaries highlighted direct subprime exposure as typically about 6 to 8 percent of each fund's portfolio. However, after the funds had collapsed, the BSAM [Bear Stearns Asset Management] sales force was ultimately told that total subprime exposure—direct and indirect—was approximately 60 percent."

Whether the outsized returns are real, when investment results are extraordinary, investors need to investigate how these returns were generated. In fraudulent cases, the returns were often claimed to have been generated in the context of some obscure investment strategies. Or the strategies were relatively straightforward, but the returns were so impressive that investors might do well to recall the old saying "too good to be true." This is the case with the massive $64.8 billion Ponzi fraud scheme perpetrated by Bernie Madoff, a former NASDAQ chairman.

Madoff claimed to have followed a sell-buy options strategy called split-strike conversion. He would buy a basket of stocks, selling call options at strike prices above the prices he paid for these securities, and simultaneously buy put options for down-side protection—all of which sounds reasonable and legitimate. However, this strategy could not possibly have produced the gains he claimed, which were 10 to 12 percent a year with only three down months between 1996 and 2004, and little variations over the years. In the meantime, the huge trades he claimed he made with $13 billion in assets left no "footprints" in the options market. Any of these three feats would be impossible to achieve, much less all three concurrently. Yet among those who invested were big hedge fund and wealth management operations like Fairfield Greenwich Group, Tremont Capital, Fortis Bank, Union Bancaire Privet, and many well-known individuals.

The actor, writer, and investor Ben Stein, who did not invest with Madoff, recounted a visit from wealth management advisors of a major investment bank. "They told me that if I invested a certain sum with them, they would make sure that a large chunk of it was managed by a money manager of stupendous acumen. This genius, so they said, never lost money. He did better in up markets than in down markets, but even in down markets, he did well. They said he used a strategy of buying stocks and hedging with options. I protested that a perfect hedge would not allow making any money, because money made on the one side would be lost on the other. They assured me that this genius had found a way to spot market inefficiencies and, indeed, to make money off a perfect hedge."[25]

"Madoff's Strategy Was Just Too Good to Be True," screamed a headline in the *New York Post*.[26] The realization came too late!

Expanding Alpha

The previous cautionary tales notwithstanding, hedge funds are a strategy that should be part of the portfolios of any investors who seek absolute return to build wealth for retirement and to fund living and other lifestyle expenses. The term "strategy" is used for the specific purpose of distinguishing from hedge funds as investments. As a strategy, it is useful to think of hedge funds as "hedges" or protection against downturns in the stock market as originally conceived by Alfred Jones to protect his portfolios against market declines, such as the crash of 1929. In this sense, every portfolio of long-only strategies needs hedge funds because the market does not go up forever, especially when we think of the uncertain future after the 2008 market crash and the economic conditions in the aftermath. Reducing the chances of large losses in market declines provides not only capital protection but also the ability to wait out the downturns.

The absolute return portfolio has a 40 percent allocation to hedge funds, by reducing the same amount from the equity allocation. But the initial investment need not be all that large because there is value in starting small to gain familiarity and experience. As allocations to hedge funds grow larger, investors gain opportunities to learn about hedge fund investing firsthand and become more comfortable with the differences between hedge funds and long-only investments. However, as discussed in my book *Evaluating Hedge Fund Performance*, when allocations to hedge funds approach 50 percent and beyond, the volatility of the overall portfolio (of stocks, bonds, and hedge funds) tends to rise after having steadily declined with increasing allocations to hedge funds.

For the absolute return portfolio, we start out with an allocation to a conservative fund of hedge funds; but the allocation to hedge funds needs not stop there.

Funds of funds carry a price for providing a host of services that on their own it is difficult for investors to perform. Their basic functions are gaining access to and selection of hedge fund managers and as such allow investors instant diversification, even with relatively small amounts of investments. A good fund of funds should produce reasonable return and be able to avoid fraudulent artists like Bernie

Madoff and disasters such as Beacon Hill. Well-managed funds of funds can add value by selecting top-performing hedge funds that produce consistently strong returns regardless, as well as by managing portfolio risks and performing portfolio rebalancing from time to time.

However, it is critical that investors understand how an FoF organizes and carries out these functions. Investors need to analyze the asset allocation strategy and portfolio composition of the funds of funds, how managers are selected, when and why investments are redeemed, the infrastructure, the resources, as well as the management and staff that the FoF has in place to execute these activities. Preferably, the FoF will disclose the identities of the underlying managers prior to investment. Track records, although not predictive of future returns, can serve as a good validation for the FoF's strategy, risk management and its operation in past market upheavals. Remember that risk is persistent; risky funds will remain risky in the future. An FoF's volatile track record when compared to its peers—instances of unusual losses, investing with managers of suspect reputation, or using out-of-the-ordinary strategies—are issues that should alert prudent investors.

In addition to funds of funds, the allocation to hedge funds can be profitably supplemented with long/short equity to replicate part of the stock allocation in the traditional portfolio, while reducing market risk exposure. Likewise, certain strategies such as convertible arbitrage, event driven, and global macro can be used to manage the risks of changing market environments, as well as take advantage of emerging opportunities.

Furthermore, as discussed, strategies and performances of individual hedge funds can vary substantially, leading to large variations in their return and risk profiles. Accordingly, due diligence and evaluation of hedge funds are critical to the selection of good-performing hedge funds, and, as a result, can add value to the performance of the absolute return portfolio.

Importantly, diversification with hedge funds helps position the absolute return portfolio to manage and mitigate the overall downside risks, which is a critical objective that is absent in the traditional mutual fund world of long-only investing. With a capital preservation strategy thus in place, mixing fixed income with hedge funds, investors can have the wherewithal to withstand the vagaries of the market as well as devastating shocks of market crashes. So equipped, the absolute return portfolio can explore opportunities that are risky with the potential for substantial losses, but also entail the possibility of unusual returns.

We will discuss more of these opportunistic profits for the absolute return portfolio in the next chapter.

11

Beyond the Traditional

"Absolute return" means risks of losses are managed. It's not that the management of risks is always successful or that losses never occur. But risks are not left to the vagaries of the global markets or the inexorable certainties of pundits' predictions of a strong recovery, a new bull market, or ever-rising equity prices. If they are wrong, it is us, the investors, who will pay the piper. With the absolute return approach, we want to make sure that our needs for liquidity and income are reasonably assured to be met. For some of us, it may very well mean that fixed income is the only viable investment. For others, mixing in hedge funds with a risk-controlled focus presents opportunities to enhance return while managing the downside risks. If there is still capital set aside that can absorb substantial losses without much impact on our lives—the capital that belongs to the "opportunistic risks" bucket in the absolute return portfolio—we can deploy it when opportunities for unusual returns arise. Without lamenting again on the future of the U.S. economy or the sluggish outlook of U.S. stocks, following are some such opportunities for the next decades. The common denominators of these investments are that we should expect significantly higher returns from them. Some can be liquid securities, such as emerging markets, and relatively easy to exit, such as mutual funds investing in commodities. Others are highly illiquid and require long-term commitments, such as private equity and real assets. Above all, we should be prepared for higher risks of losses or a longer time frame to see positive returns, often years after an investment is made.

Emerging Markets

Investors have long been advised to diversify into international markets. In some periods, foreign markets have been especially rewarding.

In the 1980s, the Japanese market was a great source of return. Mutual funds specialized in international equities had to have allocations to Japanese stocks. Even after the peak in 1989, Japanese stocks continued to have special allure, both because of the hope for a comeback of past glorious returns and the large weighting of Japanese stocks in popular global equity indices like the MSCI. Managers of international equity mutual funds built their portfolios in reference to these indices; excessive underweightings in the Japanese market would expose them to the risk of underperforming the benchmark indices.

Attractive Returns

In the few years between 2003 and the market peak in 2007, the Nikkei 225 made a strong comeback, and talks of a return of a Japanese bull equity market gained currency and new believers. During this period, the Nikkei 225 actually outperformed the U.S. market, as shown in Figure 11.1, although by then the Japanese market had long lost its glitter and allure to most U.S. investors. Also, foreign stock markets in developed countries from Asia to Europe outperformed U.S. equities by wide margins (see Figure 11.2). The MSCI Europe, Australasia, and Far East (EAFE) ex. Japan index outperformed the United States by more than 50 percent.

However, emerging markets made an exceptionally strong showing. Led by the so-called BRIC countries, in addition to the Asian Tigers and the resource-rich economies, returns on emerging markets have far outpaced equity investments in the developed markets.

The MSCI Emerging Markets (EM) index contains 22 countries, dominated by those in Asia and Latin America. The BRIC countries are the giant emerging markets economies, resource rich or high growth: Brazil, Russia, India, and China. See "MSCI Emerging Markets (EM)."

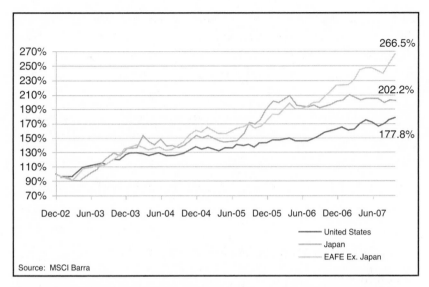

Figure 11.1   2003–2007 equity returns: U.S. and foreign developed markets

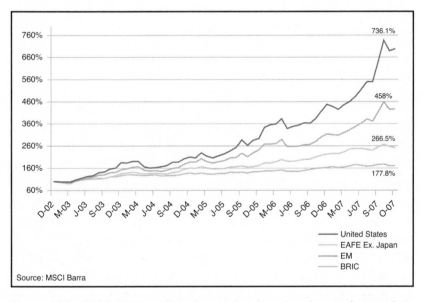

Figure 11.2   2003–2007 equity returns: developed and emerging markets

During the recovery years between 2003 and October 2007, the MSCI U.S. index rose by 77.8 percent, while the developed markets in Europe and Asia (excluding Japan) increased their values by 166.5 percent. However, the MSCI EM index rose by 358 percent, and the

BRIC countries rose by an astounding seven times. Figure 11.2 shows the performances of these international markets. With returns like these, it seemed only to make sense for emerging markets to gain greater presence in investor portfolios.

MSCI Emerging Markets (EM)

Asia:

China, India, Indonesia, Korea, Malaysia, Philippines, Taiwan, Thailand.

Europe:

Czech Republic, Hungary, Poland, Russia, Turkey.

Latin America:

Brazil, Chile, Colombia, Mexico, Peru.

Africa and Middle East:

Egypt, Israel, Morocco, South Africa.

Not for Buy-and-Hold

However, viewed over the long term, through bull and bear market cycles, the relative performances of these markets—that is, the MSCI USA, EAFE ex. Japan, emerging markets, and BRIC—are definitely more mixed. As shown in Figure 11.3, the foreign markets represented in the EAFE (ex. Japan) and Emerging Markets index fell slightly behind these U.S. returns from 1995 to June 2009; the underperformance of the two foreign indices might have been worse had it not been for the recovery in the second quarter of 2009. Even this somewhat benign picture disguised the fact that it was the BRIC that led the run-up of the emerging markets. Without the BRIC, the emerging markets were hardly worth the efforts to stray from the United States.

The emerging markets started the decade of the 1990s with a strong upward momentum. However, this advance was seriously interrupted by the Asian crisis in which George Soros and other hedge funds were reported to have profited handsomely by betting against the Thai baht. The one-two punch from the Russian currency devaluation in 1998, which brought on the collapse of the hedge fund Long Term Capital Management, was soon followed by the 2000 tech stock bubble burst in the United States. All in all, it was a hopeful beginning that turned out to be a wasted decade for emerging markets investing. Investors would have been far more satisfied with the U.S. equity market, which seemed at times like an unstoppable train—that is, until 2000.

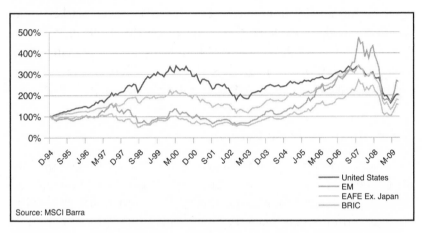

Source: MSCI Barra

Figure 11.3   U. S., developed, and emerging markets: 1994-2009 equity returns

After the 2001 recession was over, emerging markets took off like rockets. After a decade of rationalizing their economies and cleaning out the debris left from the Asian crisis, emerging markets were ready for a new phase of economic expansion, led by the BRIC countries. The imperatives for growth of these four economies fed on one another. China and India were hungry for feeding their masses of population, growing their economies, and modernizing their infra-structures and industries. Their needs for natural resources and energy were stretching the prevailing limits; Russia and Brazil stood ready to supply them with what was needed. These symbiotic relationships are still strong today. The five Asian countries (Indonesia, Malaysia, Philippines, Thailand, and Vietnam) that make up the bulk of the membership of the ASEAN (Association of Southeast Asian Nations) regional grouping reasserted themselves with an average annualized growth rate of 5.3 percent between 2000 and 2008, far surpassing the developed markets. In the country regional classifications by the IMF, these five countries are called the ASEAN 5.

All of this new economic vigor did not matter so much in the stock market crisis in 2008. As soon as the U.S. market began to lose steam in late 2007, the emerging markets and the BRIC promptly followed suit, and within three months they had lost 20 percent of their values.

It is noteworthy, however, that in this crisis, stock markets in all the major regions declined pretty much by the same magnitudes. Although the MSCI EM index lost by a few percentage points more than the United States at the lowest point in March 2009, it recovered more quickly and had outpaced the EAFE ex. Japan index.

Diversify to Increase Return

When it comes to international investing, the term "diversify" is a disservice to investors who were given advice like, "Don't put all your eggs in one basket." Diversification, with international markets in general and emerging markets in particular, increases your risks of losses; it is not risk-reducing. We don't need stastical calculations to make the point; their histories and the preceding charts are ample evidence that these markets fluctuate a lot. And they are still affected by the overall market conditions in the global economy, as well as by market conditions in the United States, especially on the downside, which would make things only worse, magnifying the losses of your portfolios in a market downturn. However, the correlations of the U.S. equity market with the BRIC and the emerging markets are lower than with the EAFE market index, bolstering the case for diversifying out of the developed markets. Thus, emerging markets represent attractive opportunities for the wary who recognize that these are opportunities for profits, not long-term holdings, nor a way to reduce portfolio risks. Looking into the future, cloudy as it is, the growth potentital of the emerging markets, expecially the select Group of 10 to be discussed next, are opportunities to supplement the moribund returns expected of the U.S. market in the coming years.

Follow the Fundamentals

This pattern of relative investment performance is not surprising given the differentials in economic growth of the United States and the developed countries as compared to the stronger growth of the emerging markets in the past decade.

As Figure 11.4 shows, when the United States began to recover in 2002, world growth followed, but the emerging markets had begun their growth spurt several years before and at a faster pace. Even the 2001 recession in the developed markets did not slow down the emerging markets by much, with China leading the way by growing at the stupendous rate of over 10 percent. As the 2008 crisis deepened, the global economy went into an abrupt slowdown, with the advanced economies slipping into a severe recession. The developing countries, however, as a group continued to eke out some growth, which the IMF estimated to be 1.6 percent in 2009, a much lower pace than the 8.3 percent growth rate in 2007, and 6.1 percent in 2008. However, China has recovered quickly with its massive stimulus program and was estimated to grow by about 8 percent in 2009—a somewhat slower pace than previously but impressive nevertheless.

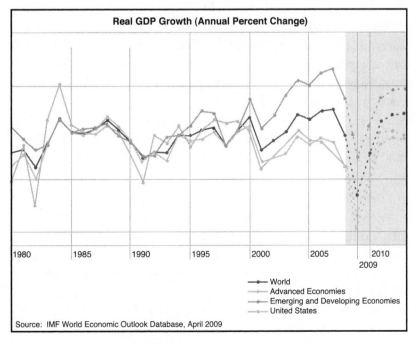

Figure 11.4   GDP growth patterns: U.S. and world economies

Opportunistic Outlook

According to the IMF,[1] the developing economies are forecasted to resume strong growth at around 6 percent, starting in 2011, and they're headed higher from there. The Euro area is projected to resume growth in 2011 but at a lethargic rate of 1.4 percent, just about half of their experience in the 2006–07 period, and improve slightly to 2.2 percent by 2014. The IMF also projects growth in the United States in 2011 at a relatively high rate of 3.5 percent, and 3.64 percent in 2013; then it's expected to taper off significantly the following two years, to 2.4 percent in 2014. These projections for the United States may likely not materialize with the high debt burden continuing to weigh in and dampen its growth prospects. In Asia, increased internal consumption and investments, state-sponsored as well as supported by continuing foreign direct investments, are expected to support and help it resume its previously high growth rates sooner than expected.

This pattern of differentiated economic growth between the developed and emerging economies has led to major shifts on the sharing of world GDP. After years of declined shares in the world economy since the mid-1980s, the U.S. economy rose to about 30 percent of world GDP in 1999. As shown in Figure 11.5, this percentage is projected by the IMF to decrease to 24 percent in 2014, after a decline to 25.2 percent in 2007. Non-U.S. developed countries are expected to fare worse, declining to just 39 percent of the world economy, from almost 47 percent in 1995 and 51 percent in 1999. The losses of the advanced economies would turn out to be the BRIC countries' gains. Their share of world GDP is expected to almost triple to 20 percent, from 7.4 percent in 1999. The other emerging economies are also expected to share in the growth, taking a 17 percent bite in 2014, from 11.5 percent in 1999.

Already the values of market capitalization of world equities have reflected these shifts in the pie of global wealth (see Figure 11.6). In the 10 years between 1999 and 2008, the equity market cap of the United States, the G7 nations, and the 16 countries in the Euro zone has declined, whereas the emerging markets' market cap has increased from 5.2 percent to 9.5 percent. The global market recovery since 2008 further accentuates the changing fortunes, with emerging

markets increasing their share to 12.3 percent by July 2009. The
Group of 10 countries' equity market cap rose even faster, from 2.2
percent in 1999 to 7 percent in July 2009.

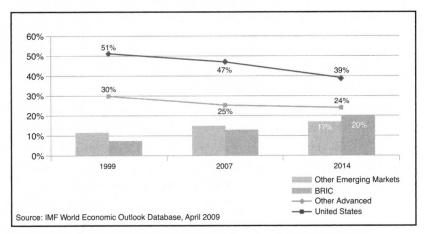

Figure 11.5   Shares of world GDP

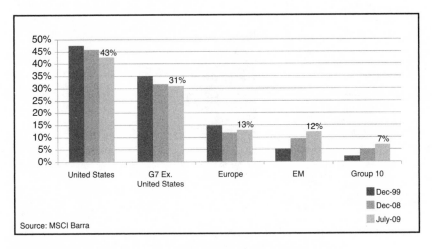

Figure 11.6   Equity market capitalizations of world regions

Group Intrigue

Of the fastest-growing emerging markets, we focus on the ten
largest countries that are projected by the IMF to experience growth
rates well above those of the developed markets. They are the four

BRIC countries and the ASEAN 5. We also include Mexico in this Group of 10 because it has a big population of over 100 million people, and its projected strong GDP growth in the years ahead rivals or exceeds Brazil's. Except for Malaysia, which used to include the dynamic nation state Singapore and is adjacent to it, each of the Group of 10 countries has the largest population among the emerging economies. As shown in Figure 11.7, the Group of 10 accounts for 52 percent of the world population. These countries, with all their flaws, already have strong records of improving their peoples' standards of living, political stability, as well as government policies that encourage economic growth and the emergence of the middle class. The expansion of the world economy can hardly take place without their participation. If anything, they might be the engine of growth, while the advanced countries are busy repairing their economies.

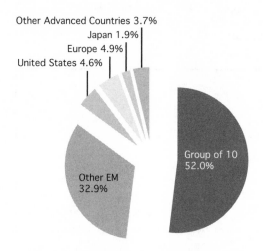

Source: IMF World Economic Outlook Database, April 2009

Figure 11.7   World population (2007)

As shown in Figure 11.8, of the ten countries, two among the BRIC (Russia and Brazil) are projected by the IMF to fall a bit short of the median growth rates of the Group between 2010 and 2014. China, India, and Vietnam have been at the top of the list, registering breakneck growth rates before the 2008 slowdown. They were forecasted to advance in 2009 at rates significantly stronger than projected by the IMF. China was on its way to clock in at 8 percent, whereas India was expected to expand at 7 percent and Vietnam at 6 percent or above. The other countries in the Group looked to fare better than the advanced economies in 2010, but significant growth will not resume until 2011.

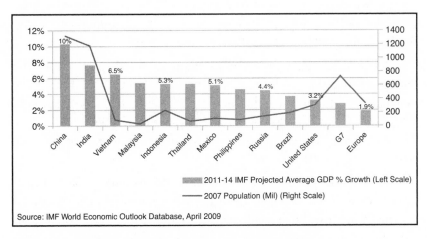

Figure 11.8   Projected GDP growth rates and population

The unexpected country on the list is Vietnam, a frontier market that is hardly on any American investor's "buy" list. Forty years ago, the United States sent war ships to Vietnam to bombard the country; now it has sent these war machines to the famous Cam Ranh Bay for friendly visits. Isolated from decades of war and the American embargo until 1994, the country embarked on a program of economic reform in 1986 and transformed itself into an open market economy. It soon was viewed by foreign investors as the Second China, where costs of doing business are lower and labor productivity is higher. Having been ravaged by a century of colonialism under the French, 40 years of war, and economic isolation, Vietnam had a poverty rate of 58 percent in 1993. By 2006, it managed to bring poverty down to 16 percent, according to the World Bank's Country Director Ajay Chibber.[2] According to the CIA FactBook, Vietnam's poverty rate was down to 14.8 percent in 2007. The country is on its way to achieve a poverty rate of around 10–11 percent by 2010. Although raw statistics can be misleading, the poverty rate in India was in excess of 25 percent in 2007, whereas in the United States, it fluctuates between 12 to 17 percent. Country Director Chibber also observed that Vietnam has achieved a literacy rate higher than 95 percent, which has been a key factor in achieving inclusive growth. The CIA Factbook showed Vietnam's literacy rate at 90.3 percent, about the same as China's 90.9 percent; India's is 61 percent.[3]

Vietnam's foreign direct investment inflows have been strong for many years. In 2008, it received pledges of $64 billion of foreign funds,[4] compared to $33.4 billion going into India.[5]

The capital, Hanoi, has more than doubled, and across the country, new cities are being built. By 2009, Ho Chi Minh City, the new name for the former southern city of Saigon, had a population of 10 million. In January 2007, Vietnam became a member of the World Trade Organization, and it now looks to Singapore as its model of economic growth for the future.

Barring war, Vietnam has the ambition to become a fully industrialized economy by 2020. A lot of growth opportunities for business and investment will materialize if the country can come close to realizing this plan.

Emerging Market Investing

Investing in emerging markets carries certain risks that are usually not issues of concern in the United States and developed markets. Aside from the usual risks stemming from markets, company fundamentals, credits, and interest rates, these securities are subject to additional risks, from unstable government policies to unexpected governmental changes, to possible currency devaluations. These risks are especially pronounced in smaller countries, although at times they also flare up in the biggest economies, like the popular demonstrations in Thailand about the premiership, or the concerns in India over its recent parliamentary elections. In China, street protests, such as those recently over job losses and ethnic strife, although contained, have been a motive in the government's policy to keep its economy growing at a fast pace, lest unrest spill over to become widespread social upheaval. Some risks that used to be a daily staple for certain countries are now less frequent, although they have no less an impact on the affected markets. A recurrent theme in Latin American countries has been sudden currency devaluations. With rising commodity prices and increased exports, these countries are no longer the pariah of international lenders. But the recent drop in oil prices has put the Russian ruble at risk of devaluation. The ongoing sparring between the United States and China over the value of the Yuan remains subdued, but any serious flare-up over the Yuan's strength or the financing of the U.S. debt load may turn into a run on the dollar with difficult-to-foresee, but surely not benign, effects on the U.S. and Chinese stock markets. Furthermore, most emerging market countries do not have viable derivatives and futures markets, regulated or over-the-counter among banks and brokers. Short selling is also often not allowed. As a result, hedging is more difficult with emerging markets.

But, unlike the old days, emerging markets investing is made easier now, especially with the proliferation of ETFs for individual markets as well as groupings of economies. Standard & Poor's has created an index for Vietnam, and its ETF is Market Vectors Vietnam (ticker: VNM). The Philippines may have an ETF soon. There are ETFs for the so-called frontier markets, emerging markets in Europe, Asia, and so on. The BRIC countries are traded under their individual markets' ETFs as well as the group, for which there are several. There are also ETFs that are designed to short sell and leverage to hedge on groups of national markets.

These securities make it simpler for investors to construct portfolios of different national markets and economic groupings that mutual fund managers who focus on individual stocks might not be able to accomplish. They also allow hedging and leveraging. It would certainly be easier to liquidate your positions with these ETFs than sell individual stocks or wait until the end of the day to put in a sell order of your mutual funds.

However, it is important to remember that not all ETFs are alike, even if their names are similar. For instance, membership in the MSCI Frontier Market Index contains 25 countries. FRN is the ticker symbol of the ETF for frontier markets sponsored by Claymore and Bank of New York (Claymore/BNY Mellon Frontier Markets ETF). It includes 16 countries, but Chile accounts for one-third of the allocation; a total of 75 percent of assets are invested in four countries: Chile, Poland, Egypt, and Colombia. The PowerShares MENA Frontier Countries ETF (Ticker: PMNA) invests in seven countries in the Middle East and North Africa. There are presently three ETFs for the BRIC countries. Their allocations to the individual countries and industry sectors, however, are quite dissimilar. Claymore/BNY Mellon BRIC (ticker: EEB) has 52 percent in Brazil, whereas the S&P BRIC 40 (BIK) is almost half dedicated to the energy sector, and geographically China accounts for 45 percent. The iShares MSCI BRIC Index Fund (BKF) is somewhat more diverse, but it also sets aside 7 percent for Hong Kong.

In addition, the availability of mutual funds of different stripes as well as hedge funds allows investors to construct portfolios of different risk levels and make-up of national markets to take advantage of the most promising of emerging markets. Figure 11.9 shows the histories of the HFRI-Emerging Markets index and the long-only MSCI Emerging Markets index since 2000. The risk-managed hedging of the HFRI index allowed it to withstand the 2000 and 2008 bear markets better than the MSCI index. In the 2000 decline, the HFRI gained 2 percent versus a loss of 40 percent by the MSCI index. The former index also experienced smaller losses in the 2008 downturn. However, it underperformed the MSCI index during the rally between 2003 and 2007. Overall, its cumulative return between 2000 and June 2009 was 139 percent, compared to 56 percent by the MSCI index.

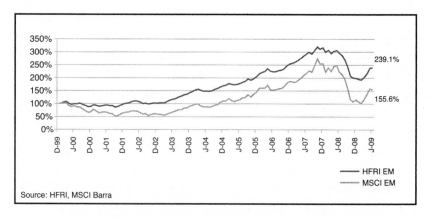

Figure 11.9   Emerging markets: hedge fund versus long-only index

One thing worth being repeated here is that investing in emerging markets, or internationally for that matter, does not constitute diversification to reduce risks. Investing outside of the United States is still an opportunistic strategy potentially bearing handsome rewards, but it also carries risk of losses that may outpace the United States in times of market upheaval. At the same time, in the context of the projected growth paths of the emerging markets, and against the backdrop of an uncertain U.S. economy and potentially unrewarding stock market, emerging markets, especially the Group of 10 countries, offer an attractive opportunity to be rewarded for taking risks.

Commodities

As the subprime mortgage debacle threatened to infect the banking system and the global economy, fears of a depression gripped the world financial markets. The growth of the most populated emerging markets came to an abrupt halt with the financial crisis and the attendant economic recession in their key export markets. All of these concerns seemed oblivious to the commodity markets. Oil prices had begun to resume their climb from around $50 a barrel early in 2007 after a brief pullback and then raced up to $144.95 by the middle of 2008, almost trebling the price in just a year.

Malthusian Risks

In early 2008, riots over rising food prices erupted in Indonesia, Mexico, Morocco, and other nations across the globe from Haiti to Bangladesh to Egypt. In Manila, the Philippines government brought in army troops to secure rice supplies. Even the United States felt the impact, with Costco and Wal-Mart rationing the amount of rice each customer could buy. Worried about its own citizens' needs, Vietnam, the world's second largest rice exporter after Thailand, cut its rice exports by nearly a quarter. Egypt imposed a six-month ban on its rice exports, whereas India effectively banned the export of all but the most expensive grades of rice. "The finance ministers [who were in Washington DC for an economic meeting] were in shock, almost in panic this weekend," Jeffrey Sachs, director of Columbia University's Earth Institute said on CNN's *American Morning*. "There are riots all over the world in the poor countries...and, of course, our own poor are feeling it in the United States."[6]

The food riots and shortage of rice felt so acutely in 2008 gradually faded away as the world turned its attention to the world's largest financial institutions teetering on the edge of total collapse and the global economy slipping into a recession. But the food price crisis exposed the Malthusian risk of the emergence and rapid growth of the emerging markets, especially the largest population countries: The earth may not be able to produce enough foodstuffs for everyone, or at least an additional two-thirds of the world's population, to eat like Americans.

Supply and Demand Imbalances

As estimated in 2008, the emerging and developing economies accounted for 84.8 percent of the world's current population of almost seven billion, and our Group of 10 countries shared 52 percent of the total. At this rate of growth, the emerging countries might add another billion mouths to feed within a decade. In the meantime, the Group of 10 members are getting richer more quickly than any time in their recent histories, growing their middle classes who are increasingly able to afford the food consumption habits of the Western countries. To this equation, add the supply constraints from rising oil prices, antiquated production technologies, and the dwindling agricultural land acreage due to mass urbanization, and the emerging picture is nothing short of alarming.

Prices of industrial commodities also rose rapidly, along with foodstuffs and oil and related fuels, until 2008. To wit, the Reuters/Jefferies CRB Index tripled in value between 2002 and 2008, before declining with the onset of the global recession (see Figure 11.10).

The imbalance between demand and supply of commodities is bound to reassert itself once the global economic recovery takes hold. Already four of the Group of 10 countries (China, India, Indonesia, and Vietnam) have continued to enjoy economic growth in 2009, albeit at rates somewhat slower than before, although probably stronger than the average 4.2 percent estimated by the IMF. China was set to achieve 8 percent growth in 2009 and was likely to have even stronger growth the next year. By 2011, the Group of 10 are expected to resume expansion, at growth rates that are high but more sustainable than in the couple of years preceding the global crisis.

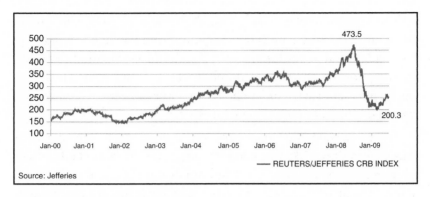

Figure 11.10   Commodity prices

Thus, the pressure on commodity prices, especially those commodities that eventually find themselves onto the family dinner tables, can only increase over time. Of course, the prospect would be even more frightening if world growth resumes at the rates of years past and inflation returns as a result of the potentially reflationary fiscal policies and easy monetary regimes now being practiced worldwide. The resulting demand pressures on commodities can only drive up prices throughout the global economy at an even faster pace. Prices of agricultural commodities will be the first to feel the impact of the price pressures, followed by their input factors, including oil and related fuels and industrial metals, which by themselves would be under a different set of price pressures.

How can investors take advantage of these developments?

Jim Rogers, who cofounded Quantum Fund with George Soros, said, "I'm convinced farmland is going to be one of the best investments of our time."[7]

Risks of Commodities

Rogers might be right, but historically, proponents of commodity investments and believers in the return of high inflation have often cited the low correlation of commodities to the stock market as a rationale for including them in a traditional stock/bond portfolio. As such, they would serve to temper the volatility of traditional portfolios. However, commodity prices have been in virtual locked steps with the equity markets, and since the middle of 2008, commodity prices and stocks have moved in tandem. From the high of 473.52 on July 2008, the Reuters/Jefferies CRB Index of 19 commodities came crashing down to 200.34 in March as the U.S. stock market hit its lows. Then, amid signs of an end to the global recession, commodity prices continued to rally along with the run-up in stock prices.

Thus, commodities may not constitute a good diversification vehicle to reduce risks as some have suggested. If commodity prices advance in response to demand and supply imbalances as well as economic growth, opportunistic profits can be harvested from commodities, but not as a strategy to reduce portfolio risks.

However, commodity investing is fraught with risks—that is, the risk of return volatility as well as the risk of large losses from sudden turns of world events. Witness the spectacular collapse of the prices of oil and the losses of mutual funds that bet on commodity prices, such as the Oppenheimer Commodity Strategy Total Return Fund. Between June 2008 and February 2009, the net asset value of this fund dropped 72.7 percent from $9.69 to $2.64. Similarly, oil prices declined by about 80 percent in an even shorter time frame. The oil ETF (Ticker: OIL) declined even more. However, the price of gold has held up well, losing 25 percent from the $1,000 top, but now it has come back close to the historic highs.

Paths to Profits from Commodities

Investors can use several vehicles to profit from the movements in commodity prices as follows:

- **Commodity exchange traded funds**—In addition to mutual funds, there are now available numerous ETFs specialized in commodities of various kinds. These commodity ETFs are derived from futures or asset-backed contracts representing the underlying commodities or baskets of several. They are easy to trade and structured so that you can go long certain commodities or go short on commodity baskets, as well as leverage on your capital.

- **Managed futures funds**—Another type of investment vehicle possibly attractive to affluent investors is the so-called managed futures fund. Run by Commodity Trading Advisors (CTAs), these managed futures funds trade on regulated futures exchanges using futures and options contracts on commodities and financial instruments. They may take opposite positions in commodities that might usually move together—say, long gold, short silver—thereby effectively building in a hedge. They can go short on any commodity, not just long. They can take positions on a large number of commodities in varying amounts, or just a few. Some CTAs concentrate in hard commodities like gold and silver, whereas others concentrate in agricultural commodities or financial instruments. A special class of assets is currencies, which some CTAs specialize in; they may bet on the direction of movements of world currencies against the dollar as well as against one another. To the extent that international equity or bond mutual funds offer a way to bet on the dollar, the bet is only one way: that of the dollar going down. The foreign exchange CTAs' trading is both ways.

The managed futures funds are required by regulatory authorities, principally the Commodity Futures Exchange, to register as CTAs, and sometimes as Commodity Pool Operators. In addition to trading on regulated exchanges, some managed futures funds may also use derivatives in over-the-counter markets with banks and brokers. They employ leverages through margins or derivatives. They are referred to as systematic traders if they use computer-generated signals that are derived from technical analyses of price movements. Discretionary managers rely on judgment to put on positions or liquidate them, although they also depend on technical analyses. In either case, they are mostly momentum players, riding on trends in the financial and commodity markets. They offer a measure of risk management to limit losses. They get stopped out—that is, they take losses or profits prematurely—when the anticipated trends fail to materialize and possibly reverse. They trade frequently and discipline themselves with rules in profit taking or liquidating positions, especially if certain limits of losses have been hit or surpassed. Some CTAs specialize in short-term trades, being content with small amounts of profits from small price movements while attempting to limit losses from individual trades.

Figure 11.11 shows the returns of the Credit Suisse/Tremont
Managed Futures Index compared to the S&P 500 and the
Barclays Aggregate Bond Index. It is interesting to note the
similar returns of the bond and the Managed Futures indices.
However, you should be aware of the higher volatility of the
Credit Suisse index, which was recorded at 12 percent, compared to 3.8 percent by the Barclays Bond Index. Dispersion of
returns of individual managed futures funds is also substantial;
they can have vastly different results depending on their styles,
investments, size of assets under management, and a host of
other factors.

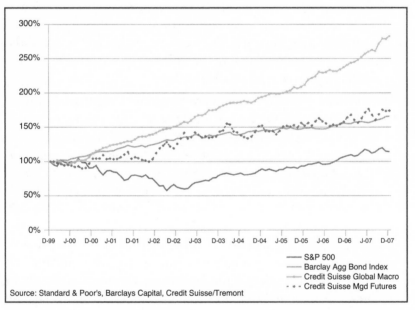

Source: Standard & Poor's, Barclays Capital, Credit Suisse/Tremont

**Figure 11.11   Returns: stocks, bonds, Managed Futures, and Global
Macro**

- **Global macro hedge funds**—Another vehicle to invest in
  commodities and broad changes in the trends of major stock
  and bond markets worldwide is the global macro hedge funds.
  The strategy space of global, macro funds is broader in scope
  than the CTAs. As a group, they place no limits on their strategies as they go long and short in stocks, bonds, currencies, and
  derivatives, including options and futures, as well as commodities. They traverse across national boundaries, among developed countries as well as emerging markets. The most well
  known of them all is the Quantum Fund owned by the financier

George Soros. To implement these views, global macro funds use multiple securities, including individual stocks and bonds, derivatives, and exchange traded futures to make their bets.

The historical returns of the Credit Suisse/Tremont Global Macro index representing global macro funds also are shown in Figure 11.11. Evidently, the Global Macro and Managed Futures indices avoided severe losses suffered by the S&P 500 in the 2000-2000 bear markets. Also, although the Futures index turned in cumulative return essentially similar to the Barclay Aggregate Bond index during the 2000–2009 period, the Global Macro index far surpassed them both. However, it should be pointed out that the Global Macro and Futures indices reflect different types of strategies, although their strategies may overlap.

Alternative Investments

Investments that are not publicly traded equity and fixed income securities are generally classified as alternative investments. Hedge funds have been considered an alternative asset class even though they invest in traditional stocks and bonds as well as other investments, such as currencies and derivatives. Calling hedge funds an alternative investment is a bit of misclassification. Why don't you want to manage risks when you are in a risky situation? Such a strategy should be the norm, a standard to assess other investments, not an alternative. Private equity, real estate, and other real assets such as timber, farm and ranch land, oil and gas properties, wine, artworks, and antiques are also considered alternative investments even though they were around long before publicly traded securities were invented.

Generally, real assets respond positively to inflation and are, therefore, favorite investments when inflationary expectations are high. Strong demand from rising income and wealth during times of economic expansion also tend to drive up returns on real assets. Specialty assets like artworks and antiques can command substantial premium for their scarcity and illiquidity, not to mention the prestige factor. At the same time, financing costs can be a significant detriment to the returns of these alternative investments, especially in times of credit shortage and when liquidity is at premium. Even valuation of publicly traded REITs and real estate ETFs are subject to these factors because their underlying assets are by nature illiquid. Conversely, in times of credit crises and economic upheavals, the lack of liquidity of real assets may prompt sellers who face financial difficulties to accept unusual discounts for their prized possessions. In such situations, investors and investment funds specializing in these asset classes may be able to take advantage of unusual opportunistic returns. However, even acquired at distressed prices, investments in these assets require patience and a willingness to forego ready liquidity.

Private equity (PE) is an alternative investment that can benefit from a long-term commitment and willingness to forego liquidity, generally from 7 to 10 years or longer. During the early years, returns on cash flows are negative due to fees and expenses of upward of 20 percent of the amounts of capital contributions. This is the so-called J-curve effect and can be a severe distraction to investors used to traditional equity investing. Private equity also depends on the general economic environment and the conditions of the equity and bond markets. This is why returns on PE show substantial correlation to equity returns, as shown in Figure 11.12.

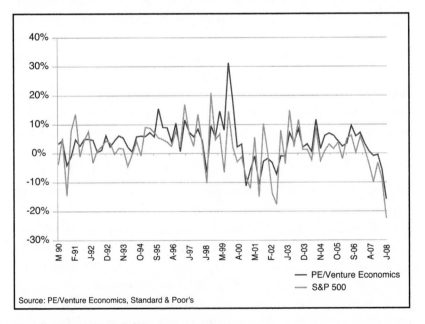

Figure 11.12 Correlation: PE and stocks

PE works best when the equity market is generally rising and providing opportunities to sell off the companies in a PE portfolio through Initial Public Offerings in the public market or mergers with other companies at favorable prices. The interest rate environment can also be a helpful factor if credit is relatively easy to obtain and rates are low, allowing PE funds to use borrowings to leverage up on their investments. As a result, returns on PE have been well ahead of the stock market. Figure 11.13 tracks the returns of PE as reported by Venture Economics since 1990. Through the end of 2008, reported PE returns were more than 12 times the 1990 value, as compared to 1.5 times by the S&P 500. At the same time, returns on PE went through rough times in the 2000 equity bear market. These return figures, however, should be used with caution because of the complications in calculating PE returns due to the uneven cash flows and other factors; they are not strictly comparable.

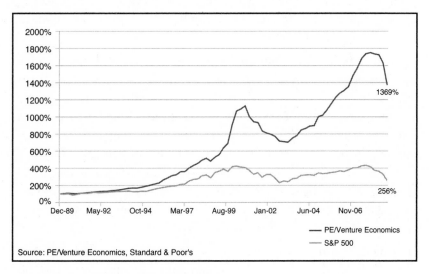

Figure 11.13   Returns: PE and stocks

Again, when market conditions turned sour in the 2008 recession, returns on PE were affected. In 2008, according to Venture Economics, PE return was reported at a loss of –21.7 percent, which is not bad compared to the public equity market. However, going forward,

PE firms are required by "fair value accounting" in Financial Accounting Standard 157 and 159 to mark-to-market the values of their portfolio holdings to comparable companies' valuations. In the past, PE firms had the leeway to account for their portfolio companies at cost until they were sold years later. As experienced with mortgage-backed and other such securities, marking-to-market is expected to cause significant increases in the volatility of private equity returns. As reported by the *Financial Times*, many leveraged buyout deals done in 2006 and 2007 may face daunting markdowns of values.[8] In these deals, PE firms paid 25 percent premium over comparable public companies in order to take their targets private. Massive amounts of debt were then used to leverage these acquisitions, "suggesting the drop in value should be more like 60 percent."[9] Expectations of valuation markdowns, depressed returns, and unfavorable economic conditions have led many PE investors to unload their investments in the secondary market. In 2008, the Harvard University endowment tried to sell a "chunk of its PE portfolio but didn't receive an acceptable offer."[10]

These unfavorable circumstances serve to remind investors that PE, although potentially attractive in the long term, needs to be approached with due regard for its requirement for long-term commitment and its lack of liquidity. In the short-term, PE investments simply cannot be sold off in the secondary market in short notice. Andrew Alper, chairman of the University of Chicago Board of Trustees and member of its endowment committee, reacting to the disappointing performance of the endowment's investments in fiscal year 2009, said that the endowment committee would have preferred to unload its stakes in PE firms.[11]

Another issue in PE investing is capital calls. Briefly, when a PE firm raises funds and obtains commitments from investors, the total commitment is not paid up front. Each investor's committed capital will be drawn down in installments over time when the PE firm issues capital calls for them to have funds to pay for their investments. It means that investors need to find temporary investments for the remainder of the committed capital, which is the difference between the paid-in or contributed capital and the commitment, be it in cash or other vehicles. Whatever these temporary investments are, the important point to remember is that funds need to be readily available when the PE firm issues capital calls; otherwise, severe penalty or for-feiture may result. The 2008 financial debacle exposed this hereto-fore-rare downside aspect of PE investing. "If you had asked me two months ago, I'd have said that in 15 years of structuring funds, I'd seen investor default only twice. But in the last two months, I've seen seven cases of either defaults arising or investors indicating to general partners that they will be unable to meet the next drawdown," said the head of a fund formation group at a law firm.[12]

Additionally, short-term negative returns in the early phase of a PE investment can be distracting to investors. This is the J-curve effect, as shown in Figure 11.14. In the early years, investors make capital contributions in response to capital calls from the PE firm as it makes new investments. Investment return is not generated in these early years; in fact, only losses are. These losses are caused by man-agement fees in the 2 percent range, which are charged on the basis of the total commitment, not on the paid-in amounts. There are also organizational expenses and possibly writedowns due to underper-foming investments, which a PE firm tends to recognize quickly as they become apparent. Depending on the amount of the contributed capital, negative returns on these cash flows can be significantly large. Thus, for years, PE investors only saw losses reported on their invest-ments. Only in later years, when gains on investments were realized through IPOs or sales, did investors receive capital distributions, hence positive returns, on contributed capital.

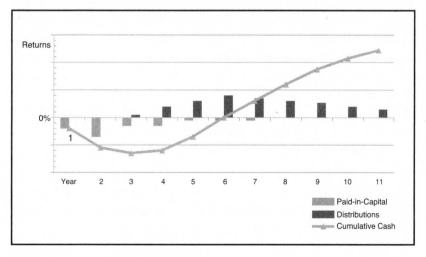

Figure 11.14   J-curve effects of PE

In the final analysis, PE is truly a long-term investment with strict liquidity demands and only negative returns in the early years. Starting perhaps in the fourth year or later, depending on a host of factors including the pace of investments, the market and economic environment, as well as the presence of early winners, will investors begin to see positive return through capital distributions. As a result, investors should have expectations of substantial return from PE, well in excess of the return of the public market, to make it worthwhile.

Absolute Return and Opportunistic Profits

We have discussed three major asset classes that potentially can enhance the return prospects of an absolute return portfolio. All are characterized by high return expectations as well as significant risks of losses. In the aftermath of the 2008 recession, emerging markets are poised to resume their prospects of strong economic growth, further fueling their increased sharing of the global economy and wealth. Commodities should also benefit from increased incremental demand from emerging markets as well as potential supply constraints. PE continues to be an asset class that has the potential to generate long-term return well in excess of public equities.

In the absolute return portfolio, the boundaries for these asset classes are suggested at 20 percent. However, their allocations can vary to some degree with individual investors' financial circumstances, including the need for liquidity, the ability and willingness to make long-term commitments, and the availability of the appropriate investment vehicles such as the qualified managers. Importantly, their role in the absolute return portfolio and asset allocation strategy is to enhance return opportunistically, but only with the expectation that any resulting losses are within the margins of affordability with little impacts on investors' financial plans and lifestyle commitments.

With the inclusion of these opportunitic investments, together with fixed income and hedge funds, the absolute return portfolio can be positioned to benefit from high return potential while preserving access to liquidity and managing the risks of losses.

Conclusion

About the time of the first anniversary of the collapse of world financial markets, the finance ministers and central bankers from the Group of Twenty developed and emerging economies met in London in 2009 to gauge the state of the world economy. The "Group of Twenty Finance Ministers and Central Bank Governors" (G20) is a loose formation that comprises the finance ministers and central bank governors of 19 countries, which account for 85 percent of world GDP and 80 percent of world trade, and the presidency of the European Union. They first praised themselves for stabilizing the financial markets amid signs that the global economy is improving, even though "public spending, like the successful cash-for-clunkers schemes, has predominantly driven recent gains."[1] U.S. Treasury Secretary Timothy Geithner said, "The financial system is showing signs of repair. Growth is now under way.... However, we still face significant challenges ahead."[2] So, the finance ministers agreed to "continue to implement decisively our necessary financial support measures and expansionary monetary and fiscal policies...until recovery is secured."[3] The British prime minister was more emphatic. "To decide now that it is time to start withdrawing and reversing the exceptional measures we have taken would in my judgment be a serious mistake," Brown said. "On the contrary, with more than half of the $5 trillion fiscal expansion committed to, yet to be spent, I believe the prudent course is for G-20 countries to deliver the fiscal plans and stimulus packages they have put in place and make sure they are implemented in full both this year and next."[4]

So for now, talks of "radical restructuring" to address "fundamental causes" of the global credit crunch, to "strengthen financial regulation to rebuild trust," or in the words of Treasury Secretary Geithner to "adopt more effective constraints" on excessive risk taking by financial institutions can remain on the agenda but get no action. Worries about the next crisis can be set aside. In the following words of participants and observers at the meeting:[5] "Much remains to be done," said the Bank of Israel governor. Even though "it would be a catastrophe not to draw all the lessons from the present crisis in terms of regulation," said European Central Bank President Jean-Claude Trichet. Unless steps are taken to reduce complexity and leverage in financial markets, "we're going to have a replay of what has just happened over the last few years," said Richard Bookstaber, chief investment officer of FrontPoint Partners LLC. "What I'm very worried about is the recovery is going to come and the political will is going to disappear to actually repair the system," said Stephen Cecchetti, head of the monetary and economic unit at Basel, Switzerland-based Bank for International Settlements, the central bank of world central banks.

The banks are rejoicing with their profits rising, thanks to taxpayers' subsidy and little restriction on their risk-taking. As cited earlier, leveraging is back on Wall Street as banks have reverted to their old ways. "Companies are selling exotic financial products that felled markets and the world economy last fall. And banks' appetite for risk has grown: The nation's top five banks collectively stood to lose more than $1 billion on average a day in the second quarter of 2009 should their trading bets go sour, a record level."[6] The banks' estimate was $1.04 billion as compared to $0.59 billion in 2007. Short sellers are also in hiding, as *Barron's* observed. "Have they taken to their beds lying comatose in shuttered rooms...? Or have they been in a perpetually frenzied rush to be first in line at the soup kitchen? Or are they wandering aimlessly on city streets, muttering 'should have covered, should have covered'?"[7] Nevertheless, merciful to the "widely despised bunch" of short sellers, *Barron's* also noted, "Our belief that what we've been seeing, for all its splendor, is a rally in a secular bear market.... [Although] valuations are already starkly elevated...we wouldn't be shocked if the market goes up another 10% before it takes another header...."[8]

Why the hand wringing? Why wait to be shocked by a market with valuations "starkly elevated"? Why should savers and long-term investors subject their financial futures, their hard-earned savings of a lifetime to what increasingly gives meaning to John Maynard Keynes' vivid description of the stock market as "the bubble on a whirlpool of speculation. When the capital development of a country becomes a by-product of the activities of a casino...," especially without taking the necessary precautions of managing and minimizing the downside risks of losses?[9]

We have reviewed the collapse of the housing speculation and the 2008 crash of the stock market from excess risk taking and leveraging across all sectors of the economy, precipitated by the unraveling of sub-prime home mortgages. In this bubble burst, the U.S. experience resembles in key aspects the twin crash of the real estate and stock markets of Japan following its equity market peak in 1989. There is one key difference, however. The U.S. equity market is starting out on an economic foundation in much worse shape than Japan's at the start of its two decades of malaise. From record government budget deficits to overleveraging in the household and financial sectors, from the unprecedented national debt burden to trade deficits and reliance on foreign countries for debt financing, from a deteriorated domestic manufacturing base and low personal saving rates to a weakened world economy, the United States has little flexibility to repair its economy and return to a healthy growth rate.

Nothing much structurally has changed since the crisis. By continuing on the same paths of leveraging and excess debt, the U.S. economy is trying to escape from a "frightful storm" at the risk of lurching into another. As the manager of a large hedge fund observed, "This is more likely a ski jump...with short-term stimulus creating a bump that will ultimately lead to a more precipitous decline later."[10] In between, with the "protective factor" of a healthy banking system severely damaged, the Federal Reserve is alone in its quest of economic growth with price stability. Yet among the principal tools available to it remains only the printing press, which has been working overtime. Can it wield sufficient power to combat the twin evils of inflation and deflation in the face of rising unemployment, a stagnant housing market, and record debt burden?

Just as Keynes counseled against putting the development of a country in the hands of casino operators, savers and long-term investors need to think about managing the risks of losses from their investments in the equity market. Although equities can and did provide handsome returns, the fundamental conditions that give rise to the strength of the market are no longer present, with headwinds gathering and favorable dynamics gone into reverse. Equity investing is no longer a game of favorable odds where winning is more or less expected for the patient and disciplined investors. The time has come for stocks to be regarded for what they are: risky assets of potential gains but also devastating losses.

There is nothing new in this observation. But the winning streak in the 1980s and 1990s has lulled the sense of vulnerability, and stocks were viewed as a must-have investment of predictable rewards. Not anymore. After almost two decades of rising prices, the stock market has gone, since 2000, through 10 years of booms and busts, leaving in its wake devastation and unfilled expectations. The continued excess of risk-taking and leveraging of the economy coupled with zero inter- est rate policy has set the equity market in a path so analogous with Japan's stocks that the risk is high and significant of U.S. stocks simi- larly experiencing that country's two decades of slumber; this risk should not be offhandedly dismissed. It's not that there were no precedents in the United States of range-bound markets lasting almost two decades, punctuated with sharp rallies and steep sudden falls. An often-referenced period was the years of rolling booms and busts between 1966 and 1982. In fact, in its 110 years of history, the popular benchmark Dow Jones Industrial Average has experienced many more years of sideways or declining prices than soaring valua- tions. When adjusted for inflation, the prospects of stocks look even more precarious—for many years.

Like games of chances, potential gains and losses of stocks need to be weighed against the odds for each outcome. But in any market condition, risks of losses need to be managed, not left to hopes of perpetual rising prices or vagaries of the market. For some, "swim- ming naked" may be fun or natural. For savers and long-term investors who do not and cannot trade in and out of the market, we outline the absolute return approach and asset allocation strategy that is designed to provide liquidity and income and preserve capital, but also is in a position to take advantage of opportunistic profits. Underlying this approach is the focus on managing the risks of losses from equities or any risky assets to limit their impacts on the savings and retirement assets of long-term investors and savers to the extent that any loss would not alter their financial well-being and futures. It is also designed to provide liquidity and a predictable source of income for those who rely on their assets to support their lifestyles and retirements.

For many savers, an absolute return portfolio may comprise only fixed income securities of laddered maturities and possibly professionally managed bond funds to enhance return and manage the interest rate risk. For others, opportunities exist to enhance return and achieve equity-like performance by adding hedge funds, which focus on risk management and alpha sources of return. There are multiple hedge fund strategies that are designed to achieve these objectives. We've discussed a few of these, from conservative fund of hedge funds to long/short equity, event driven, and others.

U.S. equities are not necessarily absent from the absolute return portfolio approach. But their riskiness should be adequately compensated by the potential return. As such, the absolute return approach and asset allocation strategy is positioned to embrace risky assets that have the risks of losses like U.S. stocks but also the potential of enhanced return as they are favored by the fundamental conditions of their asset classes. These include emerging markets, especially the so-called Group of 10 largest emerging economies with strong economic growth prospects well above those of the United States and other developed countries. Commodities are also susceptible to unusual rewards due to the Malthusian risks that cause supply and demand imbalances and drive prices higher. Alternative asset classes, such as private equity and real assets, can also be part of the absolute return portfolio that can generate opportunistic profits, although their risk of losses and restricted liquidity should be kept within the margins investors can afford.

Throughout the book, one theme is central and pervasive: Risks needs to be managed yet can be embraced to harvest handsome return. The absolute return approach and asset allocation strategy is designed for these purposes: to provide liquidity and predictable income and enhance return while preserving capital. In other words, it is to save and build wealth with minimal risks of devastating losses.

Notes

Introduction

[1]Robert J. Shiller, "Economic View: An Echo Chamber of Boom and Bust," *The New York Times*, August 30, 2009. http://www.nytimes.com/2009/08/30/business/economy/30view.html?_r=1.

[2]Ibid.

Chapter 1

[1]A loss of 30 percent or more is generally considered a bear market.

[2]Nassim Nicholas Taleb, *The Black Swan: The Impact of the Highly Improbables* (New York: Random House, 2007).

[3]"Greenspan Sees 'Seeds of Bottoming' for U.S. Housing," Reuters, May 12, 2009.

[4]"Bernanke Sees Recession Ending Soon; Warns on Debt," Reuters, June 3, 2009.

[5]David Wilson, "'Buy' Ratings Reemerge among U.S. Stock Analysts," Bloomberg.com, July 6, 2009. http://www.bloomberg.com/apps/news?pid=20601109&sid=aHo6MTmJC9Q0.

[6]Deborah Solomon, "Calls Grow to Increase Stimulus Spending," *The Wall Street Journal* (July 6, 2009): A1.

[7]Susan Cornwell and Jeremy Pelofsky, "U.S. Must Be Open to Second Economic Stimulus: Hoyer," Reuters, July 7, 2009.

[8]Edward Krudy, "Wall Street Hits 10-Week Low Amid Talk of New Stimulus," Reuters, July 7, 2009.

[9]Jeff Cox, "More Government Money Won't Stimulate Stocks: Experts," CNBC.com, July 7, 2009. http://www.cnbc.com/id/31779001.

[10]"Market Halfway through Bear Cycle: Rosenberg," CNBC.com, July 7, 2009, http://www.cnbc.com/id/31775633.

[11]Ibid.

[12]Ibid.

[13]Victoria Batchelor, "Australia Faces the 'Full Brunt' of Global Recession," Bloomberg.com, July 3, 2009. http://www.bloomberg.com/apps/news?pid=20601109&sid=aJkiwWwwe3cY.

[14]Eleanor Laise, "Pimco Says It Withdrew PPIP Application in Early June," *The Wall Street Journal*, July 8, 2009. http://online.wsj.com/article/SB124708520111513795.html.

[15]"Toxic Asset Program May Be Too Late to Help Banks," Associated Press, July 8, 2009.

[16]Richard W. Fisher and Harvey Rosenblum, "The Blob That Ate Monetary Policy," *The Wall Street Journal*, September 28, 2009, A23.

[17]Meredith Whitney, "The Credit Crunch Continues," *The Wall Street Journal* (October 2, 2009): A19.

[18]James Sterngold, "The $6 Trillion Hole in Japan's Pocket," *The New York Times*, January 21, 1994.

Chapter 2

[1]Christopher Wood, "The Bubble Economy: Japan's Extraordinary Speculative Boom of the '80's and the Dramatic Bust of the '90's," *The Atlantic Monthly Press*, 1992.

[2]Paul Krugman, "Setting Sun—Japan: What Went Wrong?," Blog, June 11, 1998. http://web.mit.edu/krugman/www/japan.html.

[3]Sebastian Moffett, "The Japanese Property Bubble: Can It Happen Here?," *The Wall Street Journal*, July 11, 2005.

[4]David J. Lynch, "U.S. Can Learn from Japan's Deflated Economy in the 1990s," *USA Today*, January 25, 2008. http://www.usatoday.com/money/economy/2008-01-21-japan-parallels_N.htm.

[5]Roger Thompson, "Rebuilding Commercial Real Estate," *Harvard Business Review*, January 9, 2006. http://hbswk.hbs.edu/item/5156.html.

[6]Ibid.

[7]Ibid.

[8]"Commercial Real Estate Is Next Bubble to Burst: Tishman," CNBC, September 21, 2009. http://www.cnbc.com/id/32952174.

[9]Dick K. Nanto, "The U.S. Financial Crisis: Lessons from Japan," CRS Report for Congress, September 29, 2008.

[10]Finbarr Flynn, "Japan Land Prices Rise for First Time in 16 Years," Bloomberg.com, March 22, 2007. http://www.bloomberg.com/apps/news?pid=20601101&sid=a5e_7OF8JvM8&refer=japan.

Chapter 3

[1]Shah Gilani, "The Credit Crisis and the Real Story Behind the Collapse of AIG," MoneyMorning.com.

[2]Basel Committee on Banking Supervision, The Joint Forum: Credit Risk Transfer, "Developments from 2005 to 2007," Bank for International Settlements, April 2008. http://www.financialstabilityboard.org/publications/r_0804c.pdf?noframes=1.

[3]"Credit Default Swaps Losses Estimated at $150 Billion," NakedCapitalism.com, May 20, 2008. http://www.nakedcapitalism.com/2008/05/credit-default-swaps-losses-estimated.html.

[4] David Evans, "Hedge Funds in Swaps Face Peril with Rising Junk Bond Defaults," Bloomberg.com, May 20, 2009. http://www.bloomberg.com/apps/news?pid=20601109&sid=aCFGw7GYxY14&refer=home.

[5] "Collaterized Debt Obligations Markets," Celent Consulting, Paris, October 31, 2005. http://reports.celent.com/PressReleases/20051031/CDOMarket.htm.

[6] "25 People to Blame for the Financial Crisis," http://www.time.com/time/specials/packages/article/0,28804,1877351_1877350_1877344,00.html.

[7] Ibid.

[8] "Collaterized Debt Obligations Markets."

[9] "Risk Transfer and Financial Stability," Remarks by Chairman Alan Greenspan to the Federal Reserve Bank of Chicago's 41ST annual conference on bank structure, May 5, 2005. http://www.federalreserve.gov/Boarddocs/Speeches/2005/20050505/default.htm.

[10] Speech by Thomas M. Hoenig, President, Federal Reserve Bank of Kansas City, January 7, 2009.

[11] "Japan's Debt Financing Program Carries Distortion Risks," *Oxford Analytica*, June 29, 2009. http://www.oxan.com/display.aspx?StoryDate=20090629&ProductCode=APDB&StoryNumber=2&StoryType=DB.

[12] Sumie Kawakamie, "Economic Bondage," *Japan Inc*, Summer 2002. http://www.japaninc.com/article.php?articleID=870.

[13] "Moody's Unifies Japan's Government Ratings at Aa2," *Global Credit Research*, Moody's Investors Service, May 18, 2009. http://www.jfm.go.jp/en/rating/pdf/en-moody090518.pdf.

[14] "Moody's Says Spending Threatens US Rating," *Financial Times*, January 10, 2008. http://www.ft.com/cms/s/0/40f3a2be-bfa9-11dc-8052-0000779fd2ac.html?nclick_check=1.

[15] Keiko Ujikane and Jason Clenfield, "Moody's Says U.S.'s Aaa Debt Rating 'Remains Solid,'" Bloomberg.com, June 23, 2009. http://www.bloomberg.com/apps/news?pid=20601009&sid=acRrvA.NM_r8.

Chapter 4

[1]Associated Press, May 10, 2009.

[2]Associated Press, May 6, 2009.

[3]Judith Burns, "'Clunkers' Lifts Foreign Cars," *The Wall Street Journal* (August 27, 2009): B9.

[4]Geoffrey T. Smith, "Germans Debate Car Trade-In Program," *The Wall Street Journal* (August 31, 2009): B3.

[5]Richard W. Fisher, "Storms on the Horizon: Remarks Before the Commonwealth Club of California," Federal Reserve Bank of Dallas, May 28, 2008. http://perotcharts.com/images/media/Storms%20Speech%20by%20Richard%20Fisher.pdf.

[6]Ibid.

[7]"The Concord Coalition Plausible Baseline," The Concord Coalition. http://www.concordcoalition.org/learn/budget/concord-coalition-plausible-baseline.

[8]Richard W. Fisher.

[9]R. Anton Braun, Daisuke Ikeda, and Douglas H. Joines, "The Saving Rate in Japan: Why It Has Fallen and Why It Will Remain Low," CIRJE Discussion Papers, December 2007. http://www.e.u-tokyo.ac.jp/cirje/research/03research02dp.html.

[10]Tom Barkley and Deborah Solomon, "Chinese Convey Concern on Growing U.S. Debt," *The Wall Street Journal*, July 29, 2009.

[11]"Yuan Deposes Dollar on China Border in Sign of Future," Bloomberg.com, July 8, 2009. http://www.bloomberg.com/apps/news?pid=newsarchive&sid=aqA9QhRSNeqM.

[12]Gabrielle Parussini, "Sarkozy: Dollar Needs Reserve Rival," *The Wall Street Journal* (August 27, 2009): C1.

[13]Nouriel Roubini, "The 'Stress Tests' Are Really 'Fudge Tests,'" *Forbes*, April 16, 2009. http://www.forbes.com/2009/04/15/gdp-stress-tests-unemployment-banks-home-prices-opinions-columnists-nouriel-roubini.html.

[14]"Statement on U.S. Economic Outlook by Dr. Nouriel Roubini," *RGE Monitor*, July 16, 2009.

[15]Bill Gross, "Investment Outlook," PIMCO, July 2009.

[16]Associated Press, March 8, 2009.

[17]Katie Kirkland, "On the Decline in Average Weekly Hours Worked," *Monthly Labor Review,* Bureau of Labor Statistics, July 2000. http://www.bls.gov/opub/mlr/2000/07/art3full.pdf.

[18]Lisa Lambert, "Waves of Job Losses Sap U.S. States' Budgets," Reuters, July 9, 2009.

[19]Iris J. Lay and Elizabeth McNicol, "State Budget Troubles Worsen," Center on Budget and Policy Priorities, June 29, 2009. http://www.cbpp.org/cms/?fa=view&id=711.

[20]Ibid.

[21]Mitch Daniels, "The Coming Reset in State Government," *The Wall Street Journal* (September 4, 2009): A17.

[22]"States Shut Down to Save Cash," *The Wall Street Journal* (September 4, 2009): A1.

[23]Bob Willis, "Home Starts, Leading Index Probably Rose: U.S. Economy Preview," Reuters, May 17, 2009. http://www.bloomberg.com/apps/news?pid=20601103&sid=aA.Q0gfraU10.

[24]Associated Press, May 19, 2009.

[25]"Greenspan Sees 'Seeds of Bottoming' for U.S. Housing," Reuters, May 12, 2009. http://www.reuters.com/article/ousiv/idUSTRE54B6AQ20090512.

[26]Associated Press, May 26, 2009.

[27]Paul Vigna, "Improving Home Sales Belie Market Reality," *The Wall Street Journal*, August 21, 2009. http://online.wsj.com/article/SB125081143925447971.html.

[28]Adrian Sainz, "RealtyTrac: April Foreclosures Rise 32 Percent," May 13, 2009. http://navigatingthestorm.blogspot.com/2009/05/realtytrac-april-foreclosures-rise-32.html.

[29]Ibid.

[30]Lynn Adler, "May Foreclosures Third Highest on Record," Reuters, June 11, 2009. http://www.reuters.com/article/newsOne/idUSTRE55A0NS20090611.

[31]"US Housing Market Could Be Facing Another Bubble: Shiller," CNBC.com, August 19, 2009.

[32]"World Markets Slide on World Bank Recovery Warning," Reuters, June 22, 2009. http://www.investmentnews.com/apps/pbcs.dll/article?AID=/20090622/REG/906229997.

[33]"Market Watch," *Barron's*, June 15, 2009.

[34]"WTO Sees 9% Global Trade Decline in 2009 as Recession Strikes," Press release, World Trade Organization, March 23, 2009. http://www.wto.org/english/news_e/pres09_e/pr554_e.htm.

[35]Ibid.

[36]"Trade Flows' Collapse Continues in First Quarter 2009," *OECD International Trade Statistics*, July 15, 2009. http://www.oecd.org/dataoecd/15/2/43319682.pdf.

[37]"World Trade Volume Climbs 2.5%," *The Wall Street Journal*, August 27, 2009.

[38]Ibid.

[39]"WTO sees 9% Global Trade Decline in 2009 as Recession Strikes," Press release, World Trade Organization, March 23, 2009. http://www.wto.org/english/news_e/pres09_e/pr554_e.htm.

[40]"RGE's Daily Top 5," *RGE Monitor*, July 30, 2009.

[41]John H. Makin, "Japan's Disastrous Keynesian Experiment," *Economic Outlook*, American Enterprise Institute, AEI Online, January 1, 2000.

[42]"Deflation—Making Sure 'It' Doesn't Happen Here," Speech by Ben S. Bernanke, Member of the Board of Governors of the U.S. Federal Reserve System, before the National Economists Club, Washington, DC, November 21, 2002.

[43]Kristen Haunss and Jody Shenn, "Leverage Rising on Wall Street at Fastest Pace Since '07 Freeze," Bloomberg.com, August 28, 2009. http://www.bloomberg.com/apps/news?pid=20601087&sid= a_XpcU5pY0f4.

Chapter 5

[1]Jason DeSena Trennert, "Remembering the Reagan Bull Market," *The Wall Street Journal* (August 13, 2009): A15.

[2]President's speech, Federal Reserve Bank of San Francisco, June 5, 2009. http://www.frbsf.org/news/speeches/2009/0605.html.

[3]Statement by Ben S. Bernanke, Chairman, Board of Governors of the Federal Reserve System, before the Committee on the Budget U.S. House of Representatives, June 3, 2009.

[4]Craig Torres and Brian Faler, "Bernanke Warns Deficits Threaten Financial Stability (Update4)," Bloomberg.com, June 3, 2009. http://www.bloomberg.com/apps/news?pid=20601087&sid= ahrOZ.gd85yc.

[5]Ariana Eunjung Cha, "China Confident in U.S., Geithner Says," *Washington Post*, June 3, 2009. http://www.washingtonpost.com/ wp-dyn/content/article/2009/06/02/AR2009060200571.html.

[6]Robert Lenzner, "Dollar Slams Up Against a (Great) Wall," *Forbes*, Friday, March 27, 2009. http://finance.yahoo.com/banking-budgeting/article/106817/Dollar-Slams-Up-Against-a-Great-Wall.

[7]Ibid.

[8]Alister Bull, "Bernanke Says Fed Has Exit Strategy from Credit Policy," Reuters, March 20, 2009. http://www.reuters.com/article/ newsOne/idUSN2028434620090320.

[9]Craig Torres and Scott Lanman, "Bernanke May Explain Exit Strategy," Bloomberg.com, July 19, 2009. http://www.bloomberg. com/apps/news?pid=20601087&sid=aNU.UkT9EB68.

[10]"Remarks by Governor Ben S. Bernanke," National Economists Club, Washington, DC. November 21, 2002. http://www. federalreserve.gov/BOARDDOCS/SPEECHES/2002/20021121/ default.htm.

[11]Mark Felsenthal and Alister Bull, "Unemployment Could Undercut U.S. Recovery: Bernanke," Reuters, July 21, 2009.

Chapter 6

[1]Tim Bond, "Insight: Learn to Love the Recovery," *Financial Times*, July 29, 2009. http://www.ft.com/cms/s/0/3c4c37ba-7c51-11de-a7bf-00144feabdc0.html.

[2]Caroline Valetkevitch, "Goldman Sachs' Cohen: New Bull Market Has Begun," Reuters, August 6, 2009.

[3]"When Buy-and-Hold Beats Bad Timing," *Investor's Business Daily*, cited at InvestorsInsight.com. http://www.investorsinsight.com/blogs/ forecasts_trends/archive/2009/03/03/beware-bear-market-brings-out-tall-tales.aspx.

[4]Harry M. Markowitz, "Portfolio Selection," *Journal of Finance* (1952) 7 (1): 77–91.

[5]For example, J. Michael Murphy, "Efficient Markets, Index Funds, Illusion, and Reality," *Journal of Portfolio Management* (Fall 1977): 5–20.

[6]Walter Hamilton, "Target-Date Retirement Funds: Not Quite 'Set It and Forget It,'" *L.A. Times*, April 12, 2009. http://articles.latimes. com/2009/apr/12/business/fi-target-date12.

[7]Ibid.

[8]Ibid.

[9]"Seniors Drawn to Mortgages That Give Back," *The Wall Street Journal* (June 11, 2009): D1.

Chapter 7

[1]RGE's Daily Top 5, *RGE Monitor,* July 24, 2009.

[2]*The Wall Street Journal,* July 24, 2009.

[3]Tara Siegel Bernard, "For Older Investors, Old Rules May Not Apply," *The New York Times,* June 19, 2009.

[4]Ibid.

[5]Adam Shell, "Stock Market Losses Take a Personal Toll on Investors," *USA Today*, March 24, 2009. http://www.usatoday.com/money/markets/2009-03-23-investor-pain_N.htm.

[6]Vince Farrell, "Farrell: We Are Overdue for a Market Correction," CNBC.com, June 5, 2009.

[7]Nassim Nicholas Taleb, *The Black Swan: The Impact of the Highly Improbables*. New York: Random House, 2007.

[8]President's speech, Janet L. Yellen, President and CEO, Federal Reserve Bank of San Francisco, for delivery on Friday, June 5, 2009 at 2:15 PM Eastern time. http://www.frbsf.org/news/speeches/2009/0605.pdf.

[9]"Revisiting T. Rowe Price's Asset Allocation Glide-Path Strategy," April 2009. http://www.troweprice.com/gcFiles/pdf/RDFs.pdf?scn=RetirementEquityExposure&src=Media_Site_Home_Page&t=lgcy.

[10]Ibid, 14.

[11]Ibid, 16.

[12]"The Eight Biggest Mistakes and How to Avoid Them," Fisher Investments.

[13]Ibid.

[14]Philip Moeller, "How Much Should You Invest in Stocks?," Yahoo News, June 5, 2009.

[15]Ibid.

[16]Ibid.

[17]Mark Veverka, "Keeping His Eyes Trained on the Long Term," *Barron's* (June 29, 2009): 34–35.

Chapter 8

[1]Mark Hulbert, "A Quarter When Mutual Fund Rankings Didn't Matter," *The New York Times*, January 24, 2009.

[2]"Standard & Poor's Indices Versus Active Funds Scorecard, Year End 2008," April 20, 2009. http://www2.standardandpoors.com/spf/pdf/index/SPIVA_Report_Year-End_2008.pdf.

[3]Ibid.

[4]Hulbert, "A Quarter When Mutual Fund Rankings Didn't Matter."

[5]Ibid.

[6]"Standard & Poor's Indices Versus Active Funds Scorecard."

[7]M. P. Dunleavey, "That Rush to Beat the Market," *The New York Times*, April 11, 2009. http://www.nytimes.com/2009/04/12/business/mutfund/12active.html.

[8]Jeremy Siegel, *Stocks for the Long Run: The Definitive Guide to Financial Market Returns & Long-Term Investment Strategies*, Third Edition. New York: McGraw-Hill, 2002.

[9]Mark Hulbert, "The Index Funds Win Again," *The New York Times*, February 21, 2009. http://www.nytimes.com/2009/02/22/your-money/stocks-and-bonds/22stra.html?_r=1.

[10]Mark Hulbert, "Why Weak Funds May Bounce Higher," *The New York Times*, April 11, 2009. http://www.nytimes.com/2009/04/12/business/mutfund/12stra.html.

[11]Dunleavey.

[12]Gary Brinson, Randolph Hood, and Gilbert Beebower, "Determinants of Portfolio Performance," *Financial Analysts Journal* (July/August 1986): 39–44.

[13]Roger G. Ibbotson and Paul D. Kaplan, "Does Asset Allocation Policy Explain 40, 90, or 100 Percent of Performance?," *Financial Analysts Journal* (January/February 2000): 26–33.

[14]All the facts and figures are from "The Big Squeeze," *Barron's* (June 29, 2009): 20–23.

[15]Yale University Office of Public Affairs, "Yale University Releases Endowment Figures," September 22, 2009. http://opa.yale.edu/news/article.aspx?id=6899.

[16]"Harvard Management Company Endowment Report: Message from the CEO," September 2009. http://www.hmc.harvard.edu/pdf/2009_HMC_Endowment_Report.pdf.

[17]"The Big Squeeze."

[18]"College Try: Chicago's Stock Sale," *The Wall Street Journal* (August 21, 2009): C1.

[19]Ibid.

[20]"The Big Squeeze."

[21]Ibid.

[22]Ibid.

Chapter 9

[1]Edward Wyatt, "Magellan Fund Chief Explains Cautious Strategy," *The New York Times*, May 15, 1996. http://www.nytimes.com/1996/05/15/business/magellan-fund-chief-explains-cautious-strategy.html.

[2]Ibid.

[3]Edward Wyatt, "Manager of Biggest Mutual Fund Quits After Recent Subpar Gains," *The New York Times*, May 24, 1996. http://www.nytimes.com/1996/05/24/business/manager-of-biggest-mutual-fund-quits-after-recent-subpar-gains.html.

[4]Ibid.

[5]Leslie Eaton, "A New Magellan Helmsman Cast from Peter Lynch's Mold; Robert Stansky Follows Mentor's 'Growth' Tack," *The New York Times*, May 24, 1996. http://www.nytimes.com/1996/05/24/business/new-magellan-helmsman-cast-peter-lynch-s-mold-robert-stansky-follows-mentor-s.html.

[6]Fidelity Investments Web site. http://personal.fidelity.com/products/funds/mfl_frame.shtml?316184100.

[7]Carol J. Loomis, "Hard Times Come to the Hedge Funds," *Fortune*, January 1970. http://www.xcv.org/misc/HardTimesForHedgeFunds.html.

[8]John Hechinger, "One College Sidesteps the Crisis," *The Wall Street Journal* (June 30, 2009): C1.

[9]"Barbara Bedway, "Stock Market Returns with No Risk!," CBSMoneywatch.com, May 28, 2009. http://moneywatch.bnet.com/investing/article/here-come-the-safe-stock-funds/305939/?tag=content;col1.

[10]"Absolute Return Investing," Putnam Investments, February 2009.

[11]Barbara Bedway.

[12]Jeff Benjamin, "Absolute-Return Trend Inspires Both Optimism and Caution," *Investment News*, June 24, 2009.

[13]Barbara Bedway.

[14]Ibid.

[15]Conrad de Aenlle, "Investing: Absolute-Return Funds: Are They Worth the Trouble?," *The New York Times*, June 29, 2007.

[16]Jeff Benjamin.

[17]Ibid.

[18]Ibid.

Chapter 10

[1]Carol J. Loomis, "The Joneses Nobody Keeps Up With," *Fortune*, April 1966.

[2]Carol J. Loomis, "Hard Times Come to the Hedge Funds," *Fortune*, January 1970. http://www.xcv.org/misc/HardTimesForHedgeFunds.html.

[3]Ibid.

[4]Ibid.

[5]Ibid.

[6]Ibid.

[7]Barry Eichengreen and Donald Mathieson, "Hedge Funds: What Do We Really Know?," International Monetary Fund, ISBN 1-55775-849-2, September 1999. http://www.imf.org/external/pubs/ft/issues/issues19/.

[8]Data provided courtesy of Hedge Fund Research, Inc.

[9]"Malaysia's Misdiagnosis," *The Economist*, July 31, 1997.

[10]Data provided courtesy of Hedge Fund Research, Inc.

[11]"Hedge Funds Took a Serious Hit in 2008," Associated Press, January 12, 2009. http://cbs5.com/national/hedge.funds.decline.2.906532.html.

[12]Benjamin N. Alpert, "Hedge Funds: Where Did That One-Star Fund Go?," Morningstar, March 23, 2009. http://news.morningstar.com/articlenet/article.aspx?id=284728.

[13]Ibid.

[14]Cyrus Sanati, "A Look at the Hedge Funds That Closed," Deal Book, March 19, 2009. http://dealbook.blogs.nytimes.com/2009/03/19/a-look-at-the-hedge-funds-that-closed/.

[15]Ibid.

[16]"First Quarter Hedge Fund Liquidations Drop by 50 Percent from Record Set in Q4 2008," Hedge Fund Research, Inc., June 16, 2009. https://www.hedgefundresearch.com/pdf/pr_20090616.pdf.

[17]"Hedge Fund Industry Assets Surge as Performance Leads Industry Recovery," Hedge Fund Research, Inc., July 21, 2009. https://www.hedgefundresearch.com/pdf/pr_20090721.pdf.

[18]View expressed by Barclays Capital strategist Robert McAdie, as quoted in "Hedge Funds Took a Serious Hit in 2008," Associated Press, January 12, 2009. http://cbs5.com/national/hedge.funds.decline.2.906532.html.

[19]"Citadel Lets Some Clients Exit as Funds Thrive," Reuters, August 4, 2009.

[20]U.S. Securities and Exchange Commission, *SEC v. Ashbury Capital Partners*, L.P. Litigation Release No. 16770, October 17, 2000.

[21]U.S. Securities and Exchange Commission, *SEC v. Higgins*, Litigation Release No. 17841, November 15, 2002.

[22]U.S. Securities and Exchange Commission, *SEC v. Ryan J. Fontaine and Simpleton Holdings a/k/a Signature Investments Hedge Fund*, Litigation Release No. 17864, November 26, 2002. http://www.sec.gov/litigation/litreleases/lr17864.htm.

[23]*SEC v. Beacon Hill Asset Management, L.L.C.* (November 15, 2002), as described in "Beacon Hill Principals Charged with Fraud, Case Expanded (Infovest21)," Altnews, June 17, 2004.

[24]U.S. Securities and Exchange Commission, "SEC Charges Two former Bear Stearns Hedge Fund Managers with Fraud," Press Release, Washington DC, June 19, 2008. The two managers were later acquitted of fraud and other charges.

[25]Ben Stein, "They Told Me That Madoff Never Lost Money," *The New York Times*, December 26, 2008. http://www.nytimes.com/2008/12/28/business/28every.html?_r=4&ref=your-money.

[26]"Madoff's Strategy Was Just Too Good to Be True," *New York Post*. December 13, 2008.

Chapter 11

[1]"World Economic Outlook Database, April 2009," International Monetary Fund, http://www.imf.org/external/pubs/ft/weo/2009/01/weodata/weoselgr.aspx.

[2]"Vietnam Leads the Way in Tackling Poverty," *VietnamNet Bridge*, February 2, 2008. http://english.vietnamnet.vn/social/2008/02/768857/.

[3]The World FactBook, U.S. Central Intelligence Agency. https://www.cia.gov/library/publications/the-world-factbook/geos/vm.html.

[4]"Foreign Direct Investment in Vietnam Triples in 2008: Gov't," *The China Post*, December 27, 2008. http://www.chinapost.com.tw/business/asia/vietnam/2008/12/27/189529/Foreign-direct.htm.

[5]Geethanjali Nataraj, "FDI and Indian Growth: The New Paradigm," *Far East Forum,* August 2, 2009. http://bx.businessweek.com/indian-economy/view?url=http%3A%2F%2Fwww.eastasiaforum.org%2F2009%2F08%2F02%2Ffdi-and-indian-growth-the-new-paradigm%2F.

[6]"Riots, Instability Spread as Food Prices Skyrocket," CNN, April 14, 2008.

[7]"Jim Rogers Discusses Agriculture, Inflation & Commodities," *Self Investors*, June 21, 2009. http://investing.typepad.com/tradingstocks/2009/06/jim-rogers-discusses-agriculture-inflation-commodities.html.

[8]Henny Sender, "Investors Braced for Private Equity Losses," *Financial Times*," January 7, 2009. http://www.ft.com/cms/s/0/8a1a2402-dc5b-11dd-b07e-000077b07658.html?nclick_check=1.

[9]Ibid.

[10]"Craig Karmin, "College Try: Chicago's Stock Sale," *The Wall Street Journal* (August 21, 2009): C1.

[11]Ibid.

[12]Oliver Smiddy, "Pressure Builds as Prospect of Investor Default Rises," Dow Jones Financial news, December 1, 2008. http://www.efinancialnews.com/homepage/content/3452635792.

Conclusion

[1]Mark Scott, "G-20 Summit: Assessing the Global Recovery," *Business Week Online*, September 4, 2009. http://www.businessweek.com/globalbiz/content/sep2009/gb2009093_270473.htm.

[2]Jane Wardell and Aoife White, "G-20 to Maintain Economic Stimulus Measures," Associated Press, September 5, 2009.

[3]"G-20 Take Aim at Executive Bonuses," CNN.com, September 7, 2009. http://edition.cnn.com/2009/BUSINESS/09/06/g20.london. meeting/.

[4]Katherine Haddon, "G20 Leaders Left To-Do List Ahead of Summit," Associated Press, September 5, 2009. http://www.google. com/hostednews/afp/article/ALeqM5gMrp0N4_j7e-HBCwthNjqiu3fMeQ.

[5]Rich Miller and Simon Kennedy, "G-20 Risks 'Catastrophe' as Push Ebbs for Regulation," Bloomberg.com, September 2, 2009. http://www.bloomberg.com/apps/news?pid=20601068&sid=akh0JQ KKbKL8.

[6]Ibid.

[7]Alan Abelson, "Time to Lighten Up," *Barron's*, September 7, 2009.

[8]Ibid.

[9]John Maynard Keynes, *The General Theory of Employment, Interest, and Money*, (New York, Harcourt, Brace & Company, 1964), p. 159.

[10]Cristina Alesci, "Goldman Sachs Wrong on Economic Recovery, Macro Hedge Funds Say," Bloomberg.com, September 1, 2009. http://www.bloomberg.com/apps/news?pid=20601109&sid=auGWG WlnohNo.

INDEX